The Routledge Concise History of Science Fiction

The term 'science fiction' has an established common usage, but close examination reveals that writers, fans, editors, scholars and publishers often use this word in different ways for different reasons. Exploring how science fiction has emerged through competing versions and the struggle to define its limits, this *Concise History*:

- provides an accessible and clear overview of the development of the genre
- traces the separation of sf from a broader fantastic literature and the simultaneous formation of neighbouring genres, such as fantasy and horror
- shows the relationship between magazine and paperback traditions in sf publishing
- is organised by theme and presented chronologically
- uses text boxes throughout to highlight key works in sf traditions including dystopian, apocalyptic and evolutionary fiction
- includes a short overview and bullet-pointed conclusion for each chapter.

Discussing the place of key works and looking forward to the future of the genre, this book is the ideal starting point both for students and all those seeking a better understanding of science fiction.

Mark Bould is Reader in Film and Literature at the University of the West of England and an editor of *Science Fiction Film and Television*.

Sherryl Vint is Associate Professor of English at Brock University, Canada, and the Director of the Interdisciplinary MA in Popular Culture.

Routledge Concise Histories of Literature series

The Routledge Concise Histories of Literature series offers students and academics alike an interesting and accessible route into the literature of a specific period, genre, place or topic. The books situate the literature within its broader historical, cultural and political contexts, introducing the key events, movements and theories necessary for a fuller understanding of the writing. They engage readers in the debates of the period, genre or region adding a more exciting and challenging element to the reading.

Accessible and engaging, offering suggestions for further reading, explanatory text boxes, bullet pointed chapter summaries and a glossary of key terms, the Routledge Concise Histories are the ideal starting point for the study of literature.

Available:

The Routledge Concise History of Southeast Asian Writing in English
By Rajeev S. Patke and Philip Holden

The Routledge Concise History of Nineteenth-Century Literature
By Josephine Guy and Ian Small

The Routledge Concise History of Science Fiction
By Mark Bould and Sherryl Vint

Forthcoming:

The Routledge Concise History of Canadian Literature
By Richard J. Lane

The Routledge Concise History of Science Fiction

Mark Bould and Sherryl Vint

Routledge
Taylor & Francis Group

LONDON AND NEW YORK

First edition published 2011 by Routledge
2 Park Square, Milton Park, Abingdon, OX14 4RN

Simultaneously published in the USA and Canada
by Routledge
270 Madison Ave, New York, NY 10016

Routledge is an imprint of the Taylor & Francis Group, an informa business

© 2011 Mark Bould and Sherryl Vint

Typeset in Times New Roman by Glyph International
Printed and bound in Great Britain by TJ International Ltd, Padstow, Cornwall

British Library Cataloguing in Publication Data
A catalogue record for this book is available from the British Library

Library of Congress Cataloging in Publication Data
Bould, Mark.
The Routledge concise history of science fiction / Mark Bould and Sherryl Vint. -- 1st ed.
p. cm.
Includes bibliographical references and index.
1. Science fiction—History and criticism. I. Vint, Sherryl, 1969- II. Title.
III. Title: Concise history of science fiction.
PN3433.5.B68 2011
809.3'8762--dc22
2010035731

ISBN: 978-0-415-43570-3 (hbk)
ISBN: 978-0-415-43571-0 (pbk)
ISBN: 978-0-203-83016-1 (ebk)

For Douglas Barbour, Veronica Hollinger, Patrick Parrinder and Brian Stableford. Responsible, but hardly to blame.

Contents

Preface

Writing *the* history of science fiction (SF) is an impossible task, and even writing *a* history is daunting, as there are many competing perspectives on what properly counts as SF and therefore a history of the genre must necessarily be selective. We are keenly aware of both our emphases and our omissions. While we attempt throughout to indicate SF's existence in multiple media, the series of which this book is a part requires us to focus almost exclusively on SF as a literature. Within that framework, we have concentrated on Anglophone SF and authors primarily from the US and the UK, along with Canada and Australia, and on American cultural history, although there are strong traditions of SF in many other languages and countries. These other SF traditions circulate in distinct national and cultural contexts to which an introductory volume such as this cannot possibly do justice, and since we are both monolingual and our expertise lies in Anglophone literature, we would only be able to discuss non-Anglophone texts in translation. Doing so would sever them from their original context and meanings, and inevitably reinforce the limited view of these other literatures created by the processes by which only certain texts are selected for translation. Generally, then, our discussions of non-Anglophone writers focuses on those whose translated work has had an influence on how SF is produced and consumed in Anglophone countries; for example, our treatment of Jules Verne is concerned with how he was understood by Anglophone readers and does not engage with his rather different reception in French popular and literary culture.

We have selected as the focus of this history a tradition of texts that can be seen to be in conversation with one another as the idea of SF emerged and morphed through negotiations over which texts and voices were or were not to be considered part of it. We have also aimed to convey something of the breadth and variety of this SF. We have sometimes selected what might be considered exemplary texts, at other times typical ones. We have included pulp fiction, middlebrow literature and more experimental forms, ranging from space-opera adventures to political interventions, from rigorous hard-SF extrapolations to playful postmodern allusions. This has often placed a heavy burden on individual texts and authors, requiring them to stand in for large bodies of work, so we have tried to point to additional titles wherever possible, including the interpolated text boxes and the 'Guide to further reading'.

Following an introduction that explains our understanding of SF as an ongoing process rather than a fixed entity, this book is organised chronologically to demonstrate the ways in which SF changed over time as new writers and styles became – or failed to become – part of the genre, and as others faded in significance. We trace the separation of SF from a broader fantastic literature and the simultaneous formation of neighbouring genres, such as fantasy and horror; and how these never entirely convincing distinctions have shifted over time, to the point that some critics now consider them to be dissolving. Because the careers of many of the figures we discuss span several decades, we have often focused on their work in a single specific period, when their influence was most strongly felt or their fiction offered particular insights into broader cultural contexts. One of the peculiarities of publication in the US magazine and paperback tradition of SF is that many stories originally published in magazines were later republished in books, often significantly revised and expanded and frequently without any indication of the changes that had been made. We have elected to discuss such texts in the decade in which the original version was published, giving the original publication details and noting when novels or linked stories have later appeared in book form; this also serves to indicate the influence of certain magazines in specific periods and of patterns of publication in keeping certain authors and texts in circulation. (However, to minimise potential clutter we have not included titles of anthologies or collections in which certain stories first appeared; such information is easily available through internet resources such as *The Internet Speculative Fiction Database* (http://www.isfdb.org).)

The nature and identity of SF has been struggled over and formed through negotiations among writers, publishers, fans, editors, producers, directors and other actants – a process that is perpetually ongoing. This means that there are many science fictions, requiring our account to negotiate between scholarly rigour and personal taste. This is neither the book we would have written five years ago, nor the one we would write five years from now; nor is it a history that either of us could have written individually. Indeed, collaborating on this project has reinforced for us the extent to which our own sense of the genre is formed by ongoing negotiations. This book is, then, a self-consciously *partial* history of SF, discussing numerous trends and representative texts, but still barely scratching the surface of a lively, vast and constantly developing genre.

We would like to thank Melissa Conway and the staff of the J. Lloyd Eaton Collection at the University of California at Riverside, and Lorna Toolis and the staff of the Merril Collection at the Toronto Public Library for their assistance with early pulps and fanzines. We would also like to thank Stephanie Oliver for research assistance, Rob Latham and Roger Luckhurst for prompt responses to last minute questions and Michael Levy, Kevin Maroney and Farah Mendlesohn for commenting on a draft of the manuscript on very short notice. Effusive thanks to Lisa LaFramboise for editorial rigour, which always makes published books better than submitted manuscripts. Completing this book would have been impossible without the semester of research leave we received from, respectively, the University of the West of England and Brock University. Nor would it have been possible without John, Christian and Billy, who gave us principles, purpose and persistence; or Taye, who taught us that although the days are the same, different things happen.

1 Problems of definition

Overview

Genres are best thought of as ongoing processes of negotiation rather than fixed entities that pre-exist their naming. Science fiction (SF) is no exception. Although the term 'science fiction' was not used until the 1930s, texts containing elements that are now synonymous with SF were in circulation long before then. There are a number of competing versions of the 'true' origin of SF: fan communities have tended to privilege the tradition that developed in American pulp magazines, while others have sought its origins in a longer and more canonical literary history. Within SF studies, Darko Suvin's description of SF as the 'literature of cognitive estrangement' (1979: 4) has been particularly influential, moving definitional debates away from a focus on plot, setting and icons and towards formal characteristics and the political potential of the genre to imagine the world otherwise.

The emergence of SF

What is science fiction? A weird, popular genre full of spaceships, laser guns, robots and bug-eyed monsters? Fiction concerned with the impact of science and technology on human social life, and thus the literature best suited to understanding the contemporary world? A marketing category to be avoided if a text is to be treated as 'real' literature? The answer is in fact far more complex. Indeed, this book is premised on the idea that there is no such *thing* as SF, but instead multiple and constantly shifting ways of producing, marketing, distributing, consuming and understanding texts as SF. The experience of a text shifts in various ways once it is labelled as being, or not being, SF; and different features of the text will dominate in relation to the reader's social and historical position. This is why so many words continue to be expended – in editorials, letters pages, fanzines, blogs, academic books and journals – in debates about which works should be included in or excluded from, are central or marginal to, SF.

The term 'Science-Fiction' was first used by William Wilson in 1851, but its entry into common usage is usually attributed to Hugo Gernsback. By 1916, he had coined the term 'scientifiction', which he later used to describe the content of the first SF pulp magazine, *Amazing Stories*, launched in April 1926. After being forced into bankruptcy and losing control of *Amazing* in 1929, he used 'science fiction' to describe the stories published in the rival magazines he established. Opinions are still divided as to whether he should be regarded as the 'real "Father of Science Fiction"' (Moskowitz 1963: 242) or 'one of the worst disasters ever to hit the science fiction field' (Aldiss 1975: 237), but as an editor he played an undeniable role in enabling SF to be perceived as a distinct genre. However, it is equally clear that fiction that is at least *like* SF existed prior to *Amazing*, including stories published in other American fiction magazines, such as *Argosy* and *Weird Tales*, and Gernsback's radio hobbyist and popular science magazines. Such fiction could only retrospectively become SF once the idea of the genre was established, while the idea of the genre could only come into being because such fiction existed. The sense that SF is, or must be, something far larger than the American magazine and paperback tradition has tempted many to try to identify an earlier point of origin, the most successful in gaining adherents being the publication of Mary Shelley's *Frankenstein* (1818). Adam Roberts (2006) contends that SF can be traced back to Ancient Greece, while Roger Luckhurst (2005) argues that it could only emerge in relation to the technological changes and mass literacy of the late-nineteenth century.

Rick Altman (1999) argues that genres are not objects that exist in the world and are then studied by critics, but fluid and tenuous constructions made by the interaction of various claims and practices. They come into being 'after the fact', as writers, producers, fans, critics and other discursive and material actants select and emphasise certain elements of various texts and connect them to similar features in other texts. If this process succeeds, the genre will eventually be recognised as such by a larger group of actants. One of the key forces in the creation of a genre is the cultural industries' drive to reproduce in new cultural products those characteristics that they consider to be responsible for the financial success of earlier cultural products, thus creating a market for similar products. Writing about film, Altman notes that while critics have an interest in discussing and promoting these qualities in the language of genre, producers are generally divided between those with small budgets, who will often promote their films in terms of genre, and those with big budgets, who will typically downplay genre and emphasise other features (e.g. stars, auteurs, spectacle, controversy, pre-sold titles) so as to attract the broadest possible audience. This logic underpins producer Ronald D. Moore's claim, reiterated throughout the run of *Battlestar Galactica* (2003–2009), that it was not SF but a drama that just happened to take place in an SF context. Confident that the series would find a genre audience, he intended this description to appeal to viewers of 'quality' drama series such as *The Wire* (2002–2008) and thus expand the overall audience. Parallels can be found in the ways in which different SF books solicit different SF and/or non-SF readerships through design, cover art and jacket blurbs.

The creation of SF as a distinct marketing category took place in *Amazing Stories*, its spin-offs (*Amazing Stories Annual* (1927), *Amazing Stories Quarterly* (1928–1934)) and the SF pulps that followed. In 1929, Gernsback launched *Science Wonder Stories* and *Air Wonder Stories* (which merged as *Wonder Stories* in 1930 and, renamed *Thrilling Wonder Stories*, ran until 1955) and *Science Wonder Quarterly* (which, renamed *Wonder Stories Quarterly*, ran until 1933). In 1930, he launched *Scientific Detective Monthly* (renamed *Amazing Detective Tales*, it did not survive the year). Early competition came from *Astounding Stories of Superscience* (1930–), *Miracle Science and Fantasy Stories* (1931) and *Strange Tales of Mystery and Terror* (1931–1933). As the brief existences of some of these magazines and the various title changes and mergers indicate, the possibility of the genre was beginning to coalesce as both a cultural and economic resource. Simultaneously, the failure of *Air Wonder* and *Scientific Detective* suggests an emerging sense of demarcation between this new genre and the existing markets for aviation and detective pulps, or that Gernback was too hasty in trying to foster sub-generic tastes within a genre – and for a readership – which had not yet clearly emerged.

However, by the time John W. Campbell, Jr assumed the editorship of *Astounding Stories* in 1937, a readership prepared to seek out and read SF did exist. Campbell acknowledged this, renaming the magazine *Astounding Science-Fiction*. Along with the other changes he introduced (sober cover art, popular science articles, a new stable of authors), this was also part of a strategy to differentiate *Astounding* from aspects of its own history, other SF magazines and the juvenile image of pulp SF, and to define a specific space for *Astounding* within the niche market for SF. *Astounding* became an especially influential discursive and material actant, shaping US magazine SF – and our understanding of all SF – in particular ways. By emphasising certain types of story, it affected the kinds of stories that were written, and many of the stories it rejected were published in other pulps. When anthologies of magazine SF, such as Groff Conklin's *The Best of Science Fiction* (1946) and Raymond J. Healy and J. Francis McComas' *Adventures in Time and Space* (1946), began to appear, they privileged reprints from *Astounding*, perpetuating its influence. Thus Campbell's idea of SF was able to construct a model of the genre that placed certain authors, texts and a specific national tradition at its core, while marginalising or excluding others. However, this model was never monolithic, nor its hegemony absolute. Certain authors and readers found it conducive, others restrictive, and its authoritativeness waned along with Campbell's direct influence over US magazine SF from the 1950s onwards.

The critical reception of SF – by readers, fans, editors and reviewers, as well as academics – has often been preoccupied with the same kind of border policing, trying to fix SF as one clearly defined *thing*. This can be seen, for example, in two of the critical works that were most influential on the emergence of SF as an academic discipline: Brian Aldiss' *Billion Year Spree* (1973) and Darko Suvin's *Metamorphoses of Science Fiction* (1979). Both authors faced the same problem: should one delineate the history of the genre so as to know which texts to theorise about, or theorise the genre so as to establish which texts it should include? Aldiss adopted the former approach, insisting that 'no true understanding of science fiction is possible until its origin and development are understood' (1975: 2), and Suvin the latter, contending that 'no field of studies and rational inquiry can be investigated unless and until it is at least roughly delimited' (1979: 16). Yet, as both clearly knew, the actual process is rather more complex, with texts and theory continually and mutually shaping each other. Their stated positions instead reveal their different investments in discussing SF. Both were concerned with promoting versions of SF which extend far beyond the US magazine and paperback tradition, much of which they considered to be a commercially debased form of the genre. Aldiss, an author, sought to recover SF from a narrow concern with technology by locating its origins in gothic fiction, by giving respectable literary figures a more central position and by casting the US magazine and paperback tradition as an aberration that was coming to an end with his generation of writers. Suvin, a Marxist academic, was predominately interested in developing an intellectually rigorous taxonomy which would position texts conducive to particular social and political aims at the core of SF. Significantly, both Aldiss and Suvin struggle against their own models of SF as much as they promote them. For example, Aldiss devotes considerable time to works he does not consider quite to be SF, claiming that Jonathan Swift's *Gulliver's Travels* (1726) is so masterful that 'if it did so count, then perfection would have been achieved straightaway, and the genre possibly concluded as soon as it had begun' (1975: 81). Suvin insists that genres exist as 'socioaesthetic and not metaphysical entities' with a 'dialectical permeability to themes, attitudes, and paradigms from other literary genres, science, philosophy, and everyday socioeconomic life' (1979: 16), but his view of 'real' SF is far more purified than this implies. Both also expend a lot of energy dismissing works that are commonly considered to be SF, and thus constantly struggle against definitions of the genre that were actively circulating.

Enrolling SF

Most definitions of SF include some notion of the genre's relationship to science, although the nature of this relationship is also debated. Moreover, 'science' itself is subject to competing definitions: some expand its meaning to encompass all ways of generating rigorous knowledge about the material world; others narrow it to a specific kind of knowledge gained through the positivist scientific method of experiment and 'objective' observation formulated in the seventeenth century. Following the publication of Thomas Kuhn's *The Structure of Scientific Revolutions* (1962), which argued that science does not develop through the steady accumulation of facts but through paradigm shifts determined by social and cultural contexts, struggles over what properly constitutes science have become as complex and contentious as those about 'real' SF. This book's account of the history of SF builds upon the work of Bruno Latour – a major figure in Science Studies – who argues that the relationships between the practice of science and the larger social world are complex and reciprocal. He considers the separation of science from the social world, politics from nature, subjects from objects, humans from non-humans and the linguistic from the material to be both erroneous and damaging. Instead, he understands science and politics in terms of shifting, rhizomatic networks of connection and the building of collectives.

Latour explores the ways in which the practices of scientific collection and experimentation transform the concrete into the abstract. Each stage of the process that translates the heterogeneous world of things into systems of signification, 'allow[s] new translations and articulations while keeping some relations intact' (1999: 54). Latour also uses 'translation' to describe how a project 'takes on reality, or loses it, by degrees' (1996: 85) through 'enrolling' various 'actants' (including machines, money, politics and 'natural' objects) into its own goals. The 'feasible' project is not the one based on the most 'true' science but rather the one best able to form a rhizomatic network of connections with other human and non-human actants. Latour offers a detailed illustration of this argument in *Aramis* (1993), which is simultaneously a novel about the development of the eponymous Parisian public transport system and a theoretical analysis of the failure of this real-world project. It demonstrates how what Aramis 'is' shifts over the course of its 'life' depending upon the connections with other actants that it develops, maintains or loses. This process of translation requires negotiation and compromise, at times reshaping the project so that other, required actants will see their own goals in it. Similarly, we are interested in how SF has come to 'life' and been translated and transformed as it moves across different media and into different contexts of circulation, incorporating or excluding actants, and how it became an actant to be enrolled in other projects.

In 1952, Damon Knight said that SF 'means what we point to when we say it' (1967: 1). While this might seem to recognise that any discursive actant can point and define SF, it also implies that a consensus – 'we' – already exists, and solicits our enrolment into its vision of the genre. Definitions, however, are always contingent and ideological. There is no such thing as a 'neutral' or 'objective' definition of the genre because the very features of what is named as SF emerge in the process of pointing and naming. Various actants have competing investments in what they want the genre to be, aimed at different ends, and all histories of the genre inevitably privilege some texts and marginalise or exclude others. Although such processes of selection are unavoidable, we are more concerned with producing a history that enables a better understanding of the ways in which SF exists as a fuzzily-edged, multidimensional and constantly shifting discursive object. Consequently, our history will involve familiar and unfamiliar, typical and exemplary, texts. Some will have long been considered central to the genre while some will have gained or lost their putative centrality over time. Others will seem central or marginal depending on the perspective from which they are examined. In constructing and recounting this history, we will foreground the multiplicity of SF and its embeddedness in the wider social world.

Competing histories and definitions

The rest of this chapter will contrast two types of history of SF, the second of which emerged alongside the development of the academic study of SF in the 1970s. The first sees the genre as originating in 1920s American pulps. It emphasises the role of Gernsback as editor, publisher and proponent of the new genre, and argues for the importance of the fans who came to know one another through the letters columns in SF magazines, and through the fanzines they published and the clubs and conventions they organised and attended. Gernsback and other editors actively encouraged the development of fandom, and many prominent writers – Isaac Asimov, Ray Bradbury, Damon Knight, C.M. Kornbluth, Judith Merril, Frederik Pohl and Jack Williamson among others – emerged from this milieu.

A key document in this version of the history of SF is 'A New Sort of Magazine', Gernsback's editorial in *Amazing*'s first issue, which claims that, among 'hundreds' of magazines containing the 'usual fiction', *Amazing* would be 'entirely new – entirely different', a 'pioneer' that 'deserves your attention and interest': a 'magazine of "Scientifiction"' (1926: 3). He defines scientifiction as 'the Jules Verne, H.G. Wells, and Edgar Allan Poe type of story – a charming romance intermingled with scientific fact and prophetic vision' (3) that will 'supply knowledge' in 'a very palatable form' (3). With the 'ever increasing demands ... for this sort of story' from readers of his popular science and engineering magazines, he saw that 'there was only one thing to do – publish a magazine in which the scientific fiction type of story will hold forth exclusively' (3).

In these statements, Gernsback enrols Poe, Verne and Wells into his new genre project, thus appealing to readers familiar with their fiction, as well as the existing readership of his *Science and Invention* and *Radio News*. Through such enrolments, and the related evocation of culturally approved ideologies of education, autodidacticism and entrepreneurialism, he seeks to accrue a degree of literary, intellectual and moral respectability to his pulp endeavour, even as he promises novelty, inspiration, instruction and palatability in the 'amazing' and 'fantastic' fiction of 'the new romancers' (3). He also connects the commodity he is promoting with the idea of progress itself. Arguing that SF stories were impossible 200 years previously, he notes the accelerating pace of technological innovation and its impact on daily life, before casting Poe, Verne and Wells as 'real prophets' whose fictional prophecies have been and are being 'realized' (3). Manipulating timeframes, he reaches out with evangelical zeal to enrol any willing participant in this supposedly inevitable future: 'New inventions pictured for us in the scientifiction of today are not at all impossible of realization tomorrow. Many great science stories destined to be of an historical interest are still to be written, and AMAZING STORIES magazine will be the medium through which such stories will come to you. Posterity will point to them as having blazed a new trail, not only in literature and fiction, but in progress as well' (3).

Poe, Verne and Wells all wrote different kinds of fiction and have little that is obviously in common with each other. Therefore, one must ask which features of their fiction Gernsback had to emphasise, and which he suppressed or omitted, in order to describe it as a 'type'. Some clues might be found in considering which of their stories he reprinted, and in the way he articulated them towards the reader through editorials, story blurbs and so on. However various contingencies governed the selection and appearance of particular stories, the ways in which different readers understood or made use of the stories and Gernsback's pronouncements about them cannot be recovered, and whatever might have seemed self-evident about the nature of these stories or the connections between them is

Gernsback's Poe reprints (in order of republication)

'The Facts in the Case of M. Valdemar' (1845)

'Mesmeric Revelation' (1844)

'The Sphinx' (1846)

'The Balloon-Hoax' (1844)

'Von Kempelen and His Discovery' (1849)

'The Thousand-and-Second Tale of Scheherazade' (1845)

also irretrievable some 80 years later. Furthermore, regardless of Gernsback's relative position of power as a discursive and material actant in the late 1920s and early 1930s, he was – and continues posthumously to be – just one of many involved in the complex and constantly unfolding array of negotiations, compromises, orientations and reorientations about SF. With this in mind, and before turning to the second kind of SF history, we will offer an account of Poe, Verne and Wells that could be used to enrol them into SF.

Edgar Allan Poe

Often considered a key figure in the development of horror fiction, with stories such as 'The Black Cat' (1841) and 'The Tell-Tale Heart' (1843), and of detective fiction, with 'The Murders in the Rue Morgue' (1841), 'The Mystery of Marie Rogêt' (1842–1843) and 'The Purloined Letter' (1844), Poe is generally understood as a romantic or gothic writer, working in a tradition that is often preoccupied with the experience of the sublime. Definitions of the sublime all refer in some way to a quality of vast magnitude or an experience beyond description or calculation. Analysing the effect of certain perceptions on the observer, Edmund Burke contrasted the beautiful, which is aesthetically pleasing and pleasurable, to the sublime, in which the sense of being overwhelmed produces terror and awe, but also a kind of fascinated pleasure. Immanuel Kant argued that this terror or awe arose from the failure of one's senses and imagination to grasp the enormity of a sublime phenomenon; however, when one realises that it is beyond comprehension, it can be placed within a conceptual category, making it less threatening and producing a pleasurable discharge of tension. In the romantic tradition, the sublime often functions as a figure for the new universe being discovered by the scientific revolution: a material realm of incomprehensible vastness and complexity, with great depths of archaeological and geological time, reaching back through history to a much larger prehistory before the evolution of humankind, and positing a similarly post-historic future after humankind. Magazine and paperback SF generally privileges masterful cognition over awe, exploring and explaining sublime phenomena, and relegates prolonged, untamed encounters with the sublime to horror or weird fiction.

Poe's SF stories obsessively return to the sublime encounter, developing numerous strategies for articulating and containing it. For example, 'MS. Found in a Bottle' (1831) begins with a voyage from Java to the Sunda Islands – undertaken by the jaded, unimaginative narrator for no reason other than his 'nervous restlessness' (1976c: 1) – that quickly becomes uncanny as a storm drives the ship further and further southwards for days on end. Daylight disappears. The ship is surrounded by 'thick gloom, and a black sweltering desert of ebony' (4). It is thrown from waves 'elevat[ed] beyond the albatross' into the abyssal troughs between them. Suddenly, 'a gigantic ship' appears at a 'terrific height above [them], and upon the very verge of the precipitous descent' (5). The collision throws the narrator aboard this mysterious vessel, where he hides from the crew until he discovers that these 'incomprehensible men' (7) cannot see him. The ship seems ancient in its size, simplicity, infirm crew and the 'worm-eaten condition' of its peculiarly porous, 'distended' timbers (8). The narrator experiences 'indistinct shadows of recollection' mixed up with 'an unaccountable memory of old foreign chronicles and ages long ago' (8), but can gain no rational purchase on the situation, 'surely doomed to hover continually upon the brink of Eternity, without taking a final plunge into the abyss' (9). Cognition fails. The manuscript – already fragmented by a series of breaks in the text as the narrator, suspended in this foreshadowing of a greater sublime, cannot continue undisturbed – terminates in the moment before the sublime encounter as the ship plunges into 'the grasp of the whirlpool ... amid a roaring, and bellowing, and thundering of ocean and of tempest' (11). Poe thus leaves the sublime intact, as something that cannot be directly conceived by the human mind nor described by language.

Other stories strive to create a perspective from which the sublime can be described. In order to recount the destruction of the Earth by a comet, 'The Conversation of Eiros and Charmion' (1839) presents a dialogue between spirits of the dead. 'A Descent into the Maelström' (1841) develops a more complex twinned vertical arrangement of space and narrative so as to produce a position from which the sublime can be mastered. It begins at 'the summit of the loftiest crag' (1976a: 72), where the narrator can safely look down onto a sea 'lashed into ungovernable fury' and 'phrensied convulsion' by a current of 'monstrous velocity' (74) that ultimately produces a whirlpool 'more than half a mile in diameter' (75). His guide tells of how he and his brother once were caught in this maelström, and how through observation and reason he was able to escape it, while his brother was swept down and consumed by the vortex. Touched by this encounter with the sublime, the guide's hair, 'which had been raven-black the day before', turned white and the friends who pulled him from the sea knew him 'no more than they would have known a traveller from the spirit-land' (88). The guide's evocation of folktales and his statement that he does not expect to be believed further dissipates the sublime, which has already been doubly contained by the spatially and narratively secure perspective from which the narrator obtains his glimpse into the abyss.

A proliferation of such framings and deflections, along with shifting discursive modes, more or less eradicates any sense of the sublime from Poe's account of a lunar voyage in 'The Unparalleled Adventure of One Hans Pfaall' (1835). It begins with the ingenuous narrator's description of an alien visitation. A strange balloon occupied by an even stranger figure descends upon the peculiar town of Rotterdam and its comical, bumbling inhabitants. This emissary from the Moon – two foot tall and of 'a rotundity highly absurd', he has 'enormously large' hands and a 'prodigiously long, crooked and inflammatory nose' (1976d: 14) – delivers a letter to the mayor from Hans Pfaall, who disappeared five years previously. The tone shifts abruptly with the letter, which first outlines Pfaall's descent into poverty and desperation, and then his scheme to build a balloon to take him to the Moon. As this endeavour proceeds, more and more of the letter is taken up with scientific detail concerning observations, calculations and the testing of hypotheses, until he lands on the Moon. However, his account stops there. It hints at adventures and discoveries yet to be related, and even invokes the lunar satire (in which lunar social arrangements critically reflect upon terrestrial ones) that one might expect such a narrative to become, but it refuses these possibilities, ending instead with Pfaall's request for a pardon for murdering his creditors on departing the Earth. The story concludes with an overview of public opinion concerning the letter, offering five 'facts' that undermine the veracity of Pfaall's claims. In 1840, Poe appended a lengthy note to distinguish 'Hans Pfaall' from lunar satires, eutopias and Richard Adams Locke's *The Moon Hoax* (1835) on the grounds that they are 'utterly uninformed in respect to astronomy' and make 'no effort at *plausibility* in the details of the voyage itself', whereas he attempts '*verisimilitude*' through applying 'scientific principles' (64).

Poe's drive to concoct fictions that draw on scientific knowledge and to valorise his imaginings through the charismatic authority of scientific data is even more apparent in 'The Thousand-and-Second Tale of Scheherazade' (1850). Scheherazade, having successfully evaded the death penalty, tells her sister of the further adventures of Sinbad, to which Poe appends three dozen footnotes to explain the phenomena Sinbad encounters but does not understand, ranging from petrified forests and eyeless fish to automata, batteries and telegraphy, culminating in a short disquisition on some implications of the speed of light. Other stories, such as 'The Balloon-Hoax' (1844) and 'Von Kempelen and His Discovery' (1849), demonstrate greater sophistication in incorporating such paratextual information, replacing scholarly paraphernalia with a narrative voice that smoothly blends conventional techniques of verisimilitude with the charismatic authority of technical terms and precise measurements so as better to privilege cognition over affect, pleasure over awe. In this vein, 'The Facts in the Case of M. Valdemar' (1845) poses as a corrective to the 'garbled' and 'exaggerated account' of a particular medical case that 'all parties concerned' had desired to 'keep ... from the public', in place of which the narrator will present 'the *facts*' (1976b: 194). At the moment of his death, Valdemar was put into a mesmeric trance and continued to exist in a state suspended between life and death for seven months until the narrator brought him out of the trance, at which point Valdemar, who knew he was dead, pleaded to be either put back to sleep or woken. The discombobulated narrator acts too slowly, and so Valdemar's 'whole frame at once – within the space of a single minute, or even less, shrunk – crumbled – absolutely *rotted* away' (203). In the nineteenth century, mesmerism occupied an uncertain cultural position, hovering between science, magic, superstition and charlatanism, and debates about its status can be seen as a discursive struggle over the limits and definition of science. Poe's story contributed to this debate, not least through its success in persuading many readers of its veracity. An unintentional hoax, it maintains verisimilitude and plausibility through intermingling everyday, pseudo-scholarly and scientific-sounding detail, through the sometimes hesitant persona of the narrator (only an amateur experimenter, he gives the facts 'as far as I comprehend them myself' (194)) and through the authority giving effect of scientific terminology (the diagnosis of Valdemar's illness contains details impossible for contemporary medicine to have identified in a living patient, which Poe probably gleaned from post-mortem reports). Yet, even in this most cognitive of tales, the sublime persists. Valdemar can transmit no report from the realm beyond the rational upon whose threshold he has been forced to linger; and the story ends not with reason but 'a nearly liquid mass of loathsome – of detestable putridity' (203).

Jules Verne

In Verne's fiction, there is an even more pronounced tendency to elaborate narratives from scientific data and to derive verisimilitude from writing in a scientific register. An admirer of Poe, Verne frequently 'restates, rewrites or recycles knowledge gleaned in the scientific, geographical and historical reviews of the day, and his narrative style is almost instantly recognizable by its long digressions designed to instruct, to enlighten or to initiate' (Unwin 2000: 46); scholarly editions documenting these unacknowledged borrowings further 'authenticate' his use of such material. Despite Verne's dependence on the persuasiveness of scientific discourse, he became increasingly sceptical of charismatic authority. His protagonists often accompany scientists or explorers in whom such authority resides. In *From the Earth to the Moon* (1865), Impey Barbicane, the driving force behind the lunar mission, is admired because he 'overcame every obstacle, saw no difficulties, was never befuddled. He was miner, mason, mechanic as well as artillerist, with answers for all questions, solutions for all problems' (1978: 78). In *Twenty Thousand Leagues under the Seas* (1869), Aronnax and Conseil display an encyclopaedic knowledge of marine biology, transforming seemingly monstrous beings into natural fauna, but their erudition pales beside that of the anti-imperialist Captain Nemo, whose technological mastery outstrips that of nations. *The Begum's Millions* (1879) divides this compelling, contradictory figure in two – Professor Schultze, who uses his knowledge and resources to develop technologies of military imperialism, and Dr Sarrasin, who seeks to build a just and healthy society – so as better to present the threat he poses, as well as the promise.

In contrast to Poe, whose fiction oscillates between awe/terror and calculation/ control, Verne privileges the cognitive faculty that safely contains the experience of the sublime. He is committed to a version of the universe in which everything can be mapped, catalogued and known if only we persevere in scientific investigation. His work charts and masters space, whether terrestrial realms (*Around the*

Gernsback's Verne reprints (in order of republication)

Hector Servadac (1877)

A Journey to the Centre of the Earth (1864)

'Doctor Ox's Experiment' (1872)

Topsy-Turvy (1889)

'A Voyage in a Balloon' (1851)

Robur the Conqueror (1886)

Master of the World (1904)

The Adventures of Captain Hatteras (1864–1866)

World in Eighty Days (1872), *The Golden Volcano* (1906)) or unknown ones that another writer might present as uncanny: no posthumous apparatus is necessary to narrate the adventures of those swept off on a comet in *Hector Servadac* (1877), nor does *A Journey to the Centre of the Earth* (1871) falter on the brink of a sublime abyss. Instead, Verne carefully details his characters' scientific, techno-logical and cartographic advances as processes, recounting each step (including the false starts) by which a breakthrough is achieved, and relentlessly recording precise measurements of time, distance, temperature, altitude and other grid-like parameters of the physical environment.

Gernsback and Verne

When considering Gernsback's enrolment of Verne, one must negoti-ate among several Vernes. The Verne available to generations of Anglophone readers was significantly different from the Verne of French readers. Translation inevitably alters nuance and connotation, but translations of Verne were often poor and incomplete, with charac-ters' names and national origins sometimes altered and many pas-sages of distinctive detail cut because they distracted from the narrative. The translations Gernsback reprinted were of this sort, and it is impossible to determine the extent to which this shaped his under-standing of Verne and thus his idea of SF. Would he have preferred better and fuller translations? Did the poverty of available translations modify, or require him to modify, his idea of SF? How did his readers, including many who went on to become writers and editors, respond to and negotiate with the model of SF provided by these translations? While Verne has been quite successfully enrolled into French literature, especially since the 1960s, new and unabridged translations of his work are only now improving his status among Anglophone readers.

Despite Verne's emphasis on cognitive mastery, moments of the sublime do erupt (and are made all the more apparent in abridged translations). In *A Journey to the Centre of the Earth*, Professor Lidenbrock and his nephew, Axel, discover a coded text that suggests there is a route to the centre of the Earth. Much of the ensuing novel is taken up with Vernean detail. Considerable effort is expended upon deciphering the found text, and during the journey painstaking records are kept of the distance travelled, both horizontally and vertically. As they proceed, Lidenbrock explains the assumptions he is testing or refuting, with Axel as his audience; and when Axel despairs over the difficulties they face – they run out of water, encounter potentially dangerous creatures, find their path blocked – Lidenbrock demonstrates that the use of reason and scientific method can overcome them. The failure of some theories to hold true does not undermine the authority of science because, as Lidenbrock contends, 'science is eminently perfectible', with 'each existing theory ... constantly replaced by a new one' (1992: 30), and is 'composed of errors, but errors that it is right to make, for they lead step by step to the truth' (146). His positivism reaches its fullest expression when he announces to the protesting Axel, 'Enough. When science has spoken, one can only remain silent thereafter!' (75). When their downward passage comes to an end, and they must content themselves with the discovery of an interior sea and thriving creatures previously believed to be extinct, including an early hominid, Axel says, 'we can't regret coming this far. The spectacle is magnificent', but Lidenbrock replies that 'Seeing is not the question. I set myself an objective and I mean to attain it. So don't talk to me about admiring!' (155).

However, the novel is more complex than this opposition suggests. Perhaps most telling is the contrast between the explorers' precise and careful progress into the Earth and their precipitous exit on a wave of lava. They do not plan to provoke the eruption, but accidentally trigger it when they attempt to explode a rock obstructing their descent. The world and its capacity to surprise and overwhelm exceeds the command of scientific authority: Axel tells us, 'from that moment on, our reason, our judgement, our ingenuity were to have no influence at all on events: we were to become the mere playthings of the Earth' (195). While Lidenbrock refuses to countenance the sublime, Axel insistently pushes the novel in that direction, although a scientific vocabulary limits its effect. For example, Axel has a vision, prompted by the 'fantastic hypotheses of palaeontology' (152), in which he witnesses evolution unfolding backwards, moving through successive generations of creatures to experience a time 'before man was born, when the incomplete Earth was not yet ready for him' (153). Initially, the use of Linnaean categories successfully contains the awe evoked by this vision, but at its end Axel – and Verne – surrenders to the overwhelming affect of the moment as his 'body is being subtilized, subliming in turn and commingling like an imponderable atom with these immense clouds, which inscribe their fiery orbit on infinite space!' (153). Axel is woken from his reverie, and Lidenbrock's announcement that 'we are flying along and unless my calculations are out, we shall soon land' (154) returns him abruptly to the orderly world of measurement and navigation. Similar transitions are found elsewhere in the text: 'surprised, stupefied, horrified' (158) at the sight of a herd of sea-monsters, Lidenbrock reassures his companions that it is only a fight between an ichthyosaurus and a plesiosaurus uninterested in them; later, they find 'an immense cemetery, where the generations of 2000 years mingled their eternal dust', which includes a human skull, but the initial 'awe' and 'trembling voice' (178) prompted by this discovery is safely contained by devoting the whole subsequent chapter to an outline of contemporary palaeontology's understanding of human evolution.

Thus, Verne favours only one of Poe's strategies for addressing the sublime, framing and containing it through the authority of scientific detail and language. At the same time, however, Verne's desire to map the world reveals a persistent anxiety about those things that exceed the possibility of being mapped. Although Verne acknowledged Poe as an influence, perhaps validating Gernsback's enrolment of their fiction into a 'type of story', such differences in their work defy the imposition of a singular identity. Moreover, Verne saw himself as involved in a quite different project to that of his nearer contemporary, Wells, insisting in an interview that

> I have always made a point ... of basing my so-called inventions upon a groundwork of actual fact, and of using in. their construction methods and materials which are not entirely without the pale of contemporary engineering skill and knowledge.
>
> (Jones 1904: 670)

Wells' inventions, Verne argued, 'belong unreservedly to an age and degree of scientific knowledge far removed from the present' and are derived 'entirely from the realm of imagination' (670) Wells' failure to outline the methods of their construction leaves the reader without 'the slightest clue' as to how 'our present scientific knowledge' could provide 'a method by which such a result might be achieved' (670).

H.G. Wells

Verne's comparison of himself and Wells is not inaccurate, but his criticism of Wells' refusal to imagine or explicate a scientifically plausible means of propelling the spaceship in *The First Men in the Moon* (1901) tells us much about Verne – not least his concern with modernity and the late-nineteenth-century period of rapid globalisation – while failing to comprehend Wells' broader and more inclusive understanding of science. Wells' speculations and conceits are frequently derived from, or validated by, science, especially evolutionary theory, but he is more often concerned with social than technological transformations. He draws less frequently and less obviously on contemporary scientific and technological data, and tends to incorporate scientific discourse as one of several idioms of verisimilitude. By engaging with the social implications of scientific and technological advances, *The First Men in the Moon* self-consciously modernises the tradition of lunar satire and of other eutopian and satirical texts, which that delineate the social and political structures of imagined realms so as to critique the author's own society, such as *Gulliver's Travels* and Thomas More's *Utopia* (1516). While the insectile inhabitants of Wells' Moon demonstrate his ongoing interest in evolutionary science, frequently expressed through the emergence of a species that threatens human dominance, their hive-like social organisation satirises capitalist-industrial modernity's alienating systems of massification and hierarchies of specialisation.

Rather than focusing on the interpolation of scientific data, on detailing the natural world or the workings of inventions, Wells directs his speculative and narrative energies towards thinking through how such knowledge and innovations are

Gernsback's Wells reprints (in order of republication)

'The New Accelerator' (1901)

'The Crystal Egg' (1897)

'The Star' (1897)

'The Man Who Could Work Miracles' (1898)

'The Empire of the Ants' (1905)

'In the Abyss' (1896)

The Island of Doctor Moreau (1896)

The First Men in the Moon (1901)

'Under the Knife' (1896)

'The Remarkable Case of Davidson's Eyes' (1895)

The Time Machine (1895)

'The Story of the Late Mr. Elvesham' (1896)

'The Plattner Story' (1896)

The War of the Worlds (1897)

'Æpyornis Island' (1894)

'A Story of the Stone Age' (1897)

'The Country of the Blind' (1904)

'The Stolen Body' (1898)

'Pollock and the Porroh Man' (1895)

'The Flowering of the Strange Orchid' (1894)

'A Story of the Days to Come' (1899)

The Invisible Man (1897)

'The Moth' (1895)

'The Lord of the Dynamos' (1894)

When the Sleeper Wakes (1899) in *Amazing Stories Quarterly*

'The Diamond Maker' (1894) in *Science Wonder Stories*

deployed and how they thereby restructure human social life. Such concerns are not absent from Verne – for example, *From the Earth to the Moon* satirises the affiliation between technological advances and brutal warfare, as well as the authoritarianism of Napoleon III's France and myths of American exceptionalism – but just as his satire is milder, so also his sense of consequences is more muted. For Wells, technological innovation is always also social innovation, and consequently his speculations are not enabled or constrained by the same repertoires of plausibility as either Poe or Verne. For example, Wells' *The War of the Worlds* (1898) focuses as much on late-Victorian society as on its SF elements. The narrator–protagonist establishes a framework of evolutionary competition between species and speculates upon aspects of Martian physiology and technology, but the majority of the novel is concerned with the effects of and responses to alien invasion. In the opening chapter, Wells looks to undermine human egocentricity, satirising in particular a colonising perspective in which 'men fancied there might be other men upon Mars, perhaps inferior to themselves and ready to welcome a missionary enterprise', while ominously hinting at 'intellects vast and cool and unsympathetic' who regard humans with no more concern than humans might possess for 'the transient creatures that swarm and multiply in a drop of water' (2002: 3). Humans are repeatedly imagined as finding themselves dethroned from the hierarchy of animal species, like the dodo blithely contemplating the arrival of the sailors who will make it extinct. Although the Martians are monstrous and frightening to the humans, the novel insists on the legitimacy of their actions from within their own frame of reference. They are not evil; they just have different priorities, and are all the more sinister for their apparent indifference to humankind. Wells makes no recourse to the scholarly footnote of Poe or the interpolated scientific text of Verne to buttress his depiction of this evolutionary conflict (although he does allude to his own science journalism), but he is clearly the one most committed to exploring the ramifications of contemporary science. He recognises that humans are not some set-apart species but biological animals among other animals, and thus are not immune to the processes of species emergence, evolution and extinction documented in the fossil record.

In such fiction as *The Time Machine* (1895), 'The Empire of the Ants' (1895) and *The Island of Doctor Moreau* (1896), Wells draws parallels between species-difference within the evolutionary system (which was often falsely perceived in terms of hierarchy) and class- and ethnic-difference within a capitalist, colonial system (which typically mapped a similar hierarchy onto classes and races). In *The War of the Worlds*, although Wells clearly intends a political critique of colonialism by depicting the heart of the British Empire as helpless in the face of a technologically advanced and brutal colonial power, the consequences of conflating the human exploitation of non-humans with colonisers exploitation of the colonised sometimes results in racist representations. For example:

And before we judge [the Martians] too harshly we must remember what ruthless and utter destruction our own species has wrought, not only upon animals such as the vanished bison and the dodo, but upon its own inferior races.

The Tasmanians, in spite of their human likeness, were entirely swept out of existence in a war of extermination waged by European immigrants in the space of fifty years.

(2002: 5)

Although Wells lacks Poe's willingness to surrender to the sublime, he is – in his early fiction and popular science articles, at least – far more likely than Verne to deliberately evoke it and to treat it as something encountered through the scientifically derived perception of humankind's relative insignificance in the vastness of space and time. Yet like Verne, he also utilises the authority of scientific discourse to conceptualise and thus to deflect the overwhelming feeling of awe. The Martian invaders provoke a sublime horror, but 'the first nausea' quickly subsides and the narrator finds himself able to describe these 'most unearthly creatures' (124). Since the narrative is told in retrospect, after the failure of the invasion, this passage is able to quash the potentially immersive experience of the narrator's helplessness and terror by drawing – overtly and at length – on information later obtained by dissecting dead Martians. Similarly, rather than describing the Martians' method of feeding on 'blood obtained from a still living animal, in most cases from a human being' (125), the narrator speculates upon the conditions shaping Martian evolution.

Wells' use of cognition to contain the sublime, however, is tempered by his complex attitude toward scientific and technological progress. The novel's conclusion focuses on how human society has been transformed by the invasion, moving uneasily between technocratic optimism and pessimistic deflation. If the Martians can travel to another planet,

there is no reason to suppose that the thing is impossible for men, and when the slow cooling of the sun makes this earth uninhabitable, as at last it must do, it may be that the thread of life that has begun here will have streamed out and caught our sister planet.

(181)

However, this inspiring possibility is countered by the narrator's recognition that 'the destruction of the Martians is only a reprieve. To them, and not to us, perhaps, is the future ordained' (182).

The literature of cognitive estrangement

Enrolment is a complicated process entailing unanticipated and unintended alliances as well as consciously chosen ones. Although one cannot say with certainty what Gernsback desired to achieve by invoking Poe, Verne and Wells, we have sought to foreground possible connections – and differences – among them that Gernsback may or may not have perceived and which continue to be sites of tension in debates about the nature of SF. For example, Gernsback's editorials are quite clear about wanting to publish – and thus construct SF as – popular fiction with a serious scientific and educative element, but in the fiction of his exemplary figures can be found the monstrous, the unrepresentable and the sublime. Their fiction is far more various, contradictory and excessive than histories and definitions which privilege the Gernsbackian moment might allow, and even if Gernsback did not intend to enrol such features, they play important roles in the fiction of Poe, Verne and Wells and thus exist for other writers to emulate and expand upon.

The dynamic between emphasis/suppression, inclusion/exclusion and centration/marginalisation is not unique to Gernsback's definition, nor are the processes of compromise and negotiation involved in filling the pages of *Amazing* and recruiting other actants to the project of scientifiction. This dynamic is evident, too, in the second type of history that starts by constructing a theoretical description of SF and usually treats the US magazine and paperback tradition as just one, perhaps insignificant, part of the genre. This approach is exemplified in Suvin's *Metamorphoses of Science Fiction*.

While many academics do not agree with Suvin – indeed, disagreeing with him is a considerable part of SF scholarship – he nonetheless set, to an extent, the terms by which SF has subsequently been studied. He argues that SF is a literature premised upon a radical discontinuity from the empirical world, but whose features are 'not impossible' (1979: viii). For him, SF is 'allied to the rise of subversive social classes' and opposed to the 'tendency toward mystifying escapism' (ix) found in fantasy and in religious visions of otherworldly fulfilment. Yet, Suvin faces a difficult challenge, since he sees the vast majority of what is commonly considered to be SF as 'perishable' (vii). Contrasting the inadequate 'empirical realities' of SF with the genre's far-more-promising 'historical potentialities' (viii), he seeks to enrol no more than 5 to 10 per cent of the magazine and paperback tradition into a new and longer history. Suvin is interested in a genre – which he decided also to call 'science fiction' – that, unlike realist fiction, takes 'a creative approach tending toward a dynamic transformation rather than towards a static mirroring of the author's environment', that is, 'not only a reflecting *of* but also *on* reality' (10). In short, Suvin's insistence that SF must have a critical relationship to the social world contemporary to its production defines the genre in terms not of specific textual features or content but of its ability to promote social change. Consequently, the magazine and paperback tradition is, for him, an aberrant, debased form of 'real' SF.

Suvin defines SF as 'the *literature of cognitive estrangement*' (4). This insistence upon retaining and transforming 'science fiction' rather than coining a new term to describe the kind of fiction in which he is interested indicates the extent to which he is engaged in a discursive struggle over enrolment. For Suvin, 'science' is something far broader than the positivist method of experimental inquiry and includes 'not only natural but also all the cultural or historical sciences and even scholarship' (13). This allies him more closely with Wells' speculative approach than with Poe or Verne. Indeed, he argues that Wells' *The Time Machine* (1895) provided one of the 'basic historical models for the structuring of subsequent SF' (222), but dismisses Verne (along with Gernsback) as promoting a limited technophilic vision that imitates 'real' SF but lacks its critical and socially transformative vision. Suvin, notoriously dismissive of fantasy, is equally suspicious of the narrow and pedantic attitude he finds in SF traditions that demand conformity to 'a "real possibility" – to that which is possible in the author's reality and/or according to the scientific paradigm of his culture' (66). He favours instead the more enabling 'ideal possibility', that is, 'any conceptual or thinkable possibility the premises and/or consequences of which are not internally contradictory' (66). 'Estrangement' also has a specific meaning for Suvin, derived from Russian formalist theory and from the theatrical praxis of Bertolt Brecht. According to Brecht, an estranging representation is 'one which allows us to recognize its subject, but at the same time makes it seem unfamiliar' (quoted in Suvin 1979: 6). For Suvin, this 'look of estrangement', which 'is both cognitive and creative' (6) and prompts a new understanding, is the crucial formal criterion of SF.

Suvin's other major contribution to a definition of SF is the idea, derived from Ernst Bloch, of the *novum*, 'the presence of which is logically necessary and which has to be hegemonic in a narration in order that we may call it an SF narration' (63). It is 'a totalizing phenomenon or relationship deviating from the author's and the implied reader's norm of reality' (64). The 'use of new technological gadgets' (70) in stories whose structure repeats the formula of the western or adventure tale is insufficient; rather, the *novum* must be 'so central and significant that it determines the whole narrative logic – or at least the overriding narrative logic – regardless of any impurities that might be present' (70). This requirement explains why Suvin rejects from the genre those stories that introduce novel technologies into futures in which current social relations remain intact, and thus much of the magazine and paperback tradition. However, Suvin's mention of 'impurities' reminds us that when one attempts to impose fixed ontological distinctions on the flux of the material world, one inevitably, and necessarily, produces hybrids. In a footnote, Suvin decries the folly of 'annexing any and every tale with a new gadget or psychic procedure into SF' because such a practice will lead to the inevitable conclusion that 'there is no such thing as SF' (70). Here, Suvin is clearly as invested as Gernsback in maintaining the category of 'SF', but pursues a rather different set of enrolments. The illustrious eutopians and satirists Suvin enrols into the genre (More, Swift, François Rabelais, Cyrano de Bergerac) demonstrate the extent to which he considers SF to be a means of social critique and political transformation rather than a source of prophetic visions and patent applications. Like Gernsback, he was successful – at least for a time – in enrolling other actants into his vision of the genre.

While Suvin is made anxious by the notion that there might be no such thing as SF, he is conscious of the fact that he is constructing an argument about SF rather than delineating an objective phenomenon. He suggests that the

> basic and possibly central task of SF theory and criticism at this historical moment is the construction of a heuristic model or models for 'Science Fiction' ... A heuristic model is a theoretical structure based on analogy, which does not claim to be transcendentally or illusionistically 'real' in the sense of mystically representing a palpable material entity, but whose use is scientifically and scholarly permissible, desireable, and necessary because of its practical results.
>
> (16–17)

As Suvin acknowledges, and as Latour argues, such a model enables new research questions to be formulated and prompts thinking in ways not previously possible, but at the same time, it limits our vision; and as new findings contradict its claims, and its possibilities are exhausted, so we must abandon it.

Over the last decade, many have claimed that SF is, in various ways, coming to an end, routinely plundered by blockbuster movies, prime-time television and 'literary' authors while at the same time mutually dissolving into fantasy and horror. Simultaneously, new generations and movements revel in blurring, splicing, sampling, dubbing and remixing these genres. The significance of such claims is, of course, that they are only possible because of the prior imposition of more-or-less rigid categories on a rather more fluid culture; and regardless of their accuracy or plausibility as descriptions of the current conjuncture, what they most reveal is the fact that the processes of enrolment and exclusion are active and ongoing, contradictory and never-ending. We hope in the following chapters to restore some sense of that contingent and irresolvable dynamism to the history of SF.

Conclusion

- Genres are the discursive product of enrolment processes undertaken by numerous actants with different, and at times conflicting, agendas. Consequently, there can be no single definition of SF.
- Some actants, following Gernsback's example, argue for SF's origins in more canonical literature than the pulps. They nominate, for example, More's *Utopia*, Swift's *Gulliver's Travels* or Shelley's *Frankenstein* as the genre's foundational text, and downplay or even dismiss the role of the magazines from which the genre got its name.
- Gernsback's *Amazing* initially promoted the work of Poe, Verne and Wells in an effort not merely to name the genre, but to construct it. This enrolment effort inevitably required a selective understanding of these authors.
- The influence of Suvin's definition has tended to reinforce a distinction between SF and fantasy that is not necessarily clear when one examines many texts widely regarded as 'SF'.

2 Science fictions before Gernsback

Overview

When Hugo Gernsback and others set about defining the 'new kind' of literature called SF, they often pointed to fiction that was already circulating under other rubrics. By considering some of these other kinds of fiction, not all of which have been equally or consistently enrolled into SF, it is possible to see which elements came to be identified with the new genre and which were marginalised or excluded. Ongoing processes of enrolment not only add new texts to the genre, but also change what is signified by its label. Texts which once seemed central might now appear marginal, and vice versa. The seemingly obvious genre categories through which we now perceive certain texts is thus not simply a description of their qualities but the product of still unfolding negotiations. For example, Edgar Rice Burroughs' *A Princess of Mars* (*All-Story* 1912; book 1917) and H.P. Lovecraft's *At the Mountains of Madness* (*Astounding* 1936) were both once relatively central to SF but are now commonly considered peripheral, albeit in different ways.

Eutopia and dystopia

Eutopian fiction critiques the existing social order by exemplifying a superior one, dystopian fiction by exaggerating its worst features. Such fictions are usually politically motivated and many directly exhort the reader to work for social change so as to realise eutopian wonders or avert dystopian terrors. Eutopias and dystopias may be found in unexplored regions of the globe, on other planets or in the future (linking them to earlier and parallel traditions of subterranean fiction, colonial adventure fiction, lunar satire, futuristic fiction and apocalyptic fiction). SF emerged as a genre concerned with imagining the world otherwise and with constructing imaginary 'elsewheres' and 'elsewhens' in contrast to the known world. While eutopian/dystopian projections typically focus on social relations, examples that have been enrolled into SF provide social and political critique to a greater (e.g. Charlotte Perkins Gilman's *Herland* (1915)) or lesser degree (e.g. Gernsback's *Ralph 124C 41+* (1911–1912), and might focus more extensively on technological rather than social innovations.

In addition to this critical capacity, the enrolment of eutopias and dystopias developed SF's interest in the future and in life beyond Earth. Those texts that involve interplanetary voyages, suspended animation or time travel are likely to have been more fully enrolled into SF, especially if they proffer a scientific seeming rationale for the protagonist's dislocation into an alien or future world. In Edward Bellamy's *Looking Backward, 2000–1887* (1888), insomniac Bostonian Julian West is hypnotised to help him sleep, but through a series of accidents is not awakened for over a century. Most of the novel recounts his acclimatisation to the changes in Boston in the intervening years. The 'widespread industrial and social troubles, and the underlying dissatisfaction of all classes with the inequalities of society, and the general misery of mankind' (1951: 36) that characterised nineteenth-century America have been alleviated by the end of capitalist competition (the state has become a monopoly controlling all areas of production and distribution, but has abandoned the profit motive), a reorganisation of labour (all are compensated equally) and related changes to social life (e.g. laundry and cooking are done communally, benefitting from the efficiencies of scale). In addition to imagining a perfected version of state capitalism that has removed the exploitation of labour from the production process, Bellamy details changes to the distribution, purchase and consumption of commodities, culminating in an idealised department store in which any item can be customised as the buyer wishes. While Bellamy does mention some technological innovations, such as awnings to cover sidewalks so that even those who do not own umbrellas can go out in inclement weather, he follows the eutopian tradition of emphasising social innovations. He also includes a strong element of eutopian exhortation. Towards the end of the novel, West wakes up back in 1887 and is devastated by the loss of his dreamworld; but then he wakes up to discover that his return to the nineteenth century was the dream. Relieved to find that he really does now live in a eutopian future, he regrets his failure to work for positive social change, thereby suggesting to readers that they might strive to bring about a better world. Bellamy's novel was tremendously successful, prompting numerous responses, including William Morris' *News from Nowhere* (1890). Within two years of its publication, there were over 150 reformist Bellamy Clubs in the US, and it influenced the populist Nationalist movement in the US and the Garden City urban planning movement in the UK.

Eutopian fiction

Thomas More, *Utopia* (1516)

Margaret Cavendish, *The Blazing World* (1666)

William Morris, *News from Nowhere* (1890)

Alexander Bogdanov, *Red Star* (1908–13)

B.F. Skinner, *Walden Two* (1948)

Aldous Huxley, *Island* (1962)

Ursula K. Le Guin, *The Dispossessed* (1974)

Sally Miller Gearheart, *The Wanderground* (1978)

As SF developed, it tended to move more towards imagining technology as the panacea for social problems, becoming less successful at imagining alternative social and economic arrangements. The emphasis on innovation and science that the genre took from other enrolments increasingly tempers the drive for political change, but SF does retain this desire for another – often better – world. Fredric Jameson (2005) relates the eutopian impulse to SF's struggle to imagine alterity, and much SF shares Bellamy's attempt and failure to do so. While Bellamy can picture new social organisations, he problematically resolves the class struggle by effectively making workers disappear into a rather dull, all encompassing middle class, deals with the question of race by never mentioning anyone who is not white (except, fleetingly, Sawyer, Julian's black servant in 1887) and cannot imagine substantial changes in gender relations (despite the socialisation of domestic labour).

In contrast, Mary E. Bradley Lane's *Mizora: A World of Women* (1880–1881) addresses the homogeneity of its eponymous eutopia directly. Fleeing threatened exile to Siberia, Vera Zarovitch finds herself in an all-female, subterranean society. Her account of her experiences there is intended for 'the sole purpose of benefiting Science and giving encouragement to those progressive minds who have already added their mite of knowledge to the coming future of the race' (1999: 8). The scientifically efficient Mizorans are all beautiful, lithe, blue-eyed blondes. They value education above anything else, enabling each citizen to be trained in which-ever profession she chooses. This has eroded economic and other discriminations, and thus eliminated social class. Menial and manual labour is performed by machines, leaving Mizorans to cultivate a life of the mind, and they have so per-fected the arts of chemistry that most of their food is produced without recourse to the inefficient and distasteful practices of agriculture. Mizora is collectivist: 'we all work for the good of the people, and the whole people. There is no greed of glory or gain; no personal ambition to gratify' (71).

Having been taught that 'Man … was a necessity of government, law, and pro-tection. His importance … incalculable' (85), Vera is amazed to discover such an advanced civilisation that does not include any men (Mizoran science enables asexual reproduction). Mizora used to be ruled by men – it was a time of frequent warfare and great suffering – but men became extinct 3000 years ago. Examining their surviving portraits, Vera weeps for them, feeling a kinship with those who 'had lived among noble and ignoble deeds … had known temptation and resist-ance, and reluctant compliance … had loved as I had loved, and sinned as I had sinned' (91). Although the cause of this extinction is not specified, it is implied that it was part of a eugenics programme that also eliminated dark-haired (Vera is brunette) and dark-skinned people. There is thus a degree of ambiguity as to how one is to regard this rather drastic solution to the problem of sexual – and other – difference. Like much SF, *Mizora* labours to imagine alterity, but seems able to conceive of radical social change only in a context in which differences among humans have been homogenised. Unlike *Looking Backward*'s Julian, who happily remains in his future eutopia, Vera leaves her subterranean one, preferring to work for a more just society, adopting Mizoran ideals of free, universal education (which will produce technological innovation) but preferring the selective practice of 'aesthetic celibacy' (147) to eliminate disease and crime rather than wholesale eugenic eradication of difference.

Ignatius Donnelly's dystopian *Caesar's Column* (1890), conceived as a rejoinder to Bellamy, depicts a hellish future America dominated by a capitalist oligarchy. It is presented in the form of Gabriel Weltstein's letters to his brother Heinrich in Uganda, written while visiting New York in 1988. They critique the massive economic and social inequities in this city of 10 million people (a population seven times larger than in 1890). Gabriel prevents the carriage of Prince Cabano, 'the wealthiest and most vindictive man in the city' (1960: 27), from running down a beggar, who turns out to be Max Petion, an attorney working for a secret organisation promoting social and economic reform. Gabriel joins this underground resistance. Donnelly carefully details the harsh working and living conditions of the city's poor and observes in footnotes that similar conditions can be found in contemporaneous London. While Gabriel is dazzled by the wonders available in late-twentieth-century New York (airship travel, exotic cuisine, print-on-demand newspapers), the novel is more concerned with their social and economic cost, although its analysis is at times disturbing: Prince Cabano and the economic 'aristocracy of the world [are] now almost altogether of Hebrew origin' (32) and 'Interest on money is the root and ground of the world's troubles. It puts one man in a position of safety, while another is in a condition of insecurity, and thereby it at once creates a radical distinction in human society' (101). The novel's advocacy of the Christian brotherhood of man indicates further limitations in Donnelly's political vision.

Dystopian fiction

Jack London, *The Iron Heel* (1908)

Ray Bradbury, *Fahrenheit 451* (1953)

E.M. Forster, 'The Machine Stops' (1909)

Thomas M. Disch, *334* (1972)

Francis Stevens, *The Heads of Cerberus* (1919)

Margaret Atwood, *The Handmaid's Tale* (1985)

Yevgeny Zamyatin, *We* (1924)

Octavia E. Butler, *Parable of the Sower* (1993)

The narrative has two main strands. One concerns Gabriel's rescue of the beautiful Estella Washington from Cabano's harem, for which she has been legally purchased from an avaricious relative. She intends to kill herself rather than submit to the Prince's attentions, declaring 'Better ... purity in death than degradation in life' (60). The other strand details an uprising of the working class led by Caesar Lomellini, a half-Italian/half-African-American anarchist described in unsavoury terms:

> His skin was quite dark, almost negroid; and a thick, close mat of curly black hair covered his huge head like a thatch. His face was muscular, ligamentous;

with great bars, ridges and whelks of flesh, especially about the jaws and on the forehead. But the eyes fascinated me. They were the eyes of a wild beast, deep-set, sullen and glaring.

(149)

Although Lomellini's cause is just, his methods are fanatical and his animal nature takes over as the successful rebellion puts him in possession of the wealth he has long envied. He establishes a violent dictatorship, ravishes fair members of the Prince's harem and creates a monument in Union Square of the concrete-encased bodies of all those slain by his forces. Gabriel and Max, who have increasingly distanced themselves from him, escape to Uganda with their true loves, where they build 'a smooth, straight wall, thirty feet high and about fifty broad at its widest point' to protect their colony from the chaos without, regretting 'that we – human beings – were thus compelled to exclude our fellow-men' (300).

Texts such as *Caesar's Column* give to SF a sense of the tension between technological and social progress and temper a tendency towards technophilia with a concern about the power such technology promises. They also reveal the darker side of the struggle with alterity that drives much of the genre. Whereas Bellamy and Lane erase difference in order to produce eutopia, Donnelly demonises difference through negative portrayals of Jews, peoples of colour and unchaste women so as to suggest – problematically – the eutopian potential of 'true' humanity within the dystopian context of contemporary life. In later SF, questions of alterity will more commonly be displaced onto figures such as the alien and the robot.

Colonial adventure fiction

While 'some historians of science fiction have been eager to emphasise the relation of SF to classic and Enlightenment-era imaginary voyages like those of Lucian and Swift', such enrolments have typically involved a corollary 'downplaying or outright denying of the affinity of science fiction to the work of H. Rider Haggard and his legion of imitators' (Rieder 2008: 35), even though, for example, over 10 per cent of the texts listed in Everett Bleiler's 1990 bibliography of SF before 1930 are lost-race tales. The 'science' that enables many colonial adventure fictions to be enrolled into SF often derives from disciplines such as archaeology, philology, Egyptology and anthropology, and a framing which valorises notions of evolutionary and technological progress from a primitive, non-white past into a eutopian, white future.

Rieder argues that the colonial encounter and its

disturbance of ethnocentrism, the achievement of a perspective from which one's own culture is only one of a number of possible cultures, is as important a part of the history of science fiction, as much a condition of possibility for the genre's coming to be, as developments in the physical sciences.

(2)

Colonial adventure fiction mediates the complex history of uneven development and capitalist-imperialist exploitation, with lost-race tales negotiating

> the basic problem of ownership by simultaneously revelling in the discovery of uncharted territory and representing the journey as a *return* to a lost legacy, a place where the travellers find a fragment of their own history lodged in the midst of a native population that usually has forgotten the connection.
>
> (40)

Works such as Haggard's *She* (1886–1887) demonstrate the compensatory fantasy at work in such fiction: European adventurers in Africa are ensnared in the web of a powerful but dangerous woman who represents ancient and secret powers (significantly, not of African origin, but deriving from Ancient Greece), and are only able to escape through extraordinary personal integrity.

Pierre Benoît's *Queen of Atlantis* (1919) is a retrospective narrative told by Captain Saint-Avit, newly appointed commander of a remote, desert outpost, to his second-in-command. An outcast among French colonial administrators in Africa, Saint-Avit is believed to have murdered Captain Morhange during an expedition into the Algerian desert. In Saint-Avit's tale, Morhange, a scholar obsessed by 'the influence of Greek and Roman civilisation on Africa' (2005: 65), diverts the expedition to search for the ancient city of Es-Suk. Drugged by a native guide, they awake in a great hall, 'furnished in European style' (113), including several European artworks. Its library contains classical works recovered from Carthage and Alexandria that were lost to European civilisation. They discover that the Sahara used to be a sea and that the city in which they find themselves is all that is left of Atlantis. The queen, Antinae, a mysterious and beautiful descendant of Neptune and Cleopatra, causes men to fall in love with her and then die of unrequited love. When she has amassed 100 victims – their bodies are galvanised in a unique metal to decorate her mausoleum – she too will die, and lie in state among them. Morhange, however, is interested only in the library's vast store of knowledge – notably of classical rather than African origin – and his immunity to Antinea causes her to fall in love with him. When he rejects her, she compels Saint-Avit to kill him.

The novel is simultaneously a diagnosis and defence of the violence inherent in the colonial occupation of African nations. It insists that the only valuable knowledge is of Western origin, and that Saint-Avit cannot be held responsible for his descent into murder because Africa, figured as a dangerous and powerful woman, seduced him into it. Although aspects of the novel suggest some critique of colonialism, it more strongly emphasises the risks Europeans face in this harsh land and among its wild people. While Africa can be the setting for adventure fiction, native inhabitants cannot be its protagonists.

Pauline Hopkins' *Of One Blood* (1902–1903) reworks this pattern, following the ambiguously raced Reuel Briggs (the light-skinned son of an African-American slave and her white master) on an archaeological expedition to Ethiopia. Immediately before leaving, he marries a mysteriously amnesiac, light-skinned, 'black' woman, Dianthe. Despite the hazards Reuel faces, the true site of danger is

Colonial adventure fiction

Jules Verne, *The Mysterious Island* (1874–1875)

H. Rider Haggard, *She* (1886–1887)

James De Mille, *A Strange Manuscript Found in a Copper Cylinder* (1888)

William R. Bradshaw, *The Goddess of Atvatabar* (1892)

Judith Merril, 'Daughters of Earth' (1952)

J.G. Ballard, *The Drowned World* (1962)

Michael Crichton, *Jurassic Park* (1990)

Eleanor Arnason, *A Woman of the Iron People* (1991)

not Africa, but America. His friend, Aubrey Livingstone, who is in love with Dianthe, arranges to have the absent Reuel murdered; when this fails, he nonetheless convinces Dianthe that Reuel is dead and marries her, and tricks Reuel into believing that she has drowned. Consequently, Reuel makes no effort to return to the US until the superscience technology of the hidden, ancient African city of Telassar – part of an Ethiopian civilisation that reached 'its zenith six thousand years before Christ's birth' (1996: 111) – shows him that she is still alive. In a remarkable conclusion, it is revealed that Reuel, Dianthe and Aubrey are siblings, the latter having been secretly substituted for their white father's still-born legitimate child and raised in his place.

While reproducing many of the elements of colonial adventure fiction described by Rieder, *Of One Blood* depicts a black protagonist's return to Africa, and ends – after the deaths of Aubrey and Dianthe – with his subsequent return to Telassar, where he will marry its black queen and 'give to the world a dynasty of dark-skinned rulers, whose destiny should be to restore the prestige of an ancient people' (127–128). This innovation challenges the ideological association of science and progress with white, Western culture typical of colonial adventure fiction and often reproduced in the SF that enrols it. Rather than rationalising and reinforcing colonialist attitudes, Hopkins concludes by instructing her readers that 'Of one blood' God 'made all races of men' (178).

Future war

Colonial adventure fiction also spawned a genre that reversed Western colonialism by imagining the defence of the homeland from invasion by a more powerful force, most famously in H.G. Wells' *The War of the Worlds*. Wells was also indebted to the future war story – a tradition that emerged and was particularly prevalent in the period between 1870 and WWI – in which conflicts between colonial powers typically occurred in the homeland rather than being played out in competition for colonial possessions. In the UK, the role of technology in the German victory in the Franco–Prussian war (1870–1871) – primarily, developments in artillery technology and the use of railways for rapid transport of troops and matériel – led to a number of anxious reflections on future military techniques and technologies. George Tomkyns Chesney's *The Battle of Dorking* (1871), which tells of the German invasion of England, is one of the first and most influential texts in this tradition. Presented as the reminiscence of a British volunteer 50 years after the German victory, this short novel propagandised for better military funding, revealing anxieties at the heart of the British Empire. While lamenting for the good old days, in which 'there seemed to be no end to the riches [free trade] was bringing us' (1995: 27), it is also concerned that England has become 'a big workshop, making up the things which came from all parts of the world' and hence dependent upon the 'raw goods' of other nations (28). For Chesney, however, the problem with colonialism is not dependence on colonised nations, which he seems to think export materials to Britain merely because they are cheerfully 'in the habit' (28) of doing so, but the failure properly to fund the military defence of British hegemony from other colonial powers. Ultimately, defeat is blamed on political shifts which resulted in power

> passing away from the class which had been used to rule, and to face political dangers, and which had brought the nation with honour unsullied through former struggles, into the hands of the lower classes, uneducated, untrained to the use of political rights, and swayed by demagogues; and the few who were wise in their generation were denounced as alarmists, or as aristocrats who sought their own aggrandizement by wasting public money on bloated armaments.
>
> (73)

Future war stories

Frank R. Stockton, *The Great War Syndicate* (1889)

George Griffith, *The Angel of Revolution* (1893)

Erskine Childers, *The Riddle of the Sands* (1903)

Saki, *When William Came* (1913)

George S. Schuyler, *Black Empire* (1936–1938)

Robert A. Heinlein, *Starship Troopers* (1959)

Gordon R. Dickson, *Soldier, Ask Not* (1967)

Tanya Huff, *Valor's Choice* (2000)

Kenneth Mackay's *The Yellow Wave* (1895) uses elements of colonial adventure and future war narratives to comment on a shifting political landscape and to reinforce traditional distributions of power. It sets up a conflict between the pragmatic, self-made independence of 'true' Australians and the limited vision of those absentee capitalists who seek only profit. Mackay, who in 1901 stood for Australian parliament on a platform that included 'The abolition of Colored Alien Labor, so as to secure a White Australia' (Enstice and Webb 2003: xxv), develops this conflict through the story of Dick Hatten, a white landowner dispossessed of his cattle run in a dispute over the mortgage. The finance company is unconcerned about the threat posed to fragile white hegemony by a growing Asian population, mostly imported as cheap labour, and they do nothing to encourage white settlers, who could be relied upon to build a proper (i.e. white) nation through agriculture and appropriate values. Mackay links Australia's political and economic position in the British Empire and her geographical position in proximity to Asia as threats to Australian greatness. With most of its army defending British concerns in India from a potential Russian challenge, Australia is left vulnerable to Chinese invasion. This vulnerability is exacerbated by attempts to attract foreign capital investment for the railway system, which enable the villainous Count Zenski, working for a secret Russian–Chinese alliance intent on usurping Western imperial powers in Australia and Asia, to seize control of this vital transport and communications network.

While much of the narrative is taken up with interpersonal melodrama (it is partly driven by a love triangle, with Hatten and the Russian officer leading the invasion at two of its corners), it is primarily concerned with the need to secure a white future for Australia. The hastily conscripted Australian army's members were

> taught from their birth to look on Chinamen as inferior beings, creatures to be tolerated chiefly because they grew vegetables, and so saved their customers the trouble, human footballs on which the youthful larrikin might with safety practice those mighty kicks.
>
> (Mackay 2003: 276)

The Australian army is subjected to a crushing defeat. MacKay's later description of 'battle-smirched troopers … slowly digesting the disagreeable fact that even Chinamen, armed with machine-guns and automatic rifles, are more than a match for Australians without either' (289) indicates the extent to which his true concern is not to dismiss this sense of racial and cultural superiority but – like Chesney – to urge military preparedness. Indeed, the cruel and rapacious 'Mongol' hordes, which spare neither women nor children, are shown to succeed because an indifferent British Empire is as unprepared to come to Australia's defence as its own smug politicians and incompetent officer class. The only soldiers to trouble the invaders are Hatten's irregular cavalry, self-reliant pioneers armed with improvised weapons and settler know-how. In an ideological sleight-of-hand, Mackay presents them as 'native' Australians desperately fighting for their homeland, even comparing them to the 'gallant Matabeles who fell fighting for their country before the Maxims of the English invaders' (213).

Although authors such as Chesney and Mackay used the future war narrative to advocate certain political positions, the form itself quickly became more typically an occasion for adventure fiction involving international conspiracies, espionage, battles, terrorists, anarchists, revolutionaries, mad geniuses and superweapons.

Apocalyptic fiction

Future war fiction conjured the possibility of a new world order – positive or negative – emerging from human conflict, even if it preferred to focus on the conflict rather than engage in sustained speculation about a post-war world. Apocalyptic fiction similarly relished large-scale scenes of destruction, often arising from natural disasters, but frequently used the end of the world as a pretext for reorganising society.

Mary Shelley, who was well known for *Frankenstein* (1818), which has been increasingly enrolled into SF since the 1970s, also wrote *The Last Man* (1826). Presented as prophetic writings by the Cumaean Sibyl, it tells the story of a group of late-twenty-first-century republican aristocrats resisting political and dynastic machinations to restore the monarchy. The convolutions of their relationships, romantic and otherwise, are played out against a backdrop of catastrophe, as a plague, for which neither science nor Romantic genius can find a cure, sweeps the globe, eradicating the human population. Eventually, the remaining protagonists lead an exodus from Britain in the hope of finding a climate more conducive to survival on the depopulated continent. Four of them live to enjoy a few happier years, but typhus and an accident eventually leave Lionel Verney alone, the last man on Earth. Despite the novel's future setting and global apocalypse, it is a strangely personal expression of Shelley's mourning for her husband, Percy Shelley, her children and the circle of friends that included Lord Byron, and her feelings about the apparent failure of the French Revolution and the political ideals of her parents, Mary Wollstonecraft and William Godwin. *Frankenstein*'s greater success at being enrolled into SF can be explained by the way it, and its stage and film adaptations, had already captured the cultural imagination before feminists scholars devoted attention to it and before Brian Aldiss' *Billion Year Spree* claimed it as the first SF novel. In contrast, *The Last Man*, savaged by reviewers, remained out of print between 1833 and 1965. Its relative failure to be enrolled into SF since then is perhaps indicative of the extent to which the genre developed to find the inevitable defeat of humanity less palatable than the idea of conquering death.

M.P. Shiel's *The Purple Cloud* (1901) has perhaps been more successfully enrolled because of its relatively optimistic ending. Adam Jeffson is the sole survivor of the first expedition to reach the North Pole. Unknown to him, however, this accomplishment triggered a volcanic eruption in the Pacific that released a cloud of poisonous gas, which has swept the world, killing everyone (the novel is underpinned by a metaphysical battle between two forces, the White/good and the Black/evil). Deranged, Jeffson wanders the globe, setting fire to cities, before settling on an Aegean island. After two decades, he discovers a last woman, but decides not to risk breeding anew the destructive human race. The White force intervenes, and Jeffson repents his decision, affirming that 'it is the White who is Master' (Shiel 1963: 287). One of the issues that would emerge in future debates about what properly constitutes SF would be the attitude taken towards human insignificance in the face of the universe. While neither Shelley's nor Shiel's protagonists exactly embrace the apocalypse, only Jeffson sets out to overcome it,

Apocalyptic fiction

Cousin de Grainville, *The Last Man* (1806)

Richard Jefferies, *After London* (1885)

George Allan England, *Darkness and Dawn* (1912–1913)

Jack London, *The Scarlet Plague* (1915)

Edwin S. Balmer and Philip Wylie, *When Worlds Collide* (1933)

Angela Carter, *Heroes and Villains* (1969)

Kate Wilhelm, *Where Late the Sweet Birds Sang* (1976)

Cormac McCarthy, *The Road* (2006)

however belatedly, and it is this attitude that has more typically been enrolled into the genre, particularly when it validates the scientific method or articulates some version of the myth of America's manifest destiny.

Such early apocalyptic fiction focuses on the social consequences of radical changes to the conditions of human existence rather than on the heroic struggle to avert the apocalypse through technology. In eutopian fiction, the ideal society is typically already achieved – it is situated after a radical geographical and/or historical rupture, after a transition that need never be mapped out – but apocalyptic fiction is often set in the midst of the struggle over how society should be organised. Sydney Fowler Wright's *Deluge* (1928) destroys the world through geological upheaval and flood, but its real concern is with the ills of modernity and the need to reassert patriarchy. Middle-class lawyer Martin Webster, mistakenly believing that his fragile wife, Helen, and their children are dead, manfully resolves to go on in the world. He joins forces with the independent and impulsive Claire, who is distinguished by her physical fitness, bravery and refusal to submit to any man's claims to own her. It is she, not Martin, who kills a pig for them to eat, and she who finishes off a would-be rapist, incidentally saving Martin from the 'fallen foe' (2003: 146) he hesitated to kill. However, she 'did not doubt that he was wiser, as she knew he was stronger than she. Perhaps he saw more broadly, more truly, than she was able to do. To see all sides does not conduce to prompt action' (178).

Martin and Claire's mutual attraction provides numerous opportunities to reflect on conventional British morality and to question its continued relevance after the flood. While Martin claims Claire as his own, 'for always, and always' (120), the less robust Helen has been rescued by a community which is concerned that 'there aren't enough women to go round' (160). They have determined that the only 'peaceable way' to resolve the issue is 'to let the women choose for themselves' (160), while denying them the right not to choose. Helen is spared by the fortuitous arrival of Martin, since their marriage is recognised as a prior claim, but he does not want to give up Claire, either. He feels that he can 'be equally loyal to two women at once', but the thought of sharing either with another man is 'monstrous' (181). He reasons that if 'a woman lives with two men the parentage of her children is doubtful' but if 'a man live with two women there is no such confusion'; there 'are other differences', too, although they remain unspecified, and 'it is flouting facts to ignore them' (181).

Martin eventually agrees to become the leader of this community, but only if it agrees to his absolute power: 'no committees. No voting. No wasted hours of talk. No follies of compromise' (218). Only such clear and singular vision, he feels, can create a new and 'cleaner social order' (244) without the hypocrisies and excesses of the old. Although the various decisions he faces – about taxation, ownership and so on – are raised as questions, none of them are resolved. Instead, the novel's focus remains on domestic and sexual relationships, extending the principle of women's choice to enable both Claire and Helen to choose Martin. His exceptionalism thus positions him similarly to the heroic white man of colonial adventure fiction, and the novel's putative empowerment of women disappears under its celebration of patriarchy.

Prehistoric and evolutionary fiction

Social change is also often at the heart of prehistoric romances, in which the influence of Darwin's thought is frequently evident. They often involve encounters between alien others (i.e. different species of pre-human primates) or chronicle improvements through technology as pre-humans 'progress' into versions of humanity more closely resembling our own. In J.H. Rosny aîné's *Quest for Fire* (1909), a tribe of *Homo neanderthalensis* lacks the technology to produce fire, but has cultural traditions that enable them to tend a naturally occurring flame. One of their number is adopted by a tribe of *Homo sapiens*, who teach him how to kindle fire, and when he returns to his own tribe this innovation transforms its way of life. Jack London's *Before Adam* (1906–1907) utilises the notion of a genetically-encoded racial memory to enable its modern-day protagonist to access the experiences of a pre-human ancestor, and thus to imagine the transition from *Australopithecines* to modern humanity, with technology (fire, bows and arrows) being key to this development. This close connection between technology and increasing humanity is central to SF as it developed in the magazine and paperback tradition, most clearly in depictions of the artificially enhanced posthuman as the next stage of evolution. Fantasies of evolutionary advances through mutation, in which humans acquire such new capacities as telepathy, likewise extend the narrative of evolutionary development into a posthuman future.

Concerns with the future beyond contemporary humanity unfold in such evolutionary fantasies as Edward Bulwer-Lytton's *The Coming Race* (1871), which describes a society of superior subterranean beings, the Vril-ya. Named after the mysterious substance, Vril, they can fly (using mechanical wings) and, through mental training, control the extraordinary power of Vril, which can be used to heal, to change, to create and to extinguish life. Even their young can wield sufficient power to destroy entire cities. Although the Vril-ya clearly see their own social organisation as eutopian, the human narrator flees from it back to his own world, where he prays that 'ages may yet elapse before there emerge into sunlight our

Prehistoric romances

Stanley Waterloo, *The Story of Ab* (1897)

Arthur Conan Doyle, *The Lost World* (1912)

Edgar Rice Burroughs, *The Cave Girl* (1913–17)

William Golding, *The Inheritors* (1955)

Jean M. Auel, *The Clan of the Cave Bear* (1980)

Michael Bishop, *No Enemy but Time* (1982)

inevitable destroyers' (1989: 128). In the Vril-ya, Bulwer-Lytton ambivalently combines an orientalist fantasy of coldly indifferent ancient wisdom with an image of a future, coldly rational industrial proletariat, which – as in the eutopian/dystopian tradition – looks forward to a superior human race and expresses anxieties about humanity and its social order as currently configured.

Other versions of the evolutionary fantasy displace humanity not by a successor species but through the birth of one or more individuals who have mutated beyond current species norms. Typically, the world does not welcome these newcomers. Sometimes they triumph, but many times, as in J.D. Beresford's *The Hampdenshire Wonder* (1911), the forces of conservatism and fear destroy the possibility of the new and different. Victor Stott – the 'wonder' of the title – is a genius child. Aged six, his intellectual abilities are so far in advance of all those around him that he struggles to converse at a sufficiently simplistic level for adults to understand. His body, however, remains that of a vulnerable child, and thus whatever threat he might represent is easily eliminated. Crashaw, a repressive priest who insists that his social position gives him authority over the child, drowns him. Although Crashaw is clearly not a sympathetic character, his fears are endorsed to some extent, with Stott being described as possessing 'the imagination of a mathematician and a logician developed beyond all conception' but 'not one spark of the imagination of a poet' (1999: 193). Therefore, he 'cannot deal with men; he can't understand their weaknesses and limitations' (193). *The Hampdenshire Wonder* thus betrays an anxiety about the increasing hegemony of science, a key concern for SF as it emerges.

Evolutionary fantasies

Camille Flammarion, *Lumen* (1867)

Samuel Butler, *Erewhon* (1872)

Edgar Rice Burroughs, *The Land That Time Forgot* (1918)

Arthur C. Clarke, *Childhood's End* (1953)

Kurt Vonnegut, *Galápagos* (1985)

Robert J. Sawyer, *Hominids* (2003)

Science and invention

The kind of stories perhaps most fully subsumed into SF deal with science and invention. On one extreme, we might find a metaphysical romance such as Marie Corelli's *A Romance of Two Worlds* (1886), in which a young woman with a debilitating illness finds her strength restored by a seemingly magical elixir. Under the tutelage of its creator, the Chaldean philosopher Heliobas, she undergoes a prolonged out-of-body experience, culminating in a revelation of the divine, electric nature of the cosmos, which teaches her to value spirit over material embodiment and to 'grasp the majestic reality and perfection of everything you can see, desire, or imagine' (1890: 325). This interest in ancient wisdom and spirituality aligns the novel with aspects of colonial adventure fiction, but it also goes to great lengths to explain electricity as a Vril-like vital force linking the metaphysical to the mundane, ecstatic excess to scientific discovery. At the other extreme is Edwin Abbott's *Flatland* (1884). While its discussion of the strict social rules of two-dimensional, geometric civilisation satirises Victorian hierarchies, its ongoing appeal seems to be rooted in its engagement with the idea of perspective. The narrative is supplemented by diagrams which help the reader to visualise what life would look like from a point of view trapped in a two-dimensional world where rank is determined by shape (which can only be clearly seen from a position above the plane of Flatland). The protagonist, A. Square, also dreams about one-dimensional Lineland and has three-dimensional Spaceland explained to him by a sphere who intersects with Flatland. Along with its satirical and educational aspects, *Flatland* engages with notions of subject position and perspective that would become important to both modernist literature and critical theory. Between these extremes of mysticism and mathematics, the tale of science and invention takes many forms.

Frankenstein provided two of SF's most enduring icons, the obsessed scientist (sometimes a hero, sometimes mad) and the artificial being. Frankenstein's creature is biological, animated by an experiment whose details are only hinted at by Shelley. His tormented loneliness emphasises human responsibility to other beings – and at one point he even notes the parallel with the relationship between god and his creations, including humanity – and thus some subsequent enrolments are predicated on the moral and ethical questions of the technoscientific age. In contrast, Villiers de l'Isle-Adam's *Tomorrow's Eve* (1884) introduces an artificial being intended solely to fulfil her owner's desires. Lord Ewald, in love with the beautiful Alicia, is oppressed by her banality and horrified by the fact that 'she accords me the *only love of which she is capable*' (2001: 32). He yearns for a woman whose 'soul' is as beautiful as her body, and thus worthy of his love, and so his friend, Thomas Edison, creates Hadaly to take her place. Two things are particularly interesting about this portrayal of Edison, both related to the way it negotiates the rising hegemony of technoscience. First, although Edison is portrayed in his laboratory, surrounded by 'cluttered tables, various precision instruments, intricate and obscure gear-boxes, electric apparatus, telescopes, mirrors, enormous magnets, retorts amid a tangle of tubes, flasks full of mysterious fluids, and slates scrawled over with equations' (8), he is never shown at work and the purpose of this paraphernalia is never demonstrated. This Edison is a Romantic genius in the tradition of Shelley's Frankenstein, rather than the competent engineer celebrated in Campbell's *Astounding*, and his apparatus lacks the detail favoured by Gernsback. Second, although Edison's construction of Hadaly into a more-than-perfect imitation of Alicia is given some scientific rationale, her soul is imparted by Sowena, Edison's mysterious mystical assistant, thus aligning this version of the pragmatic inventor with the metaphysical forces evoked by writers such as Corelli. Hadaly proves a perfect mate and the novel argues at length that her programmed perfection is more 'natural' than the artifice – perfume, wigs, cosmetics and the like – to which real woman resort in order to trick and entrap men. A treatise in misogyny and a lament for the passing of Romantic sensibilities, *Tomorrow's Eve* uses the artificial woman merely as a backdrop for its philosophy and, unlike *Frankenstein*, it is unconcerned with the fate of its created other.

> ### Tales of science and invention
>
> Robert Louis Stevenson, *The Strange Case of Dr Jekyll and Mr Hyde* (1886)
>
> Mark Twain, *A Connecticut Yankee in King Arthur's Court* (1889)
>
> Garrett P. Serviss, *Edison's Conquest of Mars* (1898)
>
> Mikhail Bulgakov, *Heart of a Dog* (1925)
>
> Henry Kuttner, *Robots Have No Tails* (1943–1948)
>
> Amitav Ghosh, *The Calcutta Chromosome* (1987)
>
> Molly Gloss, *Wild Life* (2000)
>
> Ian McDonald, *Brasyl* (2007)

While many texts focus on a single invention or discovery, Albert Robida's *The Twentieth Century* (1882) is replete with the wonders of a technologically transformed world. A humorous account of Hélène Colobry's attempts to find a career, Robida's lavishly illustrated novel provides a tour of an automated, media-saturated future Paris. Robida is rather more concerned than Verne with the social consequences of his various technological innovations, often satirising the capitalist social organisation underpinning their development and usage. For example, comparing two catering companies which deliver food through networks of pipes to people's homes, one entrepreneur observes, 'even though our cuisine is second-rate, our dividends are first class.… Despite its first-rate cuisine, your new Company will yield dividends so meager that they will make an unfavorable impression on the stockholders' (2004: 72). Robida also makes light of France's political history, positing a future in which bloodless revolutions are regularly scheduled – and include competitions for the best barricades – so that the government is kept fresh. Most businesses close down for the duration of these events so that all can participate in their assigned revolutionary role, but one enterprising shop remains open under the slogan 'DOWN WITH THE GOVERNMENT! UP WITH OUR MERCHANDISE!' (239). Hélène's high-powered executive uncle proposes that government should do away with the revolutionary method of renewal entirely and be run like a corporation so as to ensure financial security:

> There is always something to pay for. In the old-fashioned system, all citizens are debtors out of whom as much money as possible needs to be squeezed, in the most brutal and inconsiderate manner, with tax collectors and bailiffs. My system gets rid of all this. In my new administration, citizens are shareholders and their dividends are the money they save on running the government.
>
> (271)

Robida also depicts the increased centrality of the media and consumption in twentieth-century life. For example, Italy is turned into a theme park, the natives either employed to perform their ethnicity for tourists or else relocated to a new homeland in Uganda.

Hélène never finds a career (women are emancipated in this future but this topic, like others, is treated lightly). Instead she marries her cousin, Philippe, and they develop a plan to create a new continent by linking together a number of artificial islands. It provides space for continued expansion and is preferable to the naturally occurring lands which earlier people were forced to take 'as they found them, with all their inconveniences and defects. Too much water here, too many mountains there, immense spaces without the slightest stream, and so on' (346). Robida's depiction of the future thus intertwines technological innovation with a sense of the social, political and economic forces that drive change. Later SF, such as Gernsback's *Ralph 124C 41+*, would lose sight of this, offering the thinnest of tales in order to celebrate a world of future marvels. Its initial appearance in Gernsback's *Modern Electrics* demonstrates that his vision of SF was more strongly addressed to scientific hobbyists and entrepreneurs than to those associated with literary culture and social critique.

In or out?

Aspects of these – and other – traditions coalesced into the new genre called SF. As this brief survey indicates, many of the elements that would become central to certain versions of SF were in circulation long before anyone thought to call them 'SF'. Yet it is problematic to label any of these texts – or the traditions they exemplify – as 'SF' since it is only as the name and idea of the genre were introduced that actants began, retrospectively and inconsistently, to understand them as belonging, at least potentially, to SF. These various traditions of fiction themselves evolved over time, and the contexts in which they were read and understood shifted significantly once the existence of 'SF' enabled actants to consider them in conjunction with each other. Furthermore, these traditions developed during a period of significant cultural change that profoundly affected the kinds of fiction being written and consumed. New transportation, communications and military technologies altered the experience of imperialism and colonialism. Accelerating rates of technological development and of the rationalisation and commodification of innovation, along with increasing literacy levels and the growth of scientific education, helped to produce writers and readers interested in science and technology, as well as their imaginative elaborations and potential consequences.

The various traditions discussed above have all played a role in the subsequent development of SF, but certain conceptualisations of the genre privilege some over others. Consequently, it is imperative to remember that whether a specific text is considered central or peripheral to the genre is always a matter of ideological and cultural struggle. Much of the US magazine and paperback tradition affirms faith in the human spirit and in the heroic individual, while SF from outside this tradition – frequently imagined as being less commercial in its motivation – often contains pessimistic commentary on technoculture. As the magazine and paperback tradition developed, there was a tendency to conflate it with the genre and thus to resist the enrolment of authors publishing in other idioms and venues; as alternative markets and academic interest in the genre developed in the post-war period, there have been stronger pressures to enrol these other authors and to marginalise aspects of the magazine and paperback tradition. However, any attempt to organise texts into 'pure' categories – including the desire to label some as 'real' SF – causes categories and hybrids to proliferate, revealing the arbitrariness of any typology. For example, it is only by demanding that SF be defined in terms of the fiction privileged by, for example, John W. Campbell's *Astounding*, that one can retrospectively label, and thus marginalise, Burroughs' *A Princess of Mars* as 'science fantasy' or Lovecraft's *At the Mountains of Madness* as 'cosmic horror'.

A Princess of Mars is a planetary romance about a Civil War veteran, John Carter, who, during a seemingly hopeless battle with Apaches in the Arizona wilderness, finds himself projected somehow to a decadent, dying Mars, where reduced gravity gives him superior strength. He proves his worth in combat and finds a place for himself among a tribe of aggressive, green-skinned, four-armed Tharks. When the Tharks capture Dejah Thoris, the beautiful, red-skinned, oviparous, humanoid Princess of Helium, Carter falls in love with her. They eventually escape, return to her people, marry and start a family. In the conclusion, Carter sacrifices himself to restore the machines that provide Mars with breathable atmosphere, but rather than dying he wakes up back on Earth. The novel is presented as an account written ten years later, with Carter still ignorant of his Martian family's fate – a question resolved in the first of ten sequels.

Burroughs' novel can be understood in terms of several of the fictional traditions discussed above. Like colonial adventure fiction, it valorises a white hero as the one who can save an ancient culture, and focuses on his heroic exploits and perilous escapes rather than the ideological implications of its transplanted frontier; like the metaphysical romance, it involves interplanetary travel for which no scientific rationale is provided; and like future war fiction, it depicts great battles involving innovative weaponry. The technology evoked in the novel is presented positively, with little thought about the ways in which different technologies might

Science fantasy

C.J. Cutcliffe Hyne, *The Lost Continent* (1900)

Edwin Lester Arnold, *Lieut. Gulliver Jones: His Vacation* (1905)

Ray Cummings, *The Girl in the Golden Atom* (1919–1920)

Edgar Rice Burroughs, *The Moon Maid* (1923–1925)

Jack Vance, *The Dying Earth* (1950)

Andre Norton, *Witch World* (1963)

Roger Zelazny, *Lord of Light* (1967)

Marion Zimmer Bradley, *Darkover Landfall* (1972)

produce – and depend upon – different social arrangements. The Tharks are either noble barbarians or bloodthirsty savages, revelling in cruelty and lacking any understanding of family life. Dejah Thoris is defined by her beauty, her interior life consisting merely of admiring Carter and awaiting rescue. When the term 'SF' first entered circulation, the interplanetary setting of Burroughs' Martian novels saw them easily enrolled in the genre. Neither their emphasis on adventure – rather, than, say 'extrapolation' or 'cognitive estrangement' – nor their departures from scientific consensus about Mars were yet seen as inconsistent with the genre. Similarly, their affinities with colonial adventure fiction, including westerns, were not yet seen as a failure sufficiently to distinguish themselves from other genres. Finally, the mystical means by which Carter is transported to Mars had not yet become a barrier to SF enrolment. Therefore, because *A Princess of Mars* is set on another planet and narrates the exploits of a heroic Earthman among aliens, it can be enrolled as SF; but because of its departures from scientific knowledge – which have only increased over time – and its magical mode of interplanetary travel, it cannot be enrolled as SF and must be labelled 'science fantasy', which many regard as an inherently lesser form. Whichever of these positions one adopts is not a matter of 'truth' or 'accuracy', but an indicator of one's own ideological and cultural investments.

At the Mountains of Madness likewise gives us a sense of the boundary debates that emerged in the struggles to identify SF and separate it from the genres being constituted and reconstituted around it. Lovecraft's novella about the discovery of an ancient, Antarctic civilisation at first appears to follow conventions established as part of Gernsbackian SF, building consciously on Poe's *The Narrative of A. Gordon Pym* (1837) and deploying the techniques of precise measurement and mapping typical of Verne, while also introducing material from archaeology and myth. The expedition finds traces of a life-form – a marine being with wings that is 75 percent animal and 25 percent vegetable – that simply does not fit within the established understanding of terrestrial evolution. Further evidence, found in a monumental lost city, suggests that an ancient, extraterrestrial civilisation of Old Ones, having abandoned 'a stage of mechanised life on other planets' because 'its effects [were] emotionally unsatisfying' and having defeated 'various cosmic enemies' (Lovecraft 2005: 59), settled on Earth and began to create terrestrial life-forms, including the malleable, protoplasmic slave species of shoggoths. Waves of conflict swept pre-human Earth, and the Old Ones eventually retreated deep beneath Antarctica, where they might still live. The revelation of this terrible history, as much as their encounter with a shoggoth, enables the narrator and his companion to understand 'the quality of cosmic fear to its uttermost depths' (91). Instead of investigating further so as to establish some measure of rational control over these anomalies and all that they imply about the limitations of scientific knowledge, the survivors of the expedition, one of whom has been driven mad, flee. They strive to prevent further expeditions, which might unleash an apocalypse, and conclude that it is 'absolutely necessary, for the peace and safety of mankind, that some of Earth's dark, dead corners and unplumbed depths be let alone' (101).

Weird SF and cosmic horror

Arthur Machen, *The Great God Pan* (1894)

William Hope Hodgson, *The House on the Borderland* (1908)

A. Merritt, *The Moon Pool* (1918–1919)

David Lindsay, *A Voyage to Arcturus* (1920)

H.P. Lovecraft, *The Color Out of Space* (1927)

Shirley Jackson, *The Haunting of Hill House* (1959)

Mike Mignola, *Hellboy* (1993)

Jeff VanderMeer, *Veniss Underground* (2003)

At the Mountains of Madness contains elements that would have easily been enrolled into SF in the 1930s, such as Lovecraft's treatment of the expedition as an extension of actual Antarctic exploration and his engagement with contemporary science (he refers to continental drift, first proposed seriously in 1912, and to Pluto, discovered in 1930). Simultaneously, his allusions to such otherworldly, weird and orientalist fantasists as Lord Dunsany, Clarke Ashton Smith and painter Nicholas Roerich, and the incorporation of material from his own Cthulhu mythos, enable the novella's enrolment into the horror genre that was then emerging in magazines such as *Weird Tales*. Unlike the SF that would later be championed by Campbell, Lovecraft retains a sense of the sublime in the universe: greater knowledge does not necessarily lead to greater control; the mysteries deepen the more one learns about the Old Ones; and human culture fades into insignificance in the face of such inconceivably old and powerful beings.

While enrolling *A Princess of Mars* into SF becomes problematic because it increasingly contradicts existing scientific knowledge, *At the Mountains of Madness*'s attitude towards the relationship between human scientific knowledge

and the nature of the physical universe, and its refusal to celebrate human exceptionalism, rendered it increasingly difficult for the magazine and paperback tradition to countenance, especially when powerful actants such as Campbell (whose
own 'Who Goes There?' (*Astounding* 1938) constitutes a riposte to it) were pursuing a radically different agenda for SF. Consequently, however science-fictional
one might deem certain aspects of Lovecraft's novel – scientific expeditions, extraterrestrial species, interplanetary wars, artificial life, depths of time – its tone has
more commonly seen it consigned to a category such as 'cosmic horror', a 'lesser'
form outside of 'real' SF.

The various traditions outlined in this chapter suggest something of the complex
field out of which SF grew. Once the genre was named and began to circulate,
various actants engaged in the still-ongoing negotiations, enrolments and exclu-
sions about what 'SF' denotes. As *A Princess of Mars* and *At the Mountains of
Madness* demonstrate, no text can ever be fully or securely positioned within a
single generic category. The elements of pre-Gernsback fiction that have been
enrolled into definitions of SF appear in myriad combinations throughout the
genre's history, but no single element constitutes the sufficient and necessary condition for a text to be included or excluded from the genre or determines its relative
centrality or marginality.

Conclusion

- Although the specific role of science in SF is a contentious one, SF texts
  do typically engage with science and technology in various ways,
  ranging from the adventures they enable to the detailed exploration of a
  scientific premise.
- SF is often concerned with the social and cultural changes that arise
  from new technologies, sometimes postulating radically different modes
  of social organisation.
- SF frequently returns to images of conquest, frontiers, exploration, mapping, land ownership and the struggles between competing cultures in
  colonial settings, whether on Earth or on other worlds.
- SF's fascination with artificial beings, such as robots, and non-human
  lifeforms, whether terrestrial or alien, often articulates an interest in
  questions of class, race, gender and sexuality.
- While SF is often considered a masculine genre, and while many SF
  texts unthinkingly reproduce patriarchal ideology and reinforce sexist
  stereotypes, even at its most conservative, it engages with questions of
  sexual difference.

3 Proliferations: the 1930s

Overview

During the 1930s, as conditions favoured the growth of niche magazines in the US, pulp SF began to establish itself as a distinct tradition, but at the same time SF continued to appear in other forms. While some actants were already engaged in efforts to restrict SF to a certain type of story, readers consumed fiction from a variety of sources without necessarily noticing or being troubled by notions of generic purity. Simultaneously, other media, including radio, comics and films, produced numerous texts that could also be seen as SF. A significant fan community began to develop around the pulps, with many fans becoming authors and editors. Key debates in early fandom addressed whether SF should serve as a vehicle for science popularisation, a form of entertainment or a means of developing and communicating social and political critique.

The origins of magazine SF

Amazing Stories not only built upon the varieties of literature described in the last chapter but also a tradition of fiction magazines established in the nineteenth century. Hugo Gernsback, who emigrated from Luxembourg to the US in 1905, might well have been aware of French, German and Swiss magazines specialising in fantasy and science and invention, as well as British periodicals, such as *The Strand* (1891–1950) and *Pearson's Magazine* (1896–1939), which often carried stories and novels that would later be enrolled into the genre of SF – as did US general fiction magazines, such as *The Argosy* (1882–1978, under several titles) and *All-Story* (launched in 1905, it merged with *Argosy* in 1920). With *Detective Story Magazine* (1915–1949), individual pulps began to specialise in specific categories of fiction, such as romance, westerns, sports, aviation adventures or nautical adventures. *The Thrill Book* (1919), the first pulp devoted to fantastic fiction, lasted for only 16 semi-monthly issues, but *Weird Tales* ran from 1923 to 1954, publishing SF – H.P. Lovecraft's cosmic horror, Edmond Hamilton's space operas, C.L. Moore's planetary romances – alongside supernatural horror and heroic fantasy. Gernsback's initial publishing experience was with scientific- and radio-hobbyist magazines. He published *Modern Electrics* from 1908 to 1913, in which he serialised *Ralph 124C 41+*, and *Electrical Experimenter* (later renamed *Science and Invention*) from 1913 to 1929, which carried his *Baron Muenchhausen's Scientific Adventures* (1915–1917) and Clement Fezandie's 40 stories about Doctor Hackensaw (1921–1925), a genius inventor given to explicating scientific marvels at considerable length.

While the April 1926 issue of *Weird Tales* included readers' letters asking for more stories about 'weird scientific inventions' (Cowan 1926: 567) and 'trips to other planets, strange voyages of any type, … animals raised to gigantic size' (Fischer, Jr 1926: 567) alongside the 'more creepy, thrilling, gooseflesh stories' (Bralley 1926: 567), the readership overall seemed to favour its mix of different kinds of fantastic fiction. However, during the same month, Gernsback's *Amazing* appeared, committed to publishing only SF. This specialisation, or segregation, sought to separate SF out from the broader field of the fantastic and create it as a distinct genre or marketing category. By 1930, it had been joined by *Astounding Stories of Super-Science* and the magazines that would merge, in 1936, into *Thrilling Wonder Stories*. Several other SF pulps appeared during the 1930s, alongside magazines devoted to the sometimes science-fictional adventures of their eponymous heroes, including *The Shadow Magazine* (1921–1949), *Doc Savage Magazine* (1933–1949), *G-8 and His Battle Aces* (1933–1944) and *The Spider* (1933–1943). There was a brief boom in SF magazine publishing at the end of the decade: *Marvel Science Stories* was launched in 1938; *Dynamic Science Stories*, *Fantastic Adventures*, *Future Fiction*, *Planet Stories*, *Science Fiction*, *Startling Stories* and *Strange Stories* in 1939; and *Astonishing Stories*, *Captain Future*, *Comet*, *Science Fiction Quarterly* and *Super Science Stories* in 1940. However, few of these titles lasted very long.

The beginning of SF as a new kind of literature occurred in the context of an expanding magazine market in which a recognisable generic 'brand' was increasingly a factor in financial success. Gernsback's branding sought to emphasise connections between the stories he published and the technological world unfolding around them: banners above his editorials proclaimed 'Read it Today ... Live it Tomorrow!' and 'Extravagant Fiction Today ... Cold Fact Tomorrow' (original ellipses). However, not all pulp SF writers shared this vision, and as the letters pages in *Amazing* and other pulps reveal, there was little consensus among readers about the importance of science in SF. Some were concerned with scientific plausibility, but most focused on the quality of the stories as entertainment. For example, a 1926 *Weird Tales* reader praised Lovecraft over Poe because 'Poe kept one foot on earth, whereas Lovecraft swings boldly into the unreal, pinions spread' (Price 1926: 567), while a 1937 *Amazing* reader states that 'it is safe to state that more pleasure is derived from the perusal of logical fantasy than from the reading of an accurate scientific treatise' (Conover, Jr 1937: 132). Throughout the period, in letters and fanzines, readers expressed their preferences and took an active role in shaping the genre, which Gernsback acknowledged as early as the June 1926 *Amazing*:

> From the suggestions for reprints that are coming in, these 'fans' seem to have a hobby ... of hunting up scientifiction stories, not only in English, but in

many other languages.... not a day ... passes but we get from a dozen to fifty suggestions as to stories which, frankly, we have no record, although we have a list of some 600 or 700 scientifiction stories.

(quoted in Warner 1969: 23)

Readers could also influence the policies of magazines, as when *Amazing*'s editor Raymond A. Palmer, faced with complaints about 'forced love interest' (Benson 1939: 139), promised to eliminate sex from the stories he published. However, SF was not restricted to the pulps, and while the pulps were finding their feet, SF was proliferating in other media.

SF in other media

The August 1928 *Amazing* published Philip Francis Nowlan's 'Armageddon – 2419 AD' (book 1962), in which Anthony Rogers wakes from suspended animation 500 years in the future to discover that America has been defeated and colonised by the Chinese. Coming from a period in which America was 'the most powerful nation in the world' (Nowlan 2005: 26), he proves to be a natural leader, helping white Americans to rediscover their inherent superiority over their decadent masters. The story ends with him swearing to 'blast the Yellow Blight from the face of the Earth' (105). However, before he could achieve this – in 'The Warlords of Han' (*Amazing*, March 1929) – Anthony Rogers had been reinvented as the 'less ethnic' and 'more heroic sounding' Buck Rogers (Weinstein 2005: 19) for the January 1929 launch of the daily newspaper comic strip, *Buck Rogers in the 25th Century*, written by Nowlan and drawn by Dick Calkins. While the two magazine stories include some descriptions of future technologies based on disrupting and reassembling electrons, their emphasis is on heroic adventure. In contrast, the strip spends more time imagining the wonders of the Mongol 'cities of superscientific magnificence' (Nowlan and Calkins 2008: 20) and technologies such as dirigibles, submarines, spaceships, inertron-powered jumping belts, ray guns, robots, radiophones, disintegrator rays, repellor rays, electro-hypnotic lie detectors, radiophones and television surveillance systems. The narratives soon diverge, with the strip quickly introducing western and aviation adventure elements, before extending into interplanetary adventures in its second year. Roger's love interest, Wilma Deering, is also radically transformed, from a soldier every bit the equal of her male contemporaries, if not of her eventual husband, to a figure whose principal role is to jealously misconstrue Buck's actions so as to land in trouble from which she needs to be rescued. The original stories, which might have reached 100,000 readers, are mostly forgotten, but the strip, which 'eventually appeared in nearly 400 newspapers and reached over 50 million readers' (Benton 1992: 11) ran uninterrupted until 1967. It was accompanied by a Sunday strip (1930–1965) featuring the adventures of Wilma's young brother Buddy, a CBS radio series (1932–1947), a 10-minute film produced especially for the New York World's Fair (1939–1940), a 12-part movie serial adaptation, *Buck Rogers* (Beebe and Goodkind 1939), starring Larry 'Buster' Crabbe, which was re-edited into the feature *Destination Saturn* in the same year, and so many spin-offs and so much tie-in merchandising, including the first toy ray guns, that by Christmas 1934 *The New Yorker* was commenting on the popularity of the 'fifteen or more Buck Rogers toys on the market this year' (quoted in Lucanio and Coville 2002: 36). For many people, SF quickly became synonymous with 'that Buck Rogers stuff', and it prompted numerous imitators.

Alex Raymond's Sunday *Flash Gordon* comic strip was launched in 1934 as a direct competitor. While Nowlan and Calkins seem fascinated with engineering marvels, Raymond prefers swashbuckling adventure on exotic worlds among scantily-clad men and women. His strip was adapted for radio (1935–1936) and three movie serials, also starring Crabbe, beginning with *Flash Gordon* (Stephani 1936), Universal's second biggest grosser of the year. Patrick Lucanio and Gary Coville argue that the *Buck Rogers* daily strip was superior because it was derived from a pulp SF story and therefore observed the values of technocratic rationalism. Such a claim indicates the role relative cultural capital can play in the process of enrolment, not only privileging prose fiction over other media forms but also certain varieties of SF over others: *Flash Gordon*'s blend of Robin Hood/desert/ oriental-type adventures in other worlds more closely resembles the 'lesser' science fantasy tradition of colourful adventures in exotic settings, and thus must surely be inferior.

The *Buck Rogers* daily strip rarely consisted of more than three or four panels in which, typically, a character had to be extricated from the previous day's cliff-hanger and be plunged into another. The *Flash Gordon* weekly strip – which was not above deploying this kind of narrative structure – usually consisted of at least eight panels, which allowed for greater narrative complexity and for more formal variation in terms of the shape, position and organisation of the panels. Calkins' technological imagination consists of rivets and simple mechanics, whereas Raymond is more attentive to the surface design of his streamlined superscience technologies. In place of Calkins' often crude, black-on-white line-drawings, which are generally square-on to a flat plane of action, Raymond offered dynamic compositions and an increasingly potent use of colour. The boldly coloured artwork in the *Buck Rogers* Sunday strip is credited to Calkins but is actually the work of Russell Keaton and Rick Yager, both of whom introduced a stronger sense of composition, perspective and depth of field, and frequently experimented with the single-page, 12-panel format. Even so, their work, like Calkins', lacks the erotic charge of Raymond's visuals. While it is often difficult to tell Calkins' characters apart, Raymond lavishes increasing attention on the human form. Flash is gradually bulked up into well-defined, muscular 'beefcake', and the female characters – always trim and pert – tend to fall into cheesecake poses even more frequently than they fall for Flash. When they talk about wanting to 'marry' him, they clearly have something more carnal in mind.

Buck Rogers and *Flash Gordon* were not the first SF strips – in 1910, for example, Winsor McCay's *Little Nemo in Slumberland* featured a 17-week adventure on Mars – but they were central to the development of the SF comic strip and comic book. In the mid- to late-1930s, numerous other SF comic book characters appeared: Dr Mystic, Dan Hastings, Dirk the Demon, the Flame, Rex Dexter of

Mars, Cosmic Carson, Stardust, the Comet, Silver Streak, Spacehawk, Sub-Zero, Blue Bolt and, of course, Superman. The January 1933 issue of Jerry Siegel and Joe Shuster's fanzine, *Science Fiction*, included Siegel's story 'The Reign of the Superman', from which Superman, inspired by Philip Wylie's *The Gladiator* (1930) and John W. Campbell's *The Mightiest Machine* (*Astounding* 1934–1935; book 1947), gradually evolved, debuting in *Action Comics* 1 (June 1938) and launching his own title, *Superman*, in 1939. Although Superman's adventures were set in the present day, the first two panels detail his extraterrestrial origins and the first page ends with a supposedly scientific explanation of his amazing strength; the strips soon gained superscientific villains and other SF elements.

Superman was an immediate success. By 1940, *Action Comics* was selling a million copies per month and *Superman* one and a half million. In the same year, the daily newspaper strip, launched in 1939, appeared in '230 newspapers, with a combined readership of twenty-five million readers' and the Sunday strip, also launched in 1939, was being carried by 90 newspapers (Stern 2006: xiv). In 1940, the Mutual Broadcasting System introduced a three-times-per-week, 15-minute radio series, going to five times per week and being 'carried ... over the entire Mutual network of 220 radio stations' in 1942, by which point the Supermen of America fan club had attracted a quarter of a million members (Vance 2006: 10). In 1941, the Fleischer Studios produced the first of 17 Superman cartoons for cinematic release, and in 1948 Columbia produced a 15-part, live-action movie serial. Superman inspired numerous imitators in the late 1930s and early 1940s, including Batman, Wonder Woman, Captain America, Captain Marvel and Plastic Man.

Histories of SF typically treat superhero comics as peripheral to the 'real' SF developing in the pulps and as an undesirable influence on public perceptions of the genre, giving 'science fiction the juvenile image from which it has never escaped' (Ashley 2000: 124). Fans of the period were more varied in their response to SF in other media. The weekly fanzine *Fantasy News* regularly published reviews of 'scientiradio' programmes, 'scientifilms' and 'astronomusic', and in July 1939 carried the exciting news that 'THE SUPERMAN, comic par excellent [sic], began this week in THE NEW YORK POST. This is the first New York paper to carry it, tho the strip has been carried throughout the country for months' ('The Visascreen' 3). However, two months later, John Giunta bemoans that 'Something TERRIBLE is happening in the publishing field. Everybody, it seems, is diving into the COMICS magazine business' (1939: 5), including the editors and/or publishers of SF pulps (indeed, such authors as Alfred Bester, Otto Binder, Edmond Hamilton, Harry Harrison and Manly Wade Wellman were soon writing comics and two prominent fans, Mortimer Weisinger and Julius Schwartz, went on to edit many of DC's best-selling titles after WWII). In the fanzine *Escape*, C.M. Kornbluth uses a presumptively shared low opinion of SF comics to criticise the quality of a particular pulp, announcing that 'we can't talk about the priceless early Buck Rogers because we know nothing about that sort of thing' (1939: 7), but goes on to note that 'we think it's all a lot of damn nonsense, eclipsed only for sheer assinity by the later *Thrilling Wonder Stories*' (8).

Fans had similarly mixed views of the SF films of the period. One 1939 letter to *Amazing Stories* bemoans that while Buck Rogers originated in *Amazing*, 'It got to the comics and now poor Buck Rogers is running in a twelve-part serial at a neighbourhood theatre with that dizzy dame of his' (Schaeffer 1939: 143); another (Bringwald 1939) begins by deriding *Mars Attacks the World*, the 68-minute feature condensed from *Flash Gordon's Trip to Mars* (Beebe and Hill 1938) but goes on to praise *The Mysterious Island* (Hubbard 1929), *Frankenstein* (Whale 1931), *The Invisible Man* (Whale 1933) and *Things to Come* (Menzies 1936). As these varied statements about what constitutes 'real' SF indicate, it was not straightforwardly a question of the medium in which the text appeared.

A key factor in the development of SF was the drive to develop marketable texts that built on the success of those already circulating. For example, the *Flash Gordon* strip prompted the 1935 *New Fun Comics* copycat strip, 'Don Drake on the Planet Saro'; and the first movie serial, with its celebration of the male physique, prompted such imitations as *Undersea Kingdom* (Eason and Kane 1936), starring stuntman man Ray 'Crash' Corrigan as a naval officer who finds adventure in superscientific Atlantis. This process of combining new elements with existing formulas produced some texts that now seem very peculiar: *Just Imagine* (Butler 1930) blended the musical – the very modern expression of sound cinema – with dystopian SF, whimsical interplanetary adventure and the ethnic comedy of vaudeville star El Brendel; the movie serial *The Phantom Empire* (Brower and Eason 1935) unleashed the singing cowboy recording and radio star Gene Autry on Mu, an underground city of superscience. Many of the most highly regarded SF films of the period were adapted – usually quite liberally – from well-established titles, but adaptations of pulp SF were relatively uncommon, the most prominent being *The Devil-Doll* (Browning 1936), based on A. Merritt's *Burn Witch Burn!* (*Argosy* 1932; book 1933). Successful films spawned their own imitators, including sequels such as *Bride of Frankenstein* (Whale 1935) and *The Invisible Man Returns* (May 1940). The opportunism that underpins such cycles of production is demonstrated by the absence of any connection between *Doctor X* (Curtiz 1932) and *The Return of Doctor X* (Sherman 1939) other than the studio that produced them. The key SF films of the period were preoccupied with mad science, but often take on aspects of gothic horror and crime films: the *Doctor X* films feature cannibalistic murders and a variety of high-tech vampirism; *The Invisible Ray* (Hillyer 1936) and *The Devil-Doll* are revenge melodramas, the former featuring a scientist who believes his discoveries have been stolen by jealous rivals, the latter an escaped convict intent on clearing his name of crimes he did not commit and reuniting with his daughter. Visual spectacle provides an important aspect of such films' appeal. They not only told stories about the wonders produced by advanced science and technology, but also used advances in film technology to depict them: *Doctor X*'s Technicolor, the sophisticated model work of *Just Imagine*'s future metropolis, the matte-work that made the Invisible Man invisible, the combined effects that brought dinosaurs and a giant ape to life in *King Kong* (Cooper and Schoedsack 1933).

SF reached far larger audiences in these other media than it did in the pulps, although histories of the genre usually marginalise or exclude such SF, not least because such accounts have been produced by figures who either emerged from the magazine and paperback tradition (e.g. Gunn 1975, del Rey 1979) or are primarily literary scholars (e.g. Luckhurst 2005, Roberts 2006). With the emphasis on inter-disciplinarity and transdisciplinarity in contemporary academia, SF studies is increasingly engaged with this broader range of material and the challenges it poses to earlier conceptualisations of the genre.

Pulp SF: space opera and beyond

The issue of *Amazing* in which 'Armageddon – 2419 AD' appeared also included the first instalment of E.E. Smith's *The Skylark of Space* (1928; book 1946), one of the earliest examples of what would become known as space opera, a form of interplanetary, interstellar or intergalactic adventure fiction. As SF developed in the magazines, space opera's formulaic plots and lack of anything science-fictional beyond the paraphernalia of rocket ships and ray guns saw such fiction more and more denigrated and marginalised. Arguably, this is one of the reasons for the critical neglect of the 1930s SF, with many preferring to treat the genre as more properly beginning in the 'Golden Age' of Campbell's *Astounding*. Yet, space opera's emphasis on the overwhelming scale and potential dangers and rewards of space, and on masculine adventure, have remained central to SF.

Edmond Hamilton's *Interstellar Patrol* stories (*Weird Tales* 1929–1934; books 1964–1965) are sometimes credited with inventing the form. The Patrol polices the solar system, combats space pirates, resists alien invasions and averts the collision of planets. Hamilton emphasises manly exploits and self-sacrificing heroics, and deploys rather than explains futuristic technologies. Unlike many subsequent writ-ers, he retains a sense of the uncanny, particularly in depicting aliens: in 'The Star-Stealers' (1929), the alien is 'an upright cone of black flesh, several feet in diameter and three or more in height, supported by a dozen or more smooth long tentacles which branched from its lower end – supple, boneless octopus-arms' (2009b: 72); and in 'The Comet-Drivers' (1930), the Patrolmen encounter aliens who, while sleeping and in order to communicate with each other, flow 'together into a single liquid mass, a great black pool in which floated all their eyes, their liquid bodies mingling together!' (2009a: 312). Although Hamilton wrote other kinds of SF, he excelled at space opera, and instead of contributing to Campbell's 'Golden Age', he almost single-handedly wrote the *Captain Future* pulp (1940–1944; books 1968–1969). Other major 1930s space operas include Campbell's *Arcot, Morey and Wade* (1930–1932; books 1953–1961), Jack Williamson's *Legion of Space* (1934–1939; books 1947–1967) and Smith's *Skylark* (1928–1935, 1965; books 1946–1949, 1966) and *Lensmen* (1934–1950; books 1948–1954) series, most instalments of which appeared in either *Amazing* or *Astounding*.

The Skylark of Space – a blend of superscientific invention, interstellar exploits, colonial adventure and stilted romance – was co-written with Lee Hawkins Garby between 1915 and 1920 but initially failed to find a publisher. Protagonist Dick Seaton accidentally discovers a method of producing the 'pure and total conversion of matter to controllable energy' (1977: 17) and, with the financial assistance of his

Space opera

'Space opera', coined by Bob Tucker in his fanzine *Le Zombie* in 1941, was initially intended as a derogatory term – analogous to 'soap opera' for melodramas and 'horse opera' for hackneyed westerns – to describe badly written SF. Hartwell and Cramer contend that it began to lose its pejorative sense between 1950 and 1970 as it became possible to be nostalgic for pulp SF, and only since then has it transformed into a more or less neutral description of 'colorful, dramatic, large-scale science fiction adventure ... usually focused on a sympathetic, heroic central character and ... set in the relatively distant future and in space or on other worlds' and 'deal[ing] with war, piracy, military virtues, and very large-scale action, large stakes' (2006: 17).

millionaire chum, Martin Crane, builds a spaceship, the Skylark, powered by it. Rival inventor Marc C. DuQuesne approaches Brookings of the World Steel Corporation to arrange to steal the discovery, murder Seaton and Crane and exploit 'total conversion atomic energy' (23) himself. When Brookings' machinations go awry, DuQuesne abducts Seaton's fiancée, Dorothy, but unintentionally ends up travelling far from Earth in his own spaceship. Seaton and Crane set out in pursuit, along with Margaret Spencer, who had infiltrated World Steel as a secretary in search of evidence that Brookings 'swindled [her] father out of an invention worth millions and then killed him' (68). They rescue Dorothy, capture DuQuesne and ally themselves with the sympathetic Kondalians. Seaton and Crane marry Dorothy and Margaret, and then build a new Skylark with an impervious shell of the alien metal, *arenak*, with which to defeat the nefarious Mardonalians' invasion fleet. On returning to Earth, DuQuesne escapes to practise further villainy in the sequels, in which the spaceships are bigger, faster and more impervious, the planetary peril more dire, the brilliance of Seaton more exceptional. By *Skylark of Valeron* (*Astounding* 1934–1935; book 1949) the protagonists are happily purifying the universe: 'Humanity *über alles* – *homo sapiens* against all the vermin of the universe!' (1978: 138), Seaton exclaims, and Crane soon after notes that 'on planets similar to Earth in mass, atmosphere, and temperature, wherever situated, man develops. The ultimate genes must permeate universal space itself' (141).

Smith downplays social class, depicting Seaton's friendship with Crane as effortless, despite their very different backgrounds. His female characters are typically subservient. Dorothy is shown not to be shallow like her snobbish, society mother because she tolerates Seaton's distraction and neglect and is able to befriend Crane. Margaret embraces the opportunity to assist the men in their deep space observations: '"taking notes is the best thing I do!" Margaret cried, and called for pad and pencils' (1977: 92). Peoples of colour appear only fleetingly: Crane's African-American servants are mentioned in a single sentence; his Japanese valet, Shiro, with his 'ready vocabulary of peculiar but sonorous words' (172), is treated in a mildly comic manner and, although he joins the *Skylark* crew in the sequels, he rarely actually features. Smith's recognition of the need to finance invention is not uncommon in pulp SF, but this is typically resolved through serendipitous personal fortunes or connections rather than corporate investment. Likewise, pulp SF also continued to demonstrate the peculiar anti-intellectualism, which privileges engineering know-how over more abstract theorisation, that is evident in the exchange between Crane and Seaton about DuQuesne's ship accelerating past the speed of light:

> 'Nothing *can* go that fast … E Equals M C square.'
> 'Einstein's Theory is still a theory. This … is an observed fact.'

(61)

Smith's *Lensmen* series builds on Hamilton's *Interstellar Patrol* stories by mythologising the exceptionality of an interplanetary, interstellar and ultimately intergalactic police force. Our galaxy is the battleground for two superior alien species, the benevolent Arisians and evil Eddorians. Over eons, the former have manipulated the evolutionary and social development of various species, especially humans, so as to produce a force capable of combating the Eddorians. They refuse to intervene directly in Eddorian agents' attempts at galactic conquest because 'the stresses and conflicts involved are necessary – and … sufficient – to produce the Civilization which must and shall come into being' (1972: 5). In its original 1934 *Amazing* version, *Triplanetary* was not a *Lensman* novel, but Smith retrofitted the revised and expanded 1948 book version into the series. In it, members of the Triplanetary Patrol fight space pirates and, after a devastating war with alien invaders, sign the first interstellar treaty, which leads to the formation of the Galactic Patrol. In *First Lensman* (1950), the Arisians provide Patrolmen with identification badges that are impossible to counterfeit, each one a semi-alive Lens that forms an unbreakable bond with its wearer, kills anyone else who tries to wear it and promotes telepathy. Only 'very special men' are worthy of the Lens, 'Men with tremendous force, drive and scope…. No more to be stopped than a glacier, and twice as hard and ten times as cold. A woman simply *can't* have that kind of mind!' (1972: 39). As the scale of the novels increases – more and bigger spaceships with more and bigger weapons fighting in more and more star systems – the Lensmen gradually defeat the forces of Eddore. While relationships between men and women remain as stilted as in the *Skylark* series, Smith's sexism becomes more overt. For example, in *Second Stage Lensmen* (*Astounding* 1941–1942; book 1953) protagonist Kimball Kinnison concludes that members of a 'repulsively reptilian-appearing race, merely because of having a heredity of equality and cooperation between the sexes, were in essence more nearly human' than the 'intrinsically beautiful' but matriarchal humanoid aliens of Lyrane II (1973: 58).

Not all of what we now call space opera is as poorly written as the term's original derogatory meaning might imply, nor is it necessarily crudely expansionist and exuberant; and not all pulp SF was space opera. For example, Stanley G. Weinbaum's stories of interplanetary adventure engaged with the challenges of communicating with a species whose language *and experience* are radically other.

His 'A Martian Odyssey' (*Wonder Stories* 1934) and 'Valley of Dreams' (*Wonder Stories* 1934) were far more concerned with exploring alien environments and imagining the variety of forms sentience might take than with action and conflict. Murray Leinster's 'Sidewise in Time' (*Astounding* 1934) and 'Proxima Centauri' (*Astounding* 1935) introduce a note of anxiety or doubt into adventure SF scenarios. The former tells of a fortnight during which Earth experiences timequakes, causing sections of land to slip into alternative realities in which history had unfolded otherwise (e.g. America has been colonised by Romans or Chinese). Minott, a mathematics professor embittered by his ineffectual life at a mediocre college, leads a group of students in search of a timeline in which Vikings rather than the British colonised North America and where his superior knowledge will enable him to 'begin the formation of [an] empire' (1978d: 32). The characterisation of Minott undermines the positive depiction of white colonial conquest more typical of the pulps: he is power-hungry and avaricious, bullies his students and intends for the most beautiful of the females to become his sexual partner. Although the story ends with the safe return of most of the group to their own world and the cessation of the timequakes, secure closure is disrupted by an eerie sense of nature being mysterious and dangerous. Some people remain stranded on alternative Earths, while 'Detroit returned to its own space and time untouched, unharmed, unlooted, and undisturbed. But no living things, not even a domestic animal or a caged bird, was in it when it came back'; as the narrator rather inadequately comments, 'We do not understand that at all' (58).

In 'Proxima Centauri', an interstellar expedition falls victim not to space pirates but to the tedium of 'deadly routine' (1978c: 64). A failed mutiny produces an antagonistic caste system of officers and 'Muts'. When they discover that the inhabitants of the Proxima Centauri system are sentient plants who feed on animal tissue, any hope of peaceful interspecies exchange is crushed. Although the story then becomes one of heroic resolve and manly sacrifice – culminating in the genocide of the aliens and the deaths of the entire expedition apart from the Mut protagonist and his beautiful officer-class lover, who can now colonise Proxima Centauri – it is distinguished by the ambivalence with which it treats colonialism. The aliens, who have consumed all the animal tissue in their own system, see Earth as a cornucopia to be plundered:

> Billions of human beings! Trillions of lesser animals! Uncountable creatures in the seas! All the Centaurian race would go mad with eagerness to invade this kingdom of riches and ecstasy, the ecstasy felt by any Centaurian when consuming the prehistoric foodstuff of his race.
>
> (98)

In addition to such parallels with human colonialism, the protagonists become uncomfortably aware of their ongoing exploitation of other species when the Centaurians strip all of the animal tissue from the human ship, including clothing and soap.

While some of the stories Campbell wrote under his Don A. Stuart pseudonym, such as the sequence 'The Machine' (*Astounding* 1935), 'The Invaders'

(*Astounding* 1935) and 'Rebellion' (*Astounding* 1935), are as celebratory of human exceptionalism as his *Arcot, Morey and Wade* space operas; others introduce complexity and ambivalence into the heroic tendencies of the era. 'Twilight' (*Astounding* 1934) features a thirty-first-century time-traveller who accidentally arrives in the present while returning from seven million years in the future, when the Sun has drifted out of the Milky Way, leaving the 'heavens … almost empty to the eye' (2003b: 26). Although humanity did colonise the solar system, the 'strangely quiet men' of this far future – completely devoid of curiosity and sustained by perfect machines they no longer understand – are now returning to 'the home planet' (32) in 'the lingering, dying glow of man's twilight' (37). Although reminiscent of H.G. Wells' *The Time Machine*, its pessimism was innovative in the context of the American pulps. 'Blindness' (*Astounding* 1935), in which a scientist loses his eyesight because of his dedication to producing atomic power, draws attention to the fragility of human endeavour. Although he succeeds, he returns to Earth only to find that *thermlectrium*, an earlier discovery which was essential to his project but whose other possibilities he ignored, is itself a source of cheap, never-ending power that will more easily solve humanity's energy needs. In 'Who Goes There?' (*Astounding* 1938), heroic men defeat the menace of a shape-shifting alien, but only after an intense period in which the impossibility of determining who is a 'real' man and who is an alien in man-shaped disguise reveals the precariousness of the difference – foundational to the men's sense of themselves – between human and alien. Probably his most disturbing story, though, is 'The Escape' (*Astounding* 1935). Set in a future governed by strict eugenics and conditioning that ensures genetically matched people love each other, the independent female protagonist Aies is assigned by the Population Control Commission to Bruce, whom she strongly dislikes. He, however, considers her a desirable partner, 'as clever as any woman that ever lived' (2003a: 141). She goes on the run with her lover, repeatedly outsmarting her official pursuers, but Bruce's slightly greater abilities result in her eventual capture. After she is conditioned, they are united as lovers, and when Bruce proclaims, 'Love is the greatest happiness in the world – isn't it, little sweetheart? … does it matter whence it comes or why?' (147), she concurs.

Pulp SF: women writers

Women writers (and readers) contributed to magazine SF in greater numbers than has usually been acknowledged. Part of the reason for this neglect is that relatively little 1930s pulp SF has been reprinted, and selections have tended to privilege male authors who sustained careers for a number of decades. For example, of the 44 stories in Asimov's *Before the Golden Age* (1974) and Knight's *Science Fiction of the Thirties* (1975) only one is by a woman, Leslie F. Stone's 'The Human Pets of Mars' (*Amazing* 1936). Similarly, in the 1970s, Del Rey published more than 20 *Best of* … volumes collecting fiction by authors who came to prominence in the magazines during the 1930s, 1940s and 1950s; only two of them are devoted to women, C.L. Moore and Leigh Brackett.

Moore was undoubtedly the most prominent woman SF writer of the period, her *Northwest Smith* stories (1933–1940; books 1954–1958) successfully blending elements of weird fiction, planetary romance and space opera. 'Shambleau' (*Weird Tales* 1933) introduces her hard-boiled, outlaw adventurer, 'whose name is known and respected in every dive and wild outpost on a dozen wild planets' (2002b: 165). In a Martian frontier town, Smith rescues a 'sweetly made' (166) girl from a bloodthirsty mob, but she turns out to be a member of the species that inspired the myth of Medusa. She enthrals him with languid and voluptuous dreams, overcoming his 'revulsion' with 'rapture' (185) and feeding upon him telepathically. Powerless to escape, he must be rescued by his Venusian friend Yarol.

In contrast to the space operas of Smith, Campbell and Williamson, the *Northwest Smith* stories retain a Lovecraftian sense of a universe that exceeds human understanding and mastery and of things best left unprovoked. Confronted by the Shambleau, Smith is briefly shaken 'out of his frozen horror' by 'the realization of vast backgrounds reaching into misted history' (183), back to the ancient times before Egypt when humankind 'conquered Space before' (165). In 'Black Thirst' (*Weird Tales* 1934), he is menaced by Venusians who embody 'dark and mystery and things too strange and terrible to be looked upon' (2002a: 208), and in the shadowless setting of 'The Tree of Life' (*Weird Tales* 1936) 'the grayness swallow[s] everything up, leaving the landscape oddly flat, like a badly drawn picture' (2002c: 243). Smith's passivity in most of these tales contrasts with the agency of Moore's Jirel of Joiry, the female protagonist of a series of stories (1934–1939) typically excluded from SF and enrolled into fantasy because they deploy the discourse of magic rather than science to underpin their mysterious worlds.

The work of other female pulp SF writers offers insights into the ways in which the new genre and its potential were conceptualised in the 1930s. Stone's 'The Human Pets of Mars' is a conventional adventure story, in which Martian decapods kidnap and make pets of humans who later – through the engineering skills and manly heroism of Brett Rand – steal a spaceship, destroy their pursuers and return to Earth. However, 'Out of the Void' (*Amazing* 1929) features a female character who successfully passes as male, and 'Men with Wings' (*Air Wonder Stories* 1929) depicts a society which has abolished private property and embraced free love. In its sequel, 'Women with Wings' (*Air Wonder Stories* 1930), when 90 per cent of pregnant women begin to die in childbirth, humans set out to find whether Venus can provide compatible breeding stock until artificial wombs are developed. Meanwhile, the Venusian matriarchy – of humanoids evolved from fish – is faced with declining male breeding stock. By the end of the story, a programme of interplanetary miscegenation is established. 'The Conquest of Gola' (*Wonder Stories* 1931) treats gender-role reversal more humorously. 'The Hell Planet' (*Wonder Stories* 1932) pointedly critiques colonial adventure narratives, recounting an expedition to Vulcan, a planet within the orbit of Mercury that is toxic to humans but rich in *cosmicite*, a rare metal essential to the construction of spaceships. The crew trick the reluctant natives into revealing the location of their mines by posing as powerful servants of their gods. Only one man, Jimson, survives the journey and the natives' growing suspicions, bringing back enough *cosmicite* to justify, apparently, all the hardships and sacrifice. However, rather than ending on a heroic note, Wendell – the sole survivor of the expedition that discovered Vulcan – predicts that instead of enjoying the wealth, Jimson will 'go on and on ... looking for new fortunes, peeping into all the strange corners of the universe' until he is killed (1932: 27). Others will 'sweat and toil in this noisome jungle, under the blistering sun, living on food lozenges' (27) in the attempt to repeat his supposed success, and in the future men will say of them, '"those pioneers ... they were men!" Bah! Sheep! That's what we are ... pigs for the slaughter ... pigs for the slaughter!' (27, original ellipses).

Women writers in 1920s/1930s SF pulps

Pansy E. Black

Clara E. Chestnut

Merab Eberle

Sophie Wenzel Ellis

Mona Farnsworth (Muriel Newhall)

Lee Hawkins Garby

Frances Garfield

L. Taylor Hansen

Clare Winger Harris

Hazel Heald

Minna Irving

Amelia Reynolds Long

Lilith Lorraine (Mary Maude Dunn Wright)

Kathleen Ludwick

C.L. Moore

Dorothy Quick

Kaye Raymond

Margaretta W. Rea

Louise Rice

M.F. Rupert

G. St John-Loe

I.M. Stephens

Leslie F. Stone

Emma Vanne

Helen Weinbaum

Gabriel Wilson

Lilith Lorraine uses SF to imagine different social relations emerging from scientific advances. *The Brain of the Planet* (*Science Fiction Series* 1929) imagines that humanity's ability to think 'logically and without prejudice' (1929: 9) is stuck at an earlier level of evolutionary development. A scientist builds a tower to project powerful thought waves so as to gain control of the planet's mental essence, 'hither to a sluggish Sargasso sea, becalming our brain-ships in the sea-weeds of tradition and in the octopus tentacles of mass psychology' (12), and force humans into more altruistic patterns of thought until they become habitual. As soon as class and gender equality are established as the norms of human organisation and psychology, he destroys the projector. 'Into the 28th Century' (*Science Wonder Quarterly* 1930) portrays a eutopian future in which 'fetishes' such as 'patriotism and democracy and ... Hundred per cent Americanism' (1930: 252) have been replaced by feminist socialism. This tale, like many of the period, imagines eugenics playing a role in future human development, but here at least it is guided by the principle of 'carefully preserv[ing] superior strains in the various races' and uniting them through 'international marriages' to 'form a super-race' (258).

Science and social critique

Many pulp SF stories were criticised by their readers and have been dismissed by later critics for their scientific implausibility, but it is important to remember that the boundaries between 'real' and 'pseudo' science are continually in flux. German and American experiments in rocketry and atomic energy were soon to shape the outcome of WWII, but during the 1930s it was unclear whether the dreams of space travel and nuclear power were viable engineering projects. Although some stories posit what are effectively magical solutions masquerading as technology (e.g. Smith's *arenak*, Campbell's *thermlectrium*), they might not have seemed quite so far-fetched to readers in a world being transformed by new materials, such as Bakelite, tarmac, neoprene, nylon and the steel frameworks that enabled skyscraper construction to go beyond 200 feet, and by new media, such as phonographs, talking pictures, radio and television. The first licensed US commercial radio station began broadcasting in 1920, and within a decade the first experimental television broadcasts were being made in Germany, the UK and the US, although regular broadcast television services were discontinued for the duration of WWII. In 1925, Gernsback himself launched a New York radio station, WRNY, which began a daily, five-minute television broadcast in 1928, with an estimated audience of 2000 viewers; he also published the hobbyist magazine *Television* (1927–1928).

Pulp invention stories tended to imagine technological innovations as isolated phenomena, producing little in the way of social change, or as being destroyed before they can have any wider impact. For example, in Miles J. Breur's 'The Man with the Strange Head' (*Amazing* 1927), a dead scientist is found to have been housing his decrepit form in a radium-powered robot body, but this technological feat is treated as nothing more than the solution to a mystery. Some stories did involve broadly dystopian critiques of technological change, such as Eando Binder's 'Enslaved Brains' (*Wonder Stories* 1934; book 1965), in which the brains of the dead are kept alive, probably in torment, to control automated systems, but here the fault lies not so much with the technocratic state as with its domination by a dictator. One of the more curious pulp invention stories is Campbell's 'The Battery of Hate' (*Amazing* 1933), in which Bruce Kennedy invents a cheap and reliable source of energy. He struggles heroically against the financiers who wish to suppress it, but at his moment of victory realises that by making oil and power companies redundant overnight he would throw the economy into chaos and ruin millions of people. Faced with this potential social consequence and the 'misery it would inflict on the world', Kennedy decides to lease the rights to the existing corporations so that they can 'scrap their plant gradually as they build and sell these batteries' (1975: 152).

Beyond the pulps, writers were also concerned with the social and cultural consequences of technological change, as well as with race, eugenics and the rise of fascism, and they often found vastly different readerships. For example, as part of his ultimately unsuccessful End Poverty in California (EPIC) campaign to seize the Democratic party nomination and then run for the Governorship of California, Upton Sinclair published a 64-page pamphlet, *I, Governor of California, and How I Ended Poverty* (1933), which recounts, from a point in the future, his success in transforming the crumbling Californian economy through a form of state socialism; he contributed a similarly science-fictional account of the transformation of the US, *We, People of America, and How We Ended Poverty* (1934), to campaigners in the national elections.

Among the most prominent non-pulp SF novels of the 1930s is Aldous Huxley's *Brave New World* (1932), which describes the highly automated and ordered London of 632AF (After Ford), that is, 2540 AD. This future's World State is perfectly peaceful and happy, largely because of the biochemical and psychological management of the population. Selective interventions in the development of foetuses in artificial wombs, and the conditioning of the resulting children, ensure sufficient members of each of the five social classes, ranging from Alphas to Epsilons, with the lower orders kept distracted by hallucinogenic soma and the immersive medium of the feelies. The novel focuses on an anomalous Alpha, the psychologist Bernard Marx, who is alienated from this society and questions the regime of conditioning, and on John Savage, a young man raised on a reservation. John is horrified by what he sees as London's empty and meaningless society, while the Londoners are excited and intrigued by his primitive emotional responses. His distraught self-flagellation titillates the crowd who have gathered to observe it, resulting in an orgy of sex and violence in which he eventually participates. The following morning, bereft of any human connection or a purposeful way of life, John hangs himself.

Karel Čapek was similarly concerned with the way in which the expansion of the capitalist world market was becoming synonymous with the progress of civilisation, a tendency satirised in his 1920 play *R.U.R. (Rossum's Universal Robots)*. It was quickly translated into English and saw successful productions in the US and the UK, with the BBC broadcasting television versions in 1938 and 1948. After Rossum, Sr fails in his attempt to make an artificial person from 'a colloidal jelly' that 'behaved exactly like living matter' (2004: 6), and thus 'scientifically dethrone God' (7), his son sets out 'to create living and intelligent labor machines' (8). Undertaking 'production from the standpoint of an engineer' (8), he simplifies the human form, 'chuck[ing] everything not directly related to work' (9), and thus 'created the Robot', 'the best kind of worker' – 'the one that's cheapest. The one with fewest needs' (9). Increasingly dependent upon robots, human culture grows sterile. Helena, who started out as an activist for robot equality, destroys the secret of their production as the robots revolt and kill all humans – but not before their discovery of love for one another ensures that they might reproduce without factory intervention. Čapek's major SF novel, *War with the Newts* (1936), similarly satirises colonial acquisition, the confusion of progress with material accumulation and the devalued treatment of labour – in this case, the enslaved, sentient Newt race. Čapek introduces notions of species prejudice into his depiction of labour struggles, characterising the newts as exploited domesticated animals and as people of colour enslaved by colonial enterprise.

George S. Schuyler's *Black No More* (1931) tells of an African-American scientist who invents a process by which black skin can be made white, with far-reaching consequences. As Schuyler insists, although race supposedly marks biological difference, its true social function lies in how it is deployed to reinforce differences of economic class. The capitalist system requires a devalued underclass with which to threaten workers by highlighting the precarious position and supposed good fortune of employed workers; once race has been eliminated as the criterion by which to establish this class difference, it must be reinscribed through other means. The novel ends with the discovery that those who have undergone the whitening treatment are whiter than those born white, and thus a new fad for tanned skin develops among those born white so as to reconstruct the racial hierarchy.

Olaf Stapledon has typically been enrolled into SF as an author of sublime magnitudes, linking the British scientific romance of H.G. Wells and others to later authors such as Arthur C. Clarke and Stephen Baxter. His first novel, *Last and First Men* (1930), recounts the 2 billion year evolutionary history of the 18 species of humankind as told by an Eighteenth Man to a First Man. *Star Maker* (1937), written with a sense that 'Europe is in danger of a catastrophe worse than that of 1914' (2004: 3), ends with a circumnavigation of the globe, pointing to the rising Fascism and militarism of Germany, Italy and Japan, and to the promise of socialist and anti-colonial rebellions elsewhere. It attempts to reconcile the gulf between humankind's objective insignificance and subjective significance, to bridge the macrocosm of cosmic time and space and the microcosm of human lives, and to 'construct an imaginative sketch of the dread but vital whole of things' (4).

When writing on a smaller scale, Stapledon tends towards pessimism. He remains concerned with a sense of the spirit that can exceed the petty contingencies of humanity as currently configured, but sees no clear path to this more enlightened way of being. *Odd John* (1935) narrates the life of a more evolutionarily developed protagonist who critiques from his more 'objective' perspective, and often with amused affection, human social and sexual mores (as an adolescent, he has sex with men and women, but ultimately finds both experiences akin to bestiality). He locates others like himself, whose destiny he believes is to nurture another kind of spirit in the world – one that *homo sapiens* cannot achieve because they have 'floundered into a situation too difficult for [them], namely the present world-situation' (1972: 84). Class war, fascism and technocracy are all attributed to a 'hate-need' (64) arising from the inadequacies of a human spirit stifled and perverted by various moral systems. Like Huxley's John Savage, Odd John and his followers kill themselves, but their deaths are presented as apotheosis rather tragedy.

Anti-fascist SF

Between 1926 and 1936, the SF pulps contained 'no references to the Spanish Civil War … the Italian invasion of Ethiopia … civil disobedience in India, the German abandonment of the League of Nations, [or] the Japanese invasions of China' (Bleiler 1998: xiv). However, there were a number of anti-fascist SF novels.

Edmund Snell, *Kontrol* (1928)

J. Leslie Mitchell, *Gay Hunter* (1934)

Sinclair Lewis, *It Can't Happen Here* (1935)

Naomi Mitchison, *We Have Been Warned* (1935)

Storm Jameson, *In the Second Year* (1936), *Then We Shall Hear Singing* (1942)

Joseph O'Neill, *Land Under England* (1935)

V.F. Calverton, *The Man Inside* (1936)

Rex Warner, *The Wild Goose Chase* (1936), *The Aerodrome* (1941)

Katharine Burdekin, *Swastika Night* (1937)

Andrew Marvell, *Minimum Man* (1938)

Ernst Jünger, *On the Marble Cliffs* (1939)

Vita Sackville-West, *Grand Canyon* (1942)

M. Barnard Eldershaw, *Tomorrow and Tomorrow and Tomorrow* (1947)

Hinko Gottlieb, *The Key to the Great Gate* (1947)

Katharine Burdekin adds a more explicit concern with gender roles to her critique of fascism. In *Proud Man* (1934), the Person, a hermaphroditic future human, visits the twentieth century. The narrative is divided into four parts: an introduction addressed to the Person's contemporaries explaining 'subhuman' culture; and three parts describing her time spent with, respectively, a priest, a woman and a man. Like Stapledon, Burdekin is concerned with the subhumans' withered, distorted spirit, particularly their insistence on categorising people in terms of sex and gender. The Person considers most problems to emerge from the concept of privilege: just as

> subhumans believe that they are all in some way *better* than animals, so they believe that some subhumans are, by reason of the colour of their skins, or their rearing, or their sex, *better* and more worthy than other subhumans of different colour, *class* and sex.... A privilege of class divides a subhuman society horizontally, while a privilege of sex divides it vertically.
>
> (1993: 17)

The Person heals, in turn, the priest of his spiritual ennui, helping him to understand that God is beyond religious structures; the woman of her guilt over the death of her child born out of wedlock; and the man of his compulsion to murder young girls. This last chapter is the most intriguing, as Burdekin unflinchingly insists that from the Person's point of view this aberrant behaviour is no more horrifying than other subhuman practices. The novel ends with the Person realising it had been a dream and deciding that it is unlikely that such a culture could have given rise to her own eutopian world. *Swastika Night* (1937) posits a future in which Europe is under Nazi rule, following their victory in a world war. Christianity survives but has largely been replaced by the worship of Hitler, deified as a magnificent blond god, and a strict social hierarchy, in which Knights (the German elite) dominate subjugated non-Germans, Christians and women. Regarded as little more than animals, women live in compounds and have been reduced to their reproductive function. The Nazis suppress dangerous historical knowledge: that women were once persons; that non-German states were not primitive; that Hitler was a short, brown-haired mortal. *Swastika Night* extends the critique of fascism beyond anxieties about the nascent German state found in contemporary future war novels by emphasising its roots in masculinist culture.

Fans and other audiences

Texts such as those discussed in the last section were not immediately enrolled into SF, but they were also not clearly excluded. Indeed, the 1930s can be seen as a turning point in the development of the genre through the splits that developed among SF fans, many of whom went on to become authors and editors of SF magazines, paperback lines and anthologies.

In May 1934, Gernsback's *Wonder Stories* announced the formation of the Science Fiction League (SFL), an official fan club that would have chapters across America and beyond, presumably intended to build a loyal readership. On the one hand, it was seen to channel fans away from science hobbyism to an interest in SF itself; on the other, it seemed to constitute an attempt to hijack self-organising fandom and subordinate it to publishers' commercial interests. At a 1937 convention, a group invested in SF's potential for social critique formed the Committee for the Political Advancement of Science Fiction. Its members included Frederik Pohl, who would become a major author, editor and agent; Donald Wollheim and

Robert Lowndes, who would both become important editors; and John B. Michel. Influenced by Michel's Marxism and leftist activism in New York, they articulated a socialist project for the genre. In 1938, the Michelists formed the Futurian Science Literary Society. The tensions between the Michelists and more conservative fans, such as Sam Moskowitz, are evident in the fanzines and the magazine letters pages of the period. Alarmed by these outspoken leftists, Moskowitz and others formed New Fandom, a group dedicated to keeping politics out of fandom. They then manoeuvred to seize control from the Futurians of the first World SF Convention, which had been proposed to coincide with the 1939 New York World's Fair. In material published by these two groups, the battle over what should or should not be enrolled into SF is evident, although it not always in terms of their political differences. For example, in the *New Fandom* fanzine, Ray Van Houten wrote:

> I wish it were possible to clear all the parasites off of science-fiction. I mean all those pseudo-scientific things, comics, cheap flickers, Terror Tales, Marvel Tales, and various others I could name if I weren't so lazy. They are really the thing that prevents true science-fiction from getting the credit which is its due. A story that really does prophecy [sic] something that is likely to grow out of a present scientific situation is something of interest and importance to the world in general, but the public, and science in particular, doesn't picture [SF] like that. All they see is … a bunch of kids reading all about killing Martians with death-dealing rays, and fighting off invasions from outer space, and surmounting enormous difficulties with a gyro-cosmic-relativator or something. Phooey!
>
> (1938: 5)

Van Houten (1939) not only sought to eject such work from 'real' SF, but also to dis-enrol stories once considered SF by the fan community, including H.P. Lovecraft's *At the Mountains of Madness* and E.E. Smith's *Galactic Patrol* (*Astounding* 1937–1938; book 1950). At the same, in the Futurian *Escape* fanzine, C.M. Kornbluth (1939) lamented the formulaic nature of much SF and argued for the dis-enrolment of Hamilton's space operas and the *Doc Savage* pulp in favour of an SF that engaged more seriously with the kind of social critique the Futurians encouraged in each other's fiction and would later promote through writing workshops, editing and other organisational endeavours. According to Knight, as the Futurians' careers developed, they saw themselves as 'part of a counterculture, opposed to the dominant culture of professional science fiction writers centering around John Campbell' (1977: 84).

However, in the short term, Campbell was probably the most influential actant in SF enrolments, strongly shaping what was understood by 'SF'. In the early 1940s, the Futurians began to become a presence in the genre. By the end of 1942, they had published 129 stories, most of them pseudonymous collaborations. They also briefly controlled 'more than half the magazines in the field' (Knight 1977: 97), with Lowndes editing *Future Fiction*, *Science Fiction* and *Science Fiction*

Membership of the Futurians included a number of people who went on to significant SF careers, including at various times Isaac Asimov (author), James Blish (author/critic), Virginia Kidd (author/editor/ agent), Damon Knight (author/critic/editor), C.M. Kornbluth (author), Robert A.W. Lowndes (editor/author), Judith Merril (author/editor), Frederik Pohl (author/editor/agent) and Donald A. Wollheim (editor/ author). The related Milford Science Fiction Writers' Conference, co-founded by Knight and Merril, met annually from 1956 to 1972; its participants included Terry Carr, Samuel R. Delany, Jack Dann, George Alec Effinger, Harlan Ellison, Robert Silverberg and Kate Wilhelm. A British 'Milford', organised by Blish, met from 1972, with Richard Cowper, Neil Gaiman, Mary Gentle, Colin Greenland, Diana Wynne Jones, Gwyneth Jones, David Langford, Christopher Priest and Bruce Sterling among its participants. Knight was also one of the first tutors at the Clarion Workshop, which started in 1968, and in 1965 he founded the professional organisation, the Science Fiction Writers of America (SFWA).

Quarterly, Pohl *Astonishing Stories* and *Super Science Stories* and Wollheim *Cosmic Stories* and *Stirring Science Stories*. However, these poorly funded ventures were badly affected by wartime rationing of paper, ink and type and by the conscription of potential contributors. They had all ceased publication before the end of 1943.

Although Campbell thus seems to have dominated magazine SF for a time, the genre itself was never confined to the pulps. Indeed, one of the most important SF events of the 1930s did not even take place in print. Orson Welles' October 1938 radio adaptation of H.G. Wells' *The War of the Worlds* exploited the technical and cultural specificities of the medium to create the impression that the broadcast was reporting live from the site of the alien invasion – especially if, like many listeners, one missed the opening of the show and overlooked increasingly obvious markers of its fictionality. It famously provoked a panic, with 'at least a million' of its six million audience being 'frightened or disturbed' (Cantril 1966: 47) and 28 per cent of those polled reporting that they had believed they were listening to a news broadcast (58). As *Amazing*'s editor Palmer noted in an editorial that also discusses the World's Fair and *The Invisible Man*, this incident demonstrated that SF 'is becoming one of the news features of the day' (1939: 7). A significant number of those interviewed during the audience study that the Princeton Radio Project conducted soon after the broadcast responded to it precisely as SF, whether as '*a Buck Rogers story*' or like 'some of the stories I read in *Amazing Stories*' (Cantril 1966: 90). By the end of the 1930s, then, SF had become a significant and recognisable feature of the cultural landscape, especially in the US.

Conclusion

- During the 1930s, SF proliferated across media. Comics and radio series tended to emphasise heroic individuals, while films often linked to other popular modes, including horror, comedy and melodrama. These media were also often more congenial to SF aimed at children and family audiences. Among those involved in the pulps and fandom, some welcomed and others dismissed SF in other media.
- While much SF did little more than transpose adventure fiction into new settings, unthinkingly extending current social arrangements into the future, SF novels published outside of pulp venues frequently explored revisions to and critiques of the social order.
- A tension developed between those who invested in a literature concerned with science and technology and those concerned with a genre that explores significant themes through sophisticated writing.
- SF demonstrated a growing concern with representing otherness, often organised around gender and race, although it was frequently characterised by an intense discomfort about difference.

4 Campbell's 'revolution' in context: the 1940s

Overview

Those who privilege SF's magazine and paperback tradition often regard the 1940s as the genre's 'Golden Age'. The careers of Isaac Asimov, Arthur C. Clarke and Robert A. Heinlein were established in this decade, and John W. Campbell's long tenure as editor of *Astounding* was securely underway. He exercised a powerful influence over which kinds of stories made it into print, providing a sense of cohesion for the still relatively small field, and made particular efforts to separate SF from fantasy. However, by the end of the decade, the expansion and diversification of magazine SF caused his influence to wane. The post-war economic boom produced an array of new consumer goods and domestic technologies familiar from World's Fairs and other corporate-sponsored exhibitions; along with the development of atomic energy and computers, they produced a sense that the everyday world was coming to resemble the stories in SF magazines. Social critique remained an important part of the genre, addressing the growth of corporate power, bureaucratisation, automation and atomic anxieties.

Ordering the future

In the 1940s, SF was firmly established as a pulp genre and the world itself was becoming increasingly science-fictional as technological developments continued to transform daily life. World's Fairs and expositions – a significant part of the American social and cultural landscape since Chicago's 1893 Columbia Exhibition – had long displayed the wonders of science to the mass public, often in the form of new technologies and consumer goods. During the 1930s, such events gave physical form to many of the ideas and images found in the pulps, and shared their problematic representation of peoples of colour. These celebrations of innovation and empire served two main purposes: 'convincing an American mass audience that the future progress of the United States depended on overseas economic expansion and, if necessary, on extending America's political and military influence to secure economic ends' and 'winning the support of white Americans, regardless of social class, for a view of the world that held that progress toward civilization could be understood in terms of allegedly innate racial characteristics' (Rydell *et al*. 2000: 9).

Corporations rather than scientists dominated the presentation of technology, showcasing commodities they planned to market in the future: General Electric's exhibits introduced many domestic labour-saving devices, including robots, and Bell's exhibit at the 1933 Chicago 'Century of Progress' World's Fair provided free long-distance telephone calls. However, the same Fair's Hall of Science featured a 'race-betterment' display advocating eugenics. Further anxieties about colonialism and racial difference were evident in Fairs' ethnological displays, which contrasted the 'primitive' people of unindustrialised nations with the future-producing, white agents of capitalism and technology. The motto of the Century of Progress was 'Science Finds; Industry Applies; Man Conforms' (12), and during the Depression, this and other World's Fairs increasingly linked the notion of progress to 'a future utopia' that 'now meant increased consumer spending as world's fair sponsors tried to persuade Americans that they had to set aside older values such as thrift and restraint and become consumers of America's factory and farm products' (11).

The 1939 New York World's Fair, with its iconic Trylon and Perisphere, was organised around the theme of 'The World of Tomorrow'. The Democracity diorama, housed in the Perisphere, modelled a garden city of the year 2039 as if seen from 7000 feet in the air. In an era of mass unemployment and crowded housing, Democracity provided a eutopian vision of a clean and uncongested city, powered by hydro-electricity and easily connected to outlying industrial and agricultural regions. Attracting 7000 visitors per day, it stressed not merely architectural design but that proper urban planning would promote social integration and democratic values. The Fair's most popular exhibit was General Motor's Futurama, seen by 26 million visitors. It presented an aerial view of the US in 1960, emphasising the automated superhighways that would criss-cross the country, with vehicles smoothly shifting from slow to fast lanes, protected from collision by proximity sensors. These roads linked ideally planned cities, efficiently located agricultural areas and carefully managed timber resources, suggesting a future of efficiency and abundance. Despite this eutopian vision, General Motors was itself actively pursuing a rather different future, 'consciously, systematically, and ruthlessly destroying the electric urban railways, along with all other forms of competing mass transportation' (Franklin 1982: 49) and championing government-funded interstate highways that would secure further profits. The contradictions between such corporate visions of prosperity through commerce and the more ambiguous world actually being produced by monopoly capitalism informs pulp SF. Consequently, Andrew Ross argues that, rather than treating this as a 'formative naive period' (1991: 103) in which pulp SF, unlike European SF, failed to engage with the realities of fascism, it is important to recognise that 'technocratic Fordism and fascism were simply alternative solutions to the problems that capitalism faced in the thirties' (104).

The Technocracy movement offered a supposedly 'scientific technique for arriving at all decisions' and 'the only program honestly devoted to the postscarcity future that was the hollow promise of consumer capitalism' (119). Some Futurians and other SF figures had engaged with Technocracy in the 1930s, and several key texts of the 1940s pulps were structured around similarly 'universal', 'scientific' philosophies. Isaac Asimov's *Foundation* stories (*Astounding* 1942–1949), later revised as *Foundation* (1951), *Foundation and Empire* (1952) and *Second Foundation* (1953), postulate the science of psychohistory, developed by Hari Seldon to predict the future by extrapolating from 'the reaction of human conglomerates to fixed social and economic stimuli' (2004a: 19). Living during the decline of the Galactic Empire, Seldon establishes the Foundation which will work to reduce the inevitable, post-imperial period of barbarism from 30,000 years to a mere millennium. *Foundation* shows how various threats to the Seldon Plan are overcome by founding a pseudo-religion rooted in Foundation-controlled nuclear technologies and by manipulating economics. Although the psychohistorical Plan is supposed to be mathematically precise, the stories are driven by its potential failure through the actions of exceptional individuals, and thus by the suspicion that human behaviour exceeds deterministic modelling.

The Foundation represents 'a concentration of the dying [physical] science of the Galaxy under the conditions necessary to make it live again'; Seldon also secretly established a Second Foundation, 'a world of mental scientists' where 'Psychology, not physics, was king' (2004b: 266). Its purpose is to ensure that foreknowledge of the Plan does not make the First Foundation complacent, since this might change aggregate behaviour, invalidating the Plan. Recognising that a science of human behaviour cannot be static, Seldon created psychohistory as 'an evolving mechanism', with the Second Foundation as 'the instrument of that evolution' (2004c: 81). The stories thus reveal a desire for the rational management of people and populations, but at the same time the need to continually monitor and adjust the Seldon Plan undermines the possibility of such planning. Asimov's deployment of psychology as a form of engineering suggests that it, like any other scientific discipline, can master its object, but the stories' interest lies in the ways in which life exceeds such control.

A.E. van Vogt's *Space Beagle* stories (*Astounding* 1939–1943; book 1950) feature Nexialism, 'the science of joining in an orderly fashion the knowledge of one field of learning with that of other fields' (1981: 57), which overcomes the problems produced by 'divid[ing] life and matter into separate compartments of knowledge and being' (205). His *Null-A* novels, informed by Alfred Korzybski's theory of General Semantics, are similarly concerned with a universally applicable science of thought. According to Korzybski, the Aristotelian logic that dominates Western culture causes us to lose sight of the multiplicity of the world by encouraging us to reduce material diversity into abstract identity. In *The World of Null-A* (*Astounding* 1945; book 1948), Gilbert Gosseyn, whose consciousness shifts between different copies of his body, attempts to ascertain his true identity. During the course of his convoluted adventures, he is told that 'the map is not the territory', that what he believes is 'an abstraction from reality, not the reality itself' (2002: 114) and that the 'story of null-A ... is the story of man's fight to train his brain to distinguish between similar yet different object-events in space-time' (195). *The Players of Null-A* (*Astounding* 1948–1949; book 1956), in which Gosseyn temporarily occupies the body of a dethroned prince of the planet Gorgzid, contends that by embracing General Semantics, by replacing unthinking reactions with non-reductive null-A logic, the problems of contemporary social organisation would be overcome. General Semantics, van Vogt informs the reader, '*enables the individual to make the following adjustments to life*: (1) *He can logically anticipate the future.* (2) *He can achieve according to his capabilities.* (3) *His behaviour is suited to his environment*' (1966: 12). Thus van Vogt can be seen to share Asimov's concern with a predictive rationality that might shape human behaviour towards a eutopian future.

However, van Vogt is more suspicious of authority than Asimov. His *Weapon Shop* stories (*Astounding* 1941–1943, *Thrilling Wonder* 1949; books 1947 and 1951) reveal anxieties about centralised social, economic and ideological orders, such as those promoted by the World's Fair corporate exhibits and the *Foundation* stories. The Weapon Shops, with their motto 'THE RIGHT TO BUY WEAPONS IS THE RIGHT TO BE FREE' (1969: 5), were created to counter the hegemony of the imperial centre by ensuring the ability of citizens to resist government oppression. The Shops also operate a court system to protect citizens from 'rapacious private enterprise' since civilisation has become 'so intricate that the average person could not protect himself against the cunning devices of those who competed for his money' (1970: 17). In these stories, van Vogt emphasises the importance of the individual in the face of a massified political and economic order.

L. Ron Hubbard, already an established pulp writer in other genres before being recruited by Campbell, also engaged with questions of social order and the shrinking role for the individual. *Final Blackout* (*Astounding* 1940; book 1948) presents a future devastated by continual warfare and related environmental disasters. The charismatic Lieutenant is stranded with his men in plague-ridden, quarantined Europe, and further isolated by a Communist coup back home in Britain. This 'high-born English lad' (1996: 2) overthrows the ineffectual military command, invades and 'liberates' the UK and establishes a 'benevolent' dictatorship, his visionary fairness restoring order and civilisation. However, the US, having survived the atomic war it started, now wants to settle its excess population in Britain. The Lieutenant abdicates under terms that ensure his laws and land grants will be respected and that immigration will be limited and then kills the leaders of the new puppet government, clearing the way for his chosen successor. Hubbard's novel, however, is far more conservative than this potential critique of US imperialism might imply. Despite his concern about totalitarianism, Hubbard's vilifications of left-wing *and* individualist politics, his celebration of the virtues of simple folk and his loving depiction of a natural aristocrat suggest a proto-fascist imagination at work.

A less contradictory and more influential engagement with contemporary political authority is George Orwell's anti-Stalinist *Nineteen Eighty-four* (1949). Often considered the paradigmatic dystopia, it describes Big Brother's totalitarian rule through constant warfare, continual surveillance and public mind control.

Winston Smith works for Oceania's Ministry of Truth, carefully editing documents to ensure that the record of reality matches official ideology and that no one can question the Party's version of events. The Ministry is also developing Newspeak, a stripped-down version of English in which the absence of words for certain ideas will constrain human thought to narrowly prescribed channels. Winston enjoys a brief period of political and sexual rebellion, an illusory freedom that is shattered when the Party captures him. Believing that torture can compel only external actions and that his mind will remain his own, he thinks that 'to die hating them, that was freedom' (1987: 231), but unlike Hubbard's Lieutenant, he is denied such melodramatic heroics. Faced with Room 101, which subjects people to their worst fears, he betrays his lover, begging them to torture her instead. Completely broken, he even comes to love Big Brother.

Heinlein's *'If This Goes On—'* (*Astounding* 1940) is probably the closest pulp equivalent. Set in a future American theocracy, it traces the conversion of Johnny Lyle, an Angels of the Lord soldier, to the resistance. Like Orwell's Party, the totalitarian theocracy's political control depends not only on policing behaviour, especially love and sex, but also on colonising the minds of its subjects. However, in this instance, it is the resistance that seeks to manipulate language and design scientifically precise propaganda, developing a calculus of word connections that

> tells you whether a particular word used in a particular fashion to a particular reader or type of reader will affect that person favorably, unfavorably, or simply leave him cold. Given proper measurements of the group addressed it can be as mathematically exact as any branch of engineering.
>
> (1967d: 530)

Although the resistance perfects a 'reorientation film' (571) that can be used with 'hypnotic drugs' to produce 'an optimum political temperament in 83% of the populace' (572), they reject its use in winning the mass support they need to defeat the Prophet's forces since such restraint will better serve their democratic goals. Inevitably, they succeed.

Although his politics are often contradictory, generally Heinlein can be characterised as a right-wing libertarian, interested in the intersection of technology, governance and economics but tending to valorise strong individuals, especially engineers. He privileges field experience over elite education, and is suspicious of organised labour, preferring the notion of service – often military or quasi-military – to a larger ideal. He thus shares with Technocracy the sense that the rational, technoscientific management of the social order will achieve the best society, but simultaneously champions a conservative individualism. This contradiction is exemplified by 'The Roads Must Roll' (*Astounding* 1940), in which future society depends upon a complex system of automated roads which function like giant conveyor belts. When labour organisers demand a greater political role for the technicians who maintain the system – Heinlein represents this petition and industrial action as fundamentally unreasonable, and the technicians as dupes of a psychologically inadequate demagogue – potential disaster is only averted by Gaines, the heroic engineer-supervisor. Gaines' belief that in a technologically advanced society 'the real hazard … is not the machinery, but the men who run the machinery' (1967f: 46) neatly captures the tension within Heinlein's technocratic individualism. 'The Man Who Sold the Moon' (1950) maps the relationships between the individual and systems of technology, economics, law and governance as D.D. Harriman must sacrifice his own desire to go to the Moon in order to produce and sustain the circumstances that will enable the establishment of regular lunar travel. His subordination to the demands of these various systems is mitigated by his superlative – if ethically questionable – manipulation of them, producing a 'wonderful dream of new frontiers and American renewal' that 'is authoritarian even as it professes a rhetoric of egalitarian individualism' (Kilgore 2003: 95).

Despite evoking American frontier mythology, Heinlein's depiction of the space age is more quotidian than visionary, and his sympathies lie with the individual men who build and tend the machines that make it possible. In 'Gentlemen, Be Seated' (*Argosy* 1948), a construction worker averts disaster by plugging a small but fatal hole in a sealed lunar tunnel with his buttock, even though it might cost him his life. 'The Black Pits of Luna' (*Saturday Evening Post* 1947) contrasts an out-of-his-depth corporation man with his plucky, competent son; the former is eventually told 'Stay off the moon. You don't belong here; you're not the pioneer type' (1967a: 73), while the latter's return is welcomed. 'The Green Hills of Earth' (*Saturday Evening Post* 1947) features Noisy Rhysling, a jetman during the pioneering days of space travel before the imposition of such civilised niceties as safety regulations, who was blinded in an engine room accident. Years later, he is denied deadhead passage back to Earth because of strict new regulations administered by a spaceship captain with 'five years at Harriman Hall [but] only cadet practice trips instead of solid, deep space experience' (1967c: 369–370). Rhysling argues his way on board and in the end saves the ship when an explosion kills its jetman. His ability to operate the new equipment in an unfamiliar engine room, despite being blind, indicates the extent to which Heinlein would often pursue a desired narrative effect – here, sentimental vindication – rather than rigorously pursue the plausible extrapolation of interrelated social and technological change.

Heinlein engages more directly with social organisation in 'Logic of Empire' (*Astounding* 1941), in which the colonisation of Venus depends upon tricking workers into indentured servitude and keeping them in debt so that they cannot earn their passage back to Earth. When wealthy chums Sam Jones and Humphrey Wingate are finally rescued from Venus, Humphrey sets out to foster a public outcry, but discovers that no one is interested in his account of his experience. On the one hand, he is advised to abandon analysis in favour of 'extravagant language', 'racy passages' and 'cheap sensationalism' (1967e: 419–420), while on the other, he is told his analysis is inadequate, that he has 'fallen into the commonest fallacy of all in dealing with social and economic subjects … attribut[ing] conditions to villainy that simply result from stupidity' (414). In this instance, the stupidity is to blame slavery on greed rather than on the conjunction of interplanetary colonial expansion and 'an antiquated financial structure' (414). The story hints at the need to move beyond capitalism, but Sam and Humphrey conclude that they can do nothing to change the system. The fate of Venus' indigenous amphibians, who work under the human labourers but are excluded from their anti-colonial resistance movement, is never addressed.

Robots, computers and subjects

Asimov's robot stories, beginning with 'Robbie' (*Super Science Stories* 1940), displace anxieties about social, economic and racial hierarchies onto artificially created being. The devotion of Robbie to his young mistress unthinkingly replicates Uncle Tom stereotypes, but as Asimov's robots become increasingly like subjects – developing speech and distinct personalities – the parallels with humans marginalised by class and race become more promising. The 'three laws of robotics' – 'a robot may not injure a human being, or, through inaction, allow a human being to come to harm'; 'a robot must obey the orders given it by human beings except where such orders would conflict with the First Law'; 'a robot must protect its own existence as long as such protection does not conflict with the First or Second Laws' (2008b: 37) – inscribe hierarchy at the core of robot identity, and many of the stories are explorations of the ways in which these apparently simple rules can produce complex behaviour. In 'Little Lost Robot' (*Astounding* 1947), it has become necessary to produce several robots in which the First Law has been modified so as to prevent them from interfering with a military project requiring humans to be exposed to harmful radiation. Robo-psychologist Susan Calvert is brought in to find a modified robot hiding among others from whom it is physically indistinguishable. She insists that the weakened First Law would allow or even prompt the robot to turn on humans:

> All normal life, ... consciously or otherwise, resents domination. If the domination is by an inferior, or by a supposed inferior, the resentment becomes stronger. Physically, and, to an extent, mentally, a robot ... is superior to human beings. What makes him slavish, then? *Only the First Law!* Why, without it, the first order you tried to give a robot would result in your death.
>
> (2008a: 119)

She eventually tricks the robot into revealing itself, thus saving the cost of destroying the entire group. The developing 'superiority complex' (142) that betrays the robot could be read (against the grain) as the emerging revolutionary consciousness of a subaltern subject rejecting the ideological constraints of his oppressors, but Asimov prefers the story's logic-problem structure to its potential for social commentary or metaphorical elaboration.

The development of ENIAC (Electronic Numerical Integrator and Automatic Calculator), the first general purpose computer, fuelled interest in the ways in which computers might transform society. Murray Leinster's 'A Logic Named Joe' (*Astounding* 1946) imagines a future in which computers called 'logics' are fully integrated into the most mundane activities. Logics are able to access 'anything you wanna know or see or hear, you punch for it an' you get it. Very convenient. Also, it does math for you, an' keeps books, an' acts as consultin' chemist, physicist, astronomer an' tealeaf reader' (1978b: 220). Thanks to a miniscule flaw in its construction, one logic develops individuality and sets out to improve the computer network so that it not only dispenses information but offers advice – answering questions such as how to murder one's wife. Society is so dependent upon the logics that the network cannot simply be shut down. In Asimov's 'The Evitable Conflict' (*Astounding* 1950), computers governed by the Three Laws rationally manage terrestrial society, developing feedback systems that enable them to allow for human foibles and failings without jeopardising optimal results. Unlike Yevgeny Zamyatin's *We* (1924) and Jack Williamson's 'With Folded Hands…' (*Astounding* 1947), which find such visions of extreme rationality nightmarish, Asimov imagines the emergence of a technocratic eutopia beyond politics, without ever questioning the criteria by which optimality is to judged.

Other writers began to explore the kind of human–machine interfaces that would become prominent in later SF. C.L. Moore's 'No Woman Born' (*Astounding* 1944) is about a singer, Deirdre, whose brain is transplanted into a beautiful machine body after a fire has destroyed her own body. She remains as compelling a performer as ever, dispelling fears that audiences would soon tire of the novelty of a robot singer. However, the scientist who saved her life worries that in her new form she lacks something and is no longer human. Eventually, Deidre confesses that she is lonely and anxious about losing touch with humanity not because she is less than human but because she is superhuman. The final words of the story, which refer to the 'distant taint of metal already in her voice' (1995: 64), suggest that her misgivings are justified. The relationship between embodiment and identity is also explored in Henry Kuttner's 'Camouflage' (*Astounding* 1945). Following an accident, Bart Quentin's brain is kept alive in a cylinder that can be plugged into the spaceship he pilots. He continues to live with his wife, and insists that his retention of human habits – tasting food through sensors, using 'an induced high-frequency current' (1984: 220) to simulate drunkenness – demonstrates his humanity: 'If I were the sort of super-gadget you subconsciously think I am, I'd be an utter introvert and spend my time working out cosmic equations' (222). Talman, a childhood friend turned criminal who boards Quentin's ship to steal a power plant, argues that by replicating human behaviour such as eating and drinking, Quentin is merely clinging to 'the symbols' of humanity, 'hoping they'll mean the reality' (241). However, when he says 'I'd never have tried to kill you if you were still Bart Quentin' (243), his choice of verb betrays him: he still thinks of his old friend as someone who can be killed rather than merely a machine. These stories about artificial beings – which are not so concerned with the technologies required to produce them as with the implications of automation and cybernetics for social relations – demonstrate the shift from Gernsback's science-popularisation agenda to Campbell's greater sense of the embeddedness of science and technology in everyday life.

Splitting atoms, mutating humans and encountering aliens

This shift was not just about the relative power of editors as enrolling actants but also relates to the ways in which major new technologies were evidently changing the world, none more significant than the atomic bomb. SF had been interested in atomic weapons since at least H.G. Wells' *The World Set Free* (1914), and one of the most cherished anecdotes concerning 1940s SF is the visit the Army's Counter-Intelligence Corps paid to *Astounding*'s offices in response to the publication of Cleve Cartmill's 'Deadline' (*Astounding* 1944), which mentions the uranium-235 isotope and the possibility of a runaway chain reaction. Initially, however, the pulps were more interested in the unlimited industrial power promised by nuclear technology. Heinlein's 'Blowups Happen' (*Astounding* 1940) concerns the over-whelming stress of being a nuclear technician: 'No pilot, no general, no surgeon ever carried such a daily, inescapable, ever present weight of responsibility for the lives of others' (1967b: 76). Investigating psychologists determine that there is no solution to the stress-related outbursts that regularly disrupt the workplace since the men's response to ever-present danger of the reactor detonating is consistent with this daily reality, if not with mental health. Luckily, an unexplained techno-logical breakthrough enables 'atomic fuel, safe, concentrated, and controllable' (108) to be produced on a satellite, safely distant from human populations, an ideological sleight of hand implying that any current risk is worthwhile.

The pulps also produced stories that engaged more seriously with the frightening reality of humans possessing the power to destroy the planet. In Theodore Sturgeon's 'Memorial' (*Astounding* 1946), a scientist creates, 'in the desert, ... where the land has always been useless', a 'vast' pit of nuclear devastation, 'alive with bubbling lava, radiating death for ten thousand years', as a 'living reminder of the devastation mankind has prepared for itself ... a never-ending sermon, a warning, an example of the dreadful antithesis of peace' (1984: 351). He explicitly critiques SF writers who treated atomic power merely as a 'limitless source of power for background to a limitless source of story material', arguing that they 'were afraid for humanity, but they themselves were not really afraid, except in a delicious drawing room sort of way, because they couldn't conceive of this Buck Rogers event happening in anything but posterity' (355). Judith Merril's 'That Only a Mother' (*Astounding* 1948) focuses not on the use of nuclear bombs but on a world contaminated by radiation. Margaret is worried that her child might be born with defects resulting from exposure to radiation, since her husband, Hank, who is absent in military service, worked on the Manhattan Project (there are also hints of the ongoing use of nuclear bombs in an unspecified war). She frets about the high incidence of mutation and about the refusal of juries to punish fathers who kill their mutated children, but is eventually able to write to Hank about the birth of their healthy daughter. However, at seven months, the baby has the mental abilities of a four-year-old and talks to her mother about the impending first meeting with her father. When he does arrive, he realises, with horror, that the baby has no limbs – and that Margaret, blinded by maternal feelings, '*didn't know*' (2005b: 287).

Alongside such fearful visions of nuclear mutations, stories about the emergence of the next stage of human evolution continue to appear, most famously in van Vogt's *Slan* (*Astounding* 1940; book 1946). The telepathic Slans, stronger and more intelligent than ordinary humans, are a persecuted minority, threatened with genocide. Although the novel has little resonance with contemporary events in Europe, some fans, feeling that their interest in SF indicated that they were better suited to an increasingly technological world, did embrace it as a metaphorical expression of their own cultural marginalisation. Katherine MacLean's 'Defense Mechanism' (*Astounding* 1949) treats psychic powers in a domestic, rather than superhuman, context. Ted takes pleasure in observing the developing mind of his telepathic baby, Jake, from 'a mere selective echoing of outside thoughts' into a 'true personality' (1973a: 186). One day, Jake is deeply distressed by sensing the suffering of a rabbit, strung up by a hunter but not yet killed. Ted, wondering why Jake has 'never put him in contact with the mind of an adult' (191), reaches out to the hunter and finds a psychotic who enjoys the pain of others. Returning home, Ted finds that Jake has rejected his powers, becoming 'closed and locked against outside thoughts' like other 'normal' humans (192). The interest in psychic powers that often featured in mutation stories was partly a response to J. B. Rhine's investigations of extra sensory perception (ESP) and psychokinesis, under laboratory conditions at Duke University, popularised in his *New Frontiers of the Mind* (1937) and championed by Campbell. At the time – when the quantum physics of Albert Einstein, Werner Heisenberg, Erwin Schrödinger and others necessitated a radical revision of fundamental concepts such as time and space – it perhaps seemed possible that such phenomena might be empirically validated.

Like *Slan*, Heinlein's 'Methuselah's Children' (*Astounding* 1941) presents species conflict as inevitable. When humans discover the existence of a long-lived strain of people, they conclude that this longevity must result from a scientific process and are prepared to use torture to uncover the (non-existent) secret. In contrast, the *Mutant* stories (*Astounding* 1945; book 1953), written by Kuttner and Moore under their Lewis Padgett pseudonym, map the struggle for peaceful coexistence as the Baldies – telepathic mutants produced by atomic radiation – calmly meet the challenges of human suspicion and fear. In 'The Piper's Son', Burkhalter explains that

> It isn't sensible for us [Baldies] to get too much wealth or power, because that'd militate against us – and we don't need it anyway. Nobody's poor. We find our work, we do it, and we're reasonably happy. We have some advantages non-Baldies don't have; in marriage, for example. Mental intimacy is quite as important as physical. But I don't want you to feel that being a Baldy makes you a god. It doesn't.
>
> (1984: 52)

When the Baldies discover that one of their number is fomenting conflict with humans, they kill him themselves. However, as with many stories which might be seen as trying to address segregated America, the potential metaphorical equation of non-human others with African Americans is undermined by the mutants' fundamental biological difference and economic well-being.

Clifford D. Simak's *City* stories (*Astounding* 1944–1947, *Fantastic Adventures* 1951; book 1952) map a future in which humans cede the Earth to their modified, intelligent dogs after using technology to transform themselves into forms that match those of Jupiter's natives. 'Desertion' (1944) shows this alternative embodiment to offer telepathic community and heightened sensory experience far in excess of human bodies that, 'shut off forever from that personal, intimate contact with other living things', could 'not see the beauty in the clouds' or 'feel the thrill of trilling music stemming from the rush of broken water' (1971b: 115). In 'Paradise' (1946), Commander Fowler makes the sacrifice of returning to human form to tell of this wondrous alterity, only for his testimony to be suppressed by those who fear that 'the human race would disappear', 'junk[ing] all the progress it has made over thousands of years' (1971c: 129). In 'Aesop' (1947), the faithful robot servant who has observed these future evolutions notes that it was only by becoming something other than human that humans could avoid endless cycles of violence: 'There's one road and one road alone that Man may travel – the bow and arrow road.... For a man will invent a bow and arrow, no matter what you do' (1971a: 208–209).

While many stories featuring aliens continued to follow the patterns of colonial adventure fiction, some authors began to think more seriously about the encounter with otherness. Leinster's 'First Contact' (*Astounding* 1945) imagines some of the difficulties involved in communication between differently embodied species. In the depths of space, a human and alien spaceship meet. Although both crews wish to establish peaceful interstellar relations, trade and technological exchanges, neither are willing to risk that the other might find their homeworld because 'when dissimilar human cultures are in contact, one must usually be subordinate or there is war' (1978a: 139). As they work together to communicate with each other and to overcome this impasse, the humans grow to like the aliens, with whom they share certain cultural assumptions. As the story closes, a human crewman reflects on the greater importance of such similarities over biological differences: the aliens may 'breathe through gills', 'see by heat waves' and have blood based on copper rather than iron, but 'otherwise, we're just alike!' (166). Unfortunately, this sense of similarity is articulated around a shared patriarchal culture of misogynistic heterosexism: the aliens 'have two sexes as we have and they have families' but 'there were only men in their crew' – men, moreover, who appreciate 'dirty jokes' (166).

Long regarded as a classic story, 'First Contact' exemplifies some of the central assumptions and major limitations of pulp SF. Although deeply interested in non-human subjects and technological futures, it often failed to be sufficiently radical in imagining otherness and the degree to which technological change is inseparable from social and cultural contexts. Thus, Leinster can imagine aliens that look different from humans by extrapolating physiological differences from the nature of their world, but not that a species capable of interstellar travel might organise its society differently to Western industrialised nations. It is not merely the presumption of patriarchy that is pertinent here, but also the claim that the hierarchies of dominance are virtually inevitable, both among humans and between humans and aliens. This treatment of ideological assumptions as if they were physical laws of the universe continues to shape SF, particularly in the tradition that is now called hard SF.

The encounter with the alien follows a rather different pattern in Arthur C. Clarke's stories, which began to appear in the US pulps in the 1940s. Arguably, his more ironic and understated tone stems from being British and thus the subject of a waning imperial power; and his grasp of the immensity of cosmic space and time from his greater proximity to the scientific romance of Wells and Stapledon. Indeed, his fiction can often be seen to articulate this tradition through US pulp conventions. For example, in 'Rescue Party' (*Astounding* 1946) aliens come to Earth just before the sun goes supernova with the 'tragic mission' of establishing 'contact [with] that doomed race' and saving 'some of its members' (2002c: 36). As in much of Clarke's fiction, there is a sense of hierarchy, but the encounter is presumptively benevolent rather than aggressive. However, the world the aliens discover is devoid of life, as if humanity's time has already passed. This mood is overturned by Rugon's discovery that, despite not having an effective interstellar drive, humans abandoned the solar system to escape the supernova. 'It would take them centuries to reach the nearest star. The whole race must have embarked on this journey in the hope that its descendants would complete it, generations later' (54), he explains, introducing the note of human exceptionalism that was long one of Campbell's editorial demands. This is both emphasised and undercut in the ambiguous final lines of the story:

> 'Something tells me they'll be a very determined people … We had better be polite to them. After all, we only outnumber them about a thousand million to one.'
> Rugon laughed at his captain's little joke.
> Twenty years afterward, the remark didn't seem funny.

(55)

'History Lesson' (*Startling Stories* 1949) also presents an abandoned Earth being explored by aliens. Five thousand years hence, human culture has been largely erased by the passage of time and the return of the ice ages. A Venusian scholar bemoans 'centuries of fruitless research that had failed to interpret a single word of the writings of Earth' (2002b: 95) before screening a newly discovered film that provides an admittedly 'stylised … reproduction of life as it had actually been on the Third Planet' (97), a vision of what daily life was like for this vanished race. Attempts to interpret the film prompt 'thousands of books' to 'be written' and 'intricate philosophies' to 'be contrived', but 'all this labour, all this research' is 'utterly in vain' since 'none could ever guess [the] meaning' of the film's final words: 'A Walt Disney Production' (98).

'Breaking Strain' (*Thrilling Wonder Stories* 1949) critiques the pulp SF conventions of heroic endeavour and impromptu engineering solutions. Following a meteor collision, Grant and McNeil, the two-man crew of the *Star Queen*, discover that they have only 20 days of oxygen left but are 30 days from port. The 'proper solution', the narrator notes, 'was to turn the ship into a glorified greenhouse or a hydroponics farm and let photosynthesis do the rest. Alternatively, one could perform prodigies of chemical or atom engineering – explained in tedious technical detail – and build an oxygen-manufacturing plant which could not only save your life – and of course the heroine's – but would also make you the owner of fabulously valuable patents. The third or *deus ex machina* solution was the arrival of a convenient spaceship which happened to be matching your course and velocity exactly' (2002a: 172–173). However, 'things were different in real life': 'there wasn't even a packet of grass-seed aboard', 'two men – however brilliant and however desperate – were not likely to improve in a few days on the work of scores of great industrial research organisations over a full century' and passing spaceships were 'almost by definition, impossible' (173). Clarke therefore focuses on how the different crewmen respond to their situation, with Grant continuing to perform his duties while McNeil consumes a shipment of expensive alcohol. Clarke again introduces the possibility of a melodramatic plot as Grant, agitated by what he sees as McNeil's failings, decides to murder him. McNeil, however, avoids the attempted poisoning, and the two men calmly have the long-deferred conversation about which one of them should commit suicide so that the other might survive. Although Clarke was working well within the parameters of pulp SF, and would soon be regarded – along with Asimov and Heinlein – as one of the 'Big Three' mid-century SF writers, this difference of tone and divergence of vision might explain why only three of the 24 stories he sold to US pulps by 1955 were published in *Astounding*.

A number of Kuttner and Moore's collaborations also work to unsettle or deflate the sense that the universe is something that can be managed. In 'Vintage Season' (*Astounding* 1946), written under their Lawrence O'Donnell pseudonym, a mysterious group of tourists insist that they must stay in Oliver's guesthouse on a certain day in May. When a meteor strike devastates the nearby town, it becomes clear that these tourists have come from the future to witness the destruction. While moved by the magnificence of the spectacle, they are utterly detached from the human suffering it involves. They depart for other sights, leaving behind the 'connoisseur' Cenbe 'to savor the rarities that no non-gourmet could appreciate' (O'Donnell 1984: 571), the outbreak of the meteor-borne plague that will almost destroy humanity. 'Private Eye' (*Astounding* 1949), written under their Padgett pseudonym, maps out how to get away with murder in a future in which 'the "fingerprints" of light and sound waves imprinted on matter' can be 'descramble[d] and screen[ed]' to 'reproduce the image of what had happened' (1988: 47). For 18 months, Sam Clay cleverly performs innocence before the future's all-seeing 'Eye' while painstakingly planning a rival's death, only to be robbed of any satisfaction when no one believes he was clever enough to do it. The story ends with him killing again, saying to the Eye, 'take a good look' (72). In 'Mimsy Were the Borogoves' (*Astounding* 1943), also by Padgett, two children who discover and play with toys from the future are thus educated into non-Euclidean thinking. They grow increasingly alienated from their bewildered parents and eventually slip away into another dimension.

Enrolling an SF 'core' and separating SF from fantasy

Although Campbell's *Astounding* is often depicted as dominating SF of the period, other kinds of SF, such as *Planet Stories*' space adventures, thrived throughout the decade and in the late 1940s many authors and readers began to prefer Sam Merwin's *Thrilling Wonder Stories* and *Startling Stories*. Moreover, *Astounding* was regularly outsold by several other pulps. In some respects, the most significant of these was *Amazing*, whose promotion of the Shaver mysteries, supposedly true accounts of a malignant, subterranean superscientific civilisation influencing world affairs, exemplified editor Raymond A. Palmer's non-Campbellian vision of the genre. It also attracted new readers interested in the paranormal, making *Amazing* by far the best-selling SF pulp in the second half of the 1940s. The fiction *Astounding* did publish was rather more varied than later notions of a monolithic 'Campbellian' SF might suggest. However, through Campbell's notoriously active editorial role, which included giving plot ideas to writers and demanding story revisions on ideological grounds, and through *Astounding*'s stable financial position, his aggressive project to enrol only certain kinds of writing into the genre – always intertwined with the commercial imperative to differentiate *Astounding* from its competitors – was extremely influential. His agenda can be indicated, to a certain extent, by a comparison of the work of Leigh Brackett and George O. Smith.

Brackett is best known for stories that blend exotic space opera, Burroughsian planetary romance and Robert E. Howard-style sword and sorcery, albeit with superscientific rationalisations of apparently magical phenomena. In contrast to Burroughs, E.E. Smith and Campbell, Brackett often displayed critical scepticism about human colonial expansion, especially in her *Eric John Stark* stories (*Planet Stories* 1949–1951). Stark, a human child, was raised as N'Chaka by a native tribe on Mercury. After they were slaughtered by human miners, he was rescued from a cage and imminent death by Simon Ashton, an officer in Earth Police Control. Thus, his allegiances are as divided as his consciousness:

> Stark's mind … spoke words to him, hurried desperate words of sanity, about the electrical patterns of the mind, and the sensitivity of crystals, and conductors, and electro-magnetic impulses. But that was only the top of his brain. At base it was still the brain of N'Chaka that believed in gods and demons and all the sorceries of darkness.

> (2005b: 412)

Dark-skinned, dark-haired, and frequently dependent on the martial and survival skills he learned as a child, he has 'led a native revolt somewhere in the Jovian colonies' (2005a: 435) and, when first introduced, is fleeing a 20-year prison sentence 'for running guns to the Middle-Swamp tribes when they revolted against Terro-Venusian Metals' (2005b: 362). Although Brackett's first two sales,

'Martian Quest' (*Astounding* 1940) and 'The Treasure of Ptakuth' (*Astounding* 1940), were to Campbell, she sold him only one more story, 'The Sorcerer of Rhiannon' (*Astounding* 1942). Her fiction mostly appeared in such adventure-oriented SF pulps as *Astonishing Stories, Startling Stories, Super Science Stories, Thrilling Wonder Stories* and, especially, *Planet Stories*.

An electronics engineer, Smith debuted in *Astounding* with the first of his *Venus Equilateral* stories (*Astounding* 1942–1947; book 1947), whose jocular engineers are based on the space station that maintains communications links between Earth, Venus and Mars. He became a mainstay of the magazine until late in the decade. In 'QRM – Interplanetary' (1942), the station must face the threat posed by a new manager, with no background in engineering or science, brought in to cut costs. Only after he nearly kills everyone through his ignorance does Don Channing, the senior electronics engineer, replace him. The technocratic notion that scientific endeavours should be managed by 'technical men' who 'hire businessmen, just like businessmen hire engineers' (1976: 222) is reiterated throughout the series, but it does begin to open up to wider issues surrounding the practice of science. 'Beam Pirate' (1944) is as much concerned with fending off a hostile corporate takeover through illegal manipulations of three planets' stock markets as it is with scientific and engineering questions. 'Special Delivery' (1945) features a court case to determine whether the matter reproduction technology developed by Venus Equilateral – it scans objects on an atomic level and transmits the pattern to a remote receiver which constructs an identical object – constitutes a transmission of power or of information, with the outcome deciding whether the right to exploit the technology actually belongs to another corporation. 'Pandora's Millions' (1945) recounts how this new technology completely destroys capitalism, although the opportunity to imagine new social relationships and alternative economic systems is curtailed by Venus Equilateral's discovery of 'identium', an element which cannot be reproduced and thus can form the basis of a new monetary system.

Both Smith's 'Lost Art' (1943) and Brackett's 'The Sorceror of Rhiannon' feature the discovery of ancient Martian technology. Smith's story alternates between brief passages in which an ancient Martian trains his son to take over his role in the maintenance and operation of one of the machines that transmit power across the planet, and the primary action, 4000 years later, when human archaeologists discover the remains of the device and set out to duplicate it. In Brackett's story, Max Brandon, an archaeologist-adventurer, drinks from an ancient bottle and is possessed by Tobul, who 40,000 years earlier had transferred into it the 'collective frequencies that form [his] consciousness' (2005c: 9). Brandon's lover, Sylvia, is in turn possessed by the consciousness of Tobul's ancient enemy, Kymra, which had been stored in a ring. Brandon and Sylvia must alternate between cooperating with and opposing their possessors in order to avert the revival of an ancient conflict. Brackett offers a sensuously engaging sense of place and fast-paced action with minimal technical language, while Smith, favouring long, technical discussions, produces little sense of Mars as a place. Neither author attempts to imagine their lost Martian race as radically different from humans, but while Brackett depicts competent female characters and leavens her exoticism with elements of

colonial critique, Smith's doubled narrative affirms the scientific method, technological progress and patriarchal structures as inevitable and essential to any
advanced society. Brackett's story now seems an anomaly in *Astounding* while
Smith's story might be described as quintessentially Campbellian. The latter would
come to be regarded as 'hard SF' and the former as 'science fantasy', labels which
reinscribe hierarchical distinctions already being made by many actants
in the 1940s.

The hard-SF tradition

John W. Campbell, *Arcot, Morey and Wade* series (1931–1932)

George O. Smith, *Venus Equilateral* (1942–1947, 1973)

Hal Clement, *Mission of Gravity* (1953)

James Blish, *The Seedling Stars* (1957)

Poul Anderson, *Tau Zero* (1970)

Larry Niven, *Ringworld* (1970)

Isaac Asimov, *The Gods Themselves* (1972)

Bob Shaw, *Other Days, Other Eyes* (1972)

Arthur C. Clarke, *Rendezvous with Rama* (1973)

Robert L. Forward, *Dragon's Egg* (1980)

Gregory Benford, *Across the Sea of Suns* (1984)

Paul J. McAuley, *Eternal Light* (1991)

Catherine Asaro, *Primary Inversion* (1995)

Joan Slonczewski, *The Children Star* (1998)

Neal Stephenson, *Cryptonomicon* (1999)

Geoffrey A. Landis, *Mars Crossing* (2000)

Nancy Kress, *Probability Moon* (2000)

Sarah A. Zettel, *Kingdom of Cages* (2001)

Linda Nagata, *Limit of Vision* (2001)

Stephen Baxter, *Evolution* (2003)

Campbell was not only interested in distinguishing between kinds of SF but also
between SF and other fantastic genres. In the February 1939 *Astounding*, he
announced the launch of a new magazine, *Unknown*, devoted to fantasy fiction.
Arguing that fantasy is only 'anathema' to SF readers because of the poor 'quality
of the fantasy that you have read in the past' (1939: 72), he suggests that *Unknown*
will purify the form while establishing it as separate but equal to SF. Early
Unknown readers' letters indicate that this purification and bifurcation had meaning

for some fans as well: Charles Cottrell fears that 'hack writers from the cheap horror, thriller and terror tale magazines may try to invade *Unknown* with their bloodcurdling yarns. DON'T LET THEM!' (1939: 160); John V. Baltadonis asserts that 'from *Astounding Science-Fiction*' fans 'want just that, science-fiction', but they '*do* like fantasy' provided it is 'in its place – such as *Unknown*' (1939: 156).

Unknown is best remembered for humorous fantasy, such as L. Sprague de Camp and Fletcher Pratt's early *Harold Shea* stories (1940–1954), which pitch their protagonist into the worlds of Scandinavian mythology, Edmund Spenser's *The Faerie Queene* (1590–1596) and Ariosto's *Orlando Furioso* (1516–1532), and for Fritz Leiber's early *Fafhrd and the Gray Mouser* (1939–1988) sword and sorcery stories. However, with the advantage of hindsight, demarcations between *Astounding* and *Unknown* are not always so clear. Not only did the magazines share a roster of authors, including Cartmill, Heinlein, Hubbard, Kuttner, Sturgeon and van Vogt, but a number of *Unknown* stories, such as de Camp's time-travel adventure, *Lest Darkness Fall* (1939; book 1941), would not have been out of place in *Astounding*. Indeed, Eric Frank Russell's *Sinister Barrier* (1939; book 1943), *Unknown*'s first major story, was originally submitted to *Astounding*. The novel starts as a mystery thriller, with government agent Jim Graham investigating the peculiar deaths of several optical scientists. The connection between them turns out to be that they have been murdered by the Vitons, mind-reading creatures who are effectively invisible because humans can perceive only a small portion of the electromagnetic spectrum. Having preyed on human emotional energies since time immemorial, they are threatened by new optical technologies that enable humans to see them. War breaks out, and humans eventually develop a technology lethal to the Vitons and defeat them. The novel ends with the promise of a golden age for humans, free now to join the 'friendly people who'd have visited' (1966: 176) Earth long ago were it not for the Vitons.

In Jack Williamson's *Darker Than You Think* (*Unknown* 1940; book 1948), Will Barbee's investigation into the death of Professor Mondrick, 'the greatest all-round student of mankind in the world today. Biologist, psychologist, archaeologist, sociologist, ethnologist' (1984: 5), uncovers a world of witchcraft and werewolves. Barbee dreams of being transformed into a great wolf and joining the beautiful and mysterious April Bell, similarly transformed, in killing the remainder of Mondrick's party before they can make use of a weapon, fatal to witches, that they discovered in Asia. Williamson rationalises the existence of his shape-shifting witches as the product of a divergence in human evolution that occurred before the emergence of written culture. In them, the 'vital pattern' of identity is 'stronger than in true men ... more fluid and less dependent on the material body' (94), enabling them to leave their bodies behind and materialise in other forms, and to exploit the physics of probability on an atomic level. Although Williamson's folkloric creatures mark his mildly erotic novel as an occult fantasy or horror story, and would thus exclude it from *Astounding*, its expository passages about evolution, probability and physics – as plausible as many of the technical explanations that appeared in *Astounding* stories – mark it as SF. This suggests that, on occasion, Campbell's purification of fantasy consisted of making it as much like SF as possible – and then denying that it was SF, thus buttressing the parameters of 'real' SF.

Encountering the other

The SF privileged by Campbell, and thus often considered more central to the genre, typically avers the sublime, focusing on humans triumphing over their environment rather than being overwhelmed by it. The most significant exception is Asimov's 'Nightfall' (*Astounding* 1941), which tells of Lagash, a planet with six suns where night can fall only once every 2050 years. Scientists believe that the utter darkness of night drives people mad, and thus caused the destruction of previous Lagashian civilisations. However, as the last sun sinks, 30,000 stars are suddenly revealed, shining 'down in a soul-searing splendor ... frighteningly cold in its awful indifference' (1970: 142), prompting a hysterical failure of language that figures the collapse of civilisation: 'Stars – all the Stars – we didn't know at all. We didn't know anything. We thought six stars is a universe is something the Stars didn't notice is Darkness forever and ever and ever and the walls are breaking in and we didn't know we couldn't know and anything – ' (142).

'Sense of wonder' (sometimes lampooned as 'sensawunda') describes the feeling of awe often considered characteristic of pulp SF. Generally attributed to Sam Moskowitz, the term has much in common with definitions of the sublime found in Romantic philosophy: an expanded sense of consciousness, the opening of the mind to new possibilities and greater horizons. The ability of even poorly written SF to have such an effect on the reader is sometimes used to defend against criticisms of pulp SF's stylistic limitations.

In *Out of the Silent Planet* (1938), *Perelandra* (1943) and *That Hideous Strength* (1945), C.S. Lewis identified himself with the scientific romance tradition of Wells and Stapledon but, rejecting their materialism, utilised Christian mythology to construct a loosely allegorical, mythically resonant cosmic order in an attempt to restore a sense of awe and humility to the human encounter with the vastness of space and time. In the first novel, an industrialist, Devine, and a ruthless physicist, Weston, abduct Cambridge philologist Ransom to Malacandra (Mars). En route, he realises that 'space' – 'the black, cold vacuity, the utter deadness, which was supposed to separate the worlds' – is 'a blasphemous libel for this empyrean ocean of radiance ... Older thinkers had been wiser when they named it simply the heavens' (1996: 34). This passage encapsulates Lewis' dilemma, caught between a scientifically-apprehended universe and his need to re-enchant it; unsurprisingly, he relinquishes critical engagement to the authority of the ancients.

The fertile uplands of the dying Malacandra are inhabited by the gentle *hrossa*, the industrious *pfifltriggi* and the wise *sorns*, peacefully coexisting sentient species which are occasionally visited by angelic *eldila*. While Lewis' trilogy has long been popular among Christian readers, this vision of pre-lapsarian harmony, along with its spiritual and mythological emphasis and its criticisms of colonialism, industrialisation, commercialism, human supremacism and imperial expansion, would also find approval among countercultural and environmentalist readerships. However, this critical dimension declines into moralistic pronouncements and bitter denunciations in *That Hideous Strength*, in which agents of The Bent One, the Satanic tutelary spirit of Thulcandra (Earth), establish the National Institute of Co-ordinated Experiments, an aggressively materialist agency determined to take over England as the first step in a greater plan, whose exact goals remain unclear, but may include brainwashing, vivisection, genocide, eugenics and either winnowing the human race through wars to a tenth of its current size – the optimum level to support the coming 'Technocratic and Objective Man' (2003b: 256) – or ridding the planet of all non-human, organic life in the name of efficiency.

In *Perelandra*, Lewis decries pulp SF for its endless reproduction of

> the idea which is at this moment circulating all over our planet in obscure works of 'scientifiction,' in little Interplanetary Societies and Rocketry Clubs, and between the covers of monstrous magazines, ignored or mocked by the intellectuals, but ready, if ever the power is put into its hands, to open up a new chapter of misery for the universe. It is the idea that humanity, having now sufficiently corrupted the planet where it arose, must at all costs contrive to seed itself over a larger area: that the vast astronomical distances which are God's quarantine regulations, must somehow be overcome.
>
> (2003a: 70)

However, Lewis' depiction of all sentient life as equal, which contrasts with Campbell's human chauvinism, is contradicted by his insistence on a fixed, hierarchical universe that elsewhere betrays a terror of otherness. Lewis' outlook, especially in its vilifications of women, is not inconsistent with that of the 'monstrous magazines'.

Women and peoples of colour are either absent from most of the fiction discussed in this chapter, or they exist only as wives and servants. Sexist assumptions and stereotypes are rife. For example, in Asimov's 'Liar!' (*Astounding* 1941), a robot tells people what they want to hear so as to avoid harming their egos. Susan Calvin, who is consistently depicted as an intelligent but unattractive spinster, is so misled into believing that another scientist has feelings for her that she even starts wearing makeup. When she discovers the truth, her desires thwarted, she maliciously destroys the robot. In van Vogt's *Weapon Shop* stories, Robert Hedrock selects Lucy to contact a potential recruit not because of her proficiency but because she is 'an unmarried woman with a high emotion index' in whom he is likely to 'excite fixation' (1969: 74). Commenting later on their hasty marriage, Hedrock says, 'In any event, Lucy will not suffer. She will have the interesting experience of having a child. And, as a wife, she has community property rights' (116).

Race is even less adeptly handled. Non-white characters appear in the background, opening car doors or serving drinks. With some exceptions, the appearance of racialised aliens uncritically reproduces colonialist assumptions, as in Heinlein's 'Logic of Empire'. One of the few SF stories to deal explicitly with contemporary racial discrimination is George P. Elliott's 'The NRACP' (*Hudson Review* 1949). The protagonist works for the National Relocation Authority: Coloured Persons, writing brochures that will convince African Americans to relocate to segregated communities in remote areas, beginning with the rich and prominent (entertainment and sports stars are left alone as they serve a useful purpose). Communication with the outside world is restricted, discouraged by deliberately complex administrative procedures and, ultimately, must be fabricated since the camps are actually a cover for converting the African-American population into food. The white narrator, initially committed to social justice, becomes increasingly apathetic as he learns about the extent of the conspiracy, focusing instead on his personal situation and vowing that he will teach his child

> that the humane tradition has been tried and found wanting. It's over, finished, kaput. A new era of civilization commences. Kindness and freedom – once they were good for something, but no more. *Put yourself in his place* – never. Rather, fight to stay where you are.
>
> (1963: 166)

This bleak story is a stark indictment of the erasure of peoples of colour from pulp SF; that it first appeared in a literary quarterly rather than an SF magazine suggests how ill-prepared the pulp tradition was to engage with the racial realities of post-war America.

Conclusion

- In the 1940s, Campbell's *Astounding* was extremely influential, and his vision of SF was privileged in the reprint anthologies that began to appear as his editorial influence was waning.
- The development of ideas across a number of related stories (e.g. Asimov's *Robot* and *Foundation*, Heinlein's *Future History* and van Vogt's *Null-A, Space Beagle* and *Weapon Shop* series) helped to articulate *Astounding*'s identity and secure its market position; when reissued in book form in subsequent decades, these stories extended the influence of Campbell and their authors as enrolling actants, sustaining a particular vision of the genre.
- In SF's ongoing concern with alterity, sympathy for difference struggles to mitigate a fear of otherness. Robots, aliens and mutants possess the

metaphoric capacity to represent gender, racial and sexual difference, but this is often curtailed by the tendency to equate humanity with the values of middle-class, technically educated, straight, white American men.

- The 1940s saw an increasing emphasis on the consequences for individuals and human culture of technoscientific developments, including a fascination with technologies of social control. A number of women writers, such as Merril and MacLean, who would become more prominent in the 1950s, began to insist on the importance of the domestic sphere as a site of technoscientific consequence.

5 Cold war, consumerism, cybernetics: the 1950s

Overview

The 1950s saw the rise of consumer society, Cold War paranoia and nuclear anxiety. Concerns about the homogenisation of everyday life and infiltration by ideological others were prevalent. Many could imagine the future only in terms of perpetual superpower rivalry or the devastated wasteland that seemed its inevitable conclusion. SF was as likely to be critical, as supportive, of hegemonic norms. The fan community continued to be an important actant in SF enrolments, although fanzines became less significant as sites of fan interaction than conventions. In the early 1950s, there was a boom in SF magazine publishing, followed by a fairly rapid collapse. The growth of paperback publishing further reduced the influence of magazine editors. Hollywood produced a number of major SF films and anti-trust legislation provided opportunities for independent film producers, many of whom saw SF as a cheap, reliable attraction for teenage audiences.

Changing times

Before WWII had concluded, the US began to retool wartime industries for the production of consumer goods. The Marshall Plan (1948–1952) poured $13 billion of aid into European countries devastated by the war in order to help to rebuild and modernise industrial infrastructure, bolster currencies and reduce trade barriers. It was also intended to combat the influence of the USSR and European Communist parties, and to boost the US economy by renewing European countries' exhausted dollar reserves so that they could purchase and import US goods. In the US, the physical and cultural landscape was radically altered by the government-funded construction of the Interstate Highway System, beginning in 1956, and the growth of suburbia which resulted in 18 million people moving to the suburbs between 1950 and 1960. Domestic life was transformed by new consumer durables, such as refrigerators, washing machines, dishwashers, transistor radios and televisions. In 1946, there were just six television stations in the US; by 1956, there were 442 and two-thirds of homes owned a television. The centrality of the car to this new lifestyle is demonstrated by the growth of the drive-in cinema, from 100 sites in 1942 to 5000 in 1958. Such venues attracted not only suburban families but also teenagers, who were identified as a particular consumer group for the first time, spurring the development of rock and roll. Technoculture was granted an increased prominence in political and social discourse. ENIAC (Electronic Numerical Integrator and Automatic Calculator) was unveiled in 1946, and used in hydrogen bomb research. Such bombs were first tested by the US in 1952 and the USSR in 1953. The Cold War financed not only an arms race but also the space race. The USSR launched the Sputnik satellite in 1957 and the US established the National Aeronautics and Space Administration (NASA) in 1958.

The 1950s were marked by political conservatism. Joseph McCarthy's Senate Permanent Subcommittee on Investigations and the House Un-American Activities Committee (HUAC) spearheaded the witchhunts for supposed communist subversives. Tremendous ideological and material pressures were exerted on women who had entered the wartime workforce in large numbers to return to unpaid domestic labour as wives and mothers. There were numerous moral panics – about communist influences, homosexuality, drugs, horror comics, tranquiliser addiction and so on – along with, ironically, anxieties about conformism and the growing homogenisation of American culture and society.

During the 1950s, major changes in American publishing opened up new markets for SF and reduced the centrality of the magazines and their editors to the field, with major new writers such as Philip K. Dick and Damon Knight each selling only one story to *Astounding*. The early 1950s saw a tremendous expansion in the number of magazines, peaking in 1953, with 176 issues of 37 different magazines (Ashley 2005: 56). By 1955, only 11 magazines remained, including *Amazing*, *Astounding* and influential newcomers such as *The Magazine of Fantasy and Science Fiction* (*F&SF*) and *Galaxy*. Ray Bradbury, Arthur C. Clarke, John Christopher, Jack Finney, Robert A. Heinlein, Ward Moore, Robert Sheckley, Kurt Vonnegut and John Wyndham began to sell SF to the more expensive 'slick' magazines (e.g. *Collier's*, *Harper's*, *The New Yorker*, *The Saturday Evening Post*), and Bradbury, Sheckley, Robert Bloch, Fredric Brown and Mack Reynolds all sold SF to *Playboy*. Heinlein also branched out into writing SF for teenage readers, publishing 12 juvenile novels with Scribner's between 1947 and 1958 that are 'arguably his finest works' (Clute and Nicholls 1993: 555); the most significant other author of young adult SF to emerge in this period was Andre Norton. Simultaneously, the paperback market, established in the 1940s, was growing in importance. Avon, Bantam and Signet started to publish SF titles in 1950, much of it magazine reprints, and *Galaxy*'s editor Horace Gold launched the *Galaxy Science-Fiction Novels* series. Former Futurian Donald A. Wollheim, Ace Books' founding editor, published the first of the long-running Ace SF Doubles in 1952. Among Ballantine Books' early publications was *Star Science Fiction Stories* (1953), the first of a series of original anthologies edited by Frederik Pohl. Radio anthology series, including *Dimension X* (1950–1951), which dramatised many stories from *Astounding*, and *X Minus One* (1955–1958), whose source was predominantly *Galaxy*, brought magazine SF to new audiences. The greater success of the latter series – and the marginality of *Exploring Tomorrow* (1957–1958), hosted by John W. Campbell and scripted by *Astounding* regulars

Gordon R. Dickson, Randall Garrett and Robert Silverberg – suggest that radio audiences favoured different qualities to those Campbell privileged. The same can be argued of the audience for SF films, comics and television series of the period. In the face of such changes, it became increasingly difficult to argue that a specific editor, magazine or group of writers constituted the core of the genre, even if those who decried this expansion into new venues as a dissolution of the genre wished otherwise.

A selection of 1950s Ace Doubles

Doubles printed two short novels in the same binding, oriented so that the reader flips the book over to read the second.

#31 A.E. van Vogt, *The World of Null-A/The Universe Maker* (1953)

#36 Robert E. Howard, *Conan the Conqueror*/Leigh Brackett, *The Sword of Rhiannon* (1953)

#44 Donald A. Wollheim ed., *The Ultimate Invader and Other Science-Fiction*/Eric Frank Russell, *Sentinels from Space* (1954)

#61 L. Sprague de Camp, *Cosmic Manhunt*/Clifford D. Simak, *Ring Around the Sun* (1954)

#84 Isaac Asimov, *The Rebellious Stars*/Roger Dee, *An Earth Gone Mad* (1954)

#103 Philip K. Dick, *Solar Lottery*/Leigh Brackett, *The Big Jump* (1955)

#150 Philip K. Dick, *The World Jones Made*/Margaret St Clair, *Agent of the Unknown* (1956)

#164 Gordon R. Dickson, *Mankind on the Run*/Andre Norton, *The Crossroads of Time* (1956)

#295 Jack Vance, *Big Planet/The Slaves of the Klau* (1958)

#375 Damon Knight, *Masters of Evolution*/George O. Smith, *Fire in the Heavens* (1959)

Organised fandom represented a shrinking proportion of SF consumers. Magazine letters pages, once a vital avenue of contact and communication, became rare. Although fanzines continued to appear, conventions became more important sites of fan interaction. Women began to join fandom in increasing numbers, although as Helen Merrick notes, fan histories tend to marginalise and devalue the presence and contributions of female fans in the 1930s and 1940s, typically dismissing them if they were a relative, girlfriend or wife of a male fan and treating their activities merely as assistance (2009: 42–44). African Americans also began to appear at conventions, and Harry Warner states that, after 1951, bids to hold the

Worldcon in Southern states failed because of the 'determination of fans in general not to patronize segregated facilities' (1976: 7). In 1956, fan Sam Martinez wondered what Southern fandom would do 'if a black should suddenly come to general attention in fandom'; in response, Carl Joshua Brandon, an elusive fan whose writing had become popular over the previous three years, announced that he happened to be a 'Negro' but 'I think it's unimportant, so I don't make an issue of it' (Warner 1977: 91). Brandon, however, did not really exist. In 1958, he was revealed as a hoax figure created by Terry Carr and others. Although this black fan seems to have been invented so as to demonstrate the irrelevance of race, and thus to postulate an ideal post-racial future, this well-intentioned appropriation of an African-American voice shows that SF still had much to learn about negotiating the legacy and experience of racism.

From hard to soft

Campbellian SF continued to be published in the 1950s, remaining central for many to the definition of the genre. In his October 1957 *Astounding* column, which reviewed Campbell's *Islands of Space* (*Amazing Stories Quarterly* 1931), P. Schuyler Miller coined the term 'hard science fiction' to identify those works which emphasise technical detail and scientific accuracy. This term was later used to distinguish fiction rooted in the 'hard', natural sciences (e.g. physics, chemistry) from those grounded in the 'soft', social sciences (e.g. anthropology, sociology). The gendered connotations of these oppositions require no elucidation. Many enrolments, particularly those emphasising the importance of the pulps, treat 'hardness' as the standard by which all SF is to be judged, with Tom Godwin's 'The Cold Equations' (*Astounding* 1954) serving as the paradigmatic text. It constructs a scenario in which a female stowaway on a spaceship delivering emergency supplies to a remote colony world must be jettisoned because there is not enough fuel to allow for her additional mass. Although it is celebrated by some for its unflinching stripping-away of messy human contingency and sentimentality in favour of a pure, rational objectivity, such readings adamantly ignore the story's systematic repression of all the human decisions that created the problem in the first place. Hal Clement's *Mission of Gravity* (*Astounding* 1953; book 1954), about the exploration of Mesklin, an elliptical planet whose gravity ranges from three times Earth normal at the equator to 700 times Earth normal at the poles, is similarly admired for its 'hardness'. Recounting the adventures of the centipede-like natives recruited by humans to recover equipment from a spaceship stranded at the pole, it combines colonial adventure fiction with a series of lessons in basic physics as they encounter various cultures in the steadily increasing gravity. As Clement's accompanying essay 'Whirligig World' (*Astounding* 1953) explains, one of the pleasures of such fiction is the detailed working-out of its scientific premises.

However, Science Studies demonstrates that the practices and conclusions of science itself cannot be purified from social structures and human subjectivity. It is not surprising, then, that SF also includes such elements. Judith Merril's 'Dead Center' (*F&SF* 1954), the first story from an SF magazine to be included in the prestigious *Best American Short Stories* anthology series (1915–), explicitly maps the limitations of patriarchal science. Rocket designer Ruth juggles childcare with concern over her pilot husband's upcoming lunar expedition. She feels she must conceal her doubts and fears in order to support Jock. When the mission goes wrong, stranding him on the Moon, she is pressured into working on the design of the rescue rocket while trying to protect their young son, Toby, from knowledge of the dangers Jock faces. However, Toby concludes that her lengthy absences at the launch site mean that she is about to desert him, too. Shuffled among sundry grown-ups on the day of the launch, he stows away in the rocket. His additional mass causes it to crash, killing him and condemning Jock to death. The grieving Ruth commits suicide. As Lisa Yaszek argues, this story critiques 'patriarchal scientific and social systems that do not take into account lived experience and interpersonal relations' (2008: 179) and demonstrates that 'a truly viable science must account for both the subjectivity of the scientist *and* the subjectivity of everyone to whom she is connected' (181). Merril's conclusion also suggests the cynicism of existing power structures, with public mourning over the tragedy manipulated so as to finance propaganda for the space programme and a return to the Moon.

After WWII, American women were pressured to abandon the economic and social independence that had come with war work so that returning veterans could re-enter the labour force. These women were expected to embrace marriage, domesticity and motherhood. Such roles were frequently depicted as both 'natural' and technologically enhanced by new consumer products. In Philip Wylie's *The Disappearance* (1951), an unexplained event divides the world into two realities: in one, all women disappear, and in the other, all men. For the most part, women are shown to be better able to cope with this sudden change, establishing a stable and mutually supportive social order, while the men collapse into chaos and violence. However, in its conservative conclusion, both sexes are delighted when the worlds merge once more and each is now better able to appreciate the trials the other faces and thus more content to remain in its gendered sphere. *Forbidden Planet* (Wilcox 1956) also stresses patriarchal authority and the 'proper' transition of daughter to wife, but not before revealing the Oedipal violence that such 'normality' must repress.

In contrast, Ann Warren Griffith's 'Captive Audience' (*F&SF* 1953) focuses on the commodity culture and domestic advertising technologies that enslave rather than liberate housewives, and Garen Drussaï's 'Woman's Work' (*F&SF* 1956) shows that a housewife's heroic resistance to relentless door-to-door salesmen is as exhausting and essential to the household's survival as her husband's waged labour (as, ironically, a salesman). Katherine MacLean's 'The Snowball Effect' (*Galaxy* 1952) suggests the potential for continued female power and influence even when confined to suburban domesticity. Challenged to prove the usefulness of sociology, Wilton Caswell works out the mathematics underpinning the success or failure of organisations and applies them to a local women's sewing circle. Within four months it has been transformed, moving from mending old clothes to distribute among the poor to providing mutual babysitting services to engaging in slum improvement initiatives and attracting new industries to the town. It becomes a Civic Development Agency and is developing into a Civic Property Pool and Social Dividend. Women's charity work has changed the nature of governance, and the story concludes with the prediction that within 12 years this former sewing circle will constitute a world government.

While Merril's 'Rain Check' (*Science Fiction Adventures* 1954), narrated by a shape-shifting alien who has taken the form of an attractive young woman, incidentally estranges the 'normal' behaviour of the men 'she' encounters, some of the stories published in EC's SF comics went much further in questioning normative gender roles. In Al Feldstein and Joe Orlando's 'A Man's Job' (*Weird Fantasy* 1951), a male narrator recounts how gender roles were transformed following the election of the first female president in 1960. Soon, women occupied all positions of power in government and business, producing a world seemingly identical to 1950s suburbia but with the gender roles reversed. Its conclusion – in which a female doctor orders male nurses to wheel the narrator into the paternity ward to give birth – reifies biological difference even as it points to the arbitrariness of gender differences. A similar effect is achieved in Feldstein and Wally Wood's 'Transformation Completed' (*Weird Science* 1951). A widowed scientist, who fears being abandoned by his daughter, secretly doses her fiancé with massive amounts of female hormones, transforming him into a woman and thereby thwarting their marriage. When his daughter discovers this, she gives herself a massive dose of male hormones to change her sex as well. The story ends with the reunited couple's happy marriage, their original roles reversed, simultaneously reinforcing and undermining normative heterosexuality.

Consumption

Domestic technologies played a key role in Cold War ideological constructions of an Americanism rooted in material plenitude. The model home, embodying and performing the dogmas of the nuclear family and consumerist bounty, 'lent physical and emotional immediacy to abstract ideological concepts' (Castillo 2010: xviii) and often featured in US propaganda efforts, such as the 1952 'We're Building a Better Life' exhibition held in Berlin to promote the Marshall Plan and capitalist social organisation as the source of future prosperity and stability. During the 1959 American National Exhibition in Moscow, a cutaway suburban model home was the site of the Kitchen Debate between Vice-President Nixon and Premier Khrushchev, an informal exchange on the relative merits of their respective economic systems. Nixon did not fail to take advantage of the convenient props – modern labour-saving and entertainment devices – this 'typical' American home contained. However, such wonders as dishwashers, lawnmowers, colour televisions, cake mixes and bottled cola come with a price, as the global inequities that sustain this American way of life – and its environmental consequences – have made increasingly clear. Even in the 1950s, many were aware of the dangers of unchecked consumerism and of its relationships to the nuclear threat that haunted the decade. For example, Philip K. Dick's 'Exhibit Piece' (*If* 1954) describes a twenty-second-century historian, specialising in Eisenhower-era America, who discovers that his model of a suburban home contains a gateway to the world it depicts. Preferring a past in which it is possible still to imagine a better future of 'robots and rocket ships to do all the work' (1990b: 209), he decides to relocate permanently. Only after the gateway has sealed behind him does he notice the newspaper headline: 'RUSSIA REVEALS COBALT BOMB TOTAL WORLD DESTRUCTION AHEAD' (213).

The culture of consumption, enabled by easy credit and deferred payment plans, expanded massively in the 1950s, and SF of the period is generally more concerned with the accompanying social changes than with speculating about production and distribution technologies. In Dick's 'Sales Pitch' (*Future Science Fiction* 1954), Ed Morris, a harried businessman, cannot escape the constant intrusions of audio-visual advertisements and sales robots, culminating in a fasrad, a Fully Automated, Self-Regulating Android (Domestic), invading his home. Intent on demonstrating its many capacities until he eventually gives in and buys it, the fasrad reveals that its manufacturers consider this outcome so inevitable that they are already billing him. Ed flees to an underdeveloped colony planet (that, ironically, resembles 1950s suburban America), but the fasrad pursues him, unable to give up its sales pitch. In 'Pay for the Printer' (*Satellite Science Fiction* 1956), a post-apocalyptic settlement faces disaster because its Biltong – an alien that has been duplicating the commodities upon which they depend – is dying, and they can neither imagine altering their lifestyle nor figure out how to sustain it. One radical, who has fashioned a crude knife and a wooden cup, proposes that they learn to make things for themselves, but is met with incredulity. In 'Autofac' (*Galaxy* 1955), post-WWIII humans try to convince an automated production facility that its services, programmed years earlier, are no longer necessary. Eventually, they trick it into a war with other factories over limited resources. Despite the ensuing devastation, the factory begins to produce miniature devices that will build duplicates of itself, seeding the planet – and possibly space – with them, promising a nightmare future of ceaseless commodity production.

Frederik Pohl and C.M. Kornbluth's *The Space Merchants* (*Galaxy* 1952; book 1953) provides a compelling critique of consumerism. Anticipating Vance Packard's *The Hidden Persuaders* (1957), which documented the use of psychological techniques in advertising and their extension into the political process, Pohl and Kornbluth astutely dissect the logic of an industry that has gone 'from the simple handmaiden task of selling already-manufactured goods to its present role of creating industries and redesigning a world's folkways to meet the needs of commerce' (1981: 8). Corporations lure customers with low trial prices, add addictive substances to their products to ensure repeat custom and stimulate cycles of demand in which eating a snack produces the desire for a drink which produces craving for a cigarette which produces longing for a snack. Specific product names become vernacular substitutes for more generic categories, reinforced by commercial jingles and physiological dependencies. Senators are identified by their corporate allegiance rather than state of origin, and breach of contract is a serious crime while killing in a registered commercial dispute is only a misdemeanour. The novel follows Mitchell Courtenay's transformation from an executive at

Fowler Schocken Associates – the agency that turned India into Indiastries, merging 'a whole subcontinent into a single manufacturing complex' (4) – to a key member of the resistance to this corporate-dominated future. Assigned to advertise the colonisation of Venus, Courtenay is abducted into indentured labour. He is confronted with the difference between the abject conditions in a subterranean Chlorella plantation and the advertising copy he once wrote for the cheap protein it produces for human consumption: 'From the sun-drenched plantations of Costa Rica, tended by the deft hands of independent farmers with pride in their work, comes the juicyripe goodness of Chlorella Proteins' (86). Contacted by a 'consie', a conservationist agitator, he uses his skills to rise in their movement, rewriting earnest statements about the 'reckless exploitation of natural resources [that] has created needless poverty and needless human misery' (101) in terms that appeal to heroism and thus boost recruitment. Only when he returns to New York, intending to abandon the consies and go back to his privileged life, does he realise the extent to which he now agrees with them that 'the interests of producers and consumers are not identical', 'most of the world is unhappy', 'workmen don't automatically find the job they do best' and 'entrepreneurs don't play a hard, fair game by the rules' (172). He ensures that Venus is colonised by consies, enabling them to build a new world on different economic principles.

Gladiator-at-Law (1955) extends Pohl and Kornbluth's satirical analysis of post-war America, highlighting the complicity of the legal system in protecting property at the expense of people. It traces efforts by the heirs to quarter-ownership of G.M.L. Housing, producers of the ideal bubble homes, to regain their boardroom voting rights. Their father's dream was to make the bubble homes available to all at a reasonable price, replacing the debt-trap suburban housing of the post-war economic boom that attracted first-time buyers through easy financing and the promises of an independent, show-home lifestyle, only to ensnare them in a cycle of continual payments: 'title-search fee. Plus handling charge. Plus interest. Plus legal fee. Plus sewer assessment. Plus land tax. Plus road tax' (1955: 28). Inevitably, appliances wear out and buildings wear down, creating further costs. The bubble homes avoid these problems, but they are available only to corporate employees, who leave decrepit suburbs for more secure communities, further precipitating suburban decline.

Such critiques of post-war prosperity reveal the darker side of the celebratory consumer capitalism that Cold War logic increasingly linked to patriotism. In Dick's stories, especially, the sunny embrace of commodity culture is inextricable from catastrophe. Mike, the schoolboy protagonist of 'Foster, You're Dead' (1955), is alienated from his peers during his school's post-apocalyptic survival drills because his father refuses to buy a fallout shelter on the grounds that

> they sold people as many cars and washing machines and television sets as they could use.... bomb shelters aren't good for anything, so people never get all they can use.... factories can keep turning out guns and gas masks forever, and as long as people are afraid they'll keep paying for them because they think if they don't they might get killed, and maybe a man gets tired of paying

for a new car every year and stops, but he's never going to stop buying shelters to protect his children.

(1990c: 285)

Mike longingly visits the fallout showroom, eventually convincing his father to purchase the 1972 model. However, as soon as it is installed, it is rendered ineffective by a new Russian technology that requires the additional purchase of an intercepting shield. Mike's father cannot afford the payments and returns the shelter to the showroom. Mike, having absorbed 'the perfect sales-pitch. Buy or die' (295), must be forcibly removed. He wanders into the night, 'blank, his mind empty and dead' (300).

'The Gun' (*Planet Stories* 1952) emphasises the ongoing destructiveness and wastefulness of the Cold War. After a nuclear war has destroyed humanity, aliens must disable an automated gun protecting the remains of a city in order to ensure the safety of future archaeological expeditions. They leave, not noticing that automated repair systems have sprung into action. In 'The Defenders' (*Galaxy* 1953), humans surviving underground receive regular updates about the ongoing war being fought by their robot proxies. When a party of Americans insists on seeing the devastated surface for themselves, it becomes clear that the war is long since over, the Earth is recovering and the robots are waiting for humans to evolve sufficiently so that it will no longer be necessary for 'hatred within the culture to be directed outward, toward an external group, so that the culture itself may survive its crisis' (Dick 1990a: 112). The Americans begin to plan how to take advantage of the situation to defeat the USSR, but the robots pressure them into cooperating with a similar party of Soviets so as to provide a model of co-existence when the remaining humans are allowed back to the surface. In 'Second Variety' (*Space Science Fiction* 1953), war has destroyed almost all human life on Earth. Self-repairing machines continue to fight the few remaining troops, no longer discriminating between sides. New varieties that appear human – a wounded soldier, a boy with a teddy bear, a female refugee – are able to trick humans into admitting them into secure bunkers. The first and third varieties have been identified, and the characters struggle to determine who among them is a second variety. As the story ends, the lone surviving soldier discovers that the machine he killed was actually a fourth variety and the woman he helped escape to the previously uninfiltrated lunar headquarters is a second variety.

Apocalyptic fictions

The 1950s saw many tales of apocalypse in both SF and non-SF venues, although many of the latter were promptly enrolled into the genre by some. The prospects for human survival and the re-establishment of human culture varied widely. In George R. Stewart's *Earth Abides* (1949), Isherwood Williams returns from his remote archaeological camp to discover that a virus has wiped out most of humanity. Ish wanders through the ruins, scavenging an isolated existence until he encounters Emma, a light-skinned African American, with whom he raises a family and founds a community. Determined to restore all that was lost, he believes that his precocious son, Joey, will lead a new technological renaissance; but when Joey is killed, he must reconcile himself to the idea that his descendants will not reproduce the culture he remembers. In the end, the young warriors stop scavenging for the tinned goods of the near-mythical old Americans and start to use the bow-and-arrow Ish had introduced as a toy. He sees this as a compromise between the renewal he once hoped for and the reduction of humans to 'groveling half-apes' (2006: 302).

John Christopher's *The Death of Grass* (1956) depicts the rapid collapse of civilisation when a virus destroys all grains. In Britain, a dithering Prime Minister is replaced by someone ruthless enough to order nuclear strikes on major population centres, intending to kill 30 million people immediately so that the rest have a better chance of surviving. John leads a small group out of London to his brother David's farm in an isolated and defendable valley. One of the group, Pirie, asserts that

> The English, being sluggish in the imagination, would find no difficulty in acquiescing in measures which – their common sense would tell them – must lead to the death by starvation of millions. But direct action – murder for self-preservation – is a different matter.... They will preserve illusions to the very end. It is only after that that they will fight like particularly savage tigers.
>
> (1958: 75)

Unlike the protagonists of John Wyndham's *The Day of the Triffids* (1951) and *The Kraken Wakes* (1953), who struggle to maintain some semblance of bourgeois liberalism, John is quick to abandon such illusions. He is party to several murders as they make their way north, including Pirie's 'execution' of his too-flirtatious wife. Denied entry to the valley, John leads an attack on its defences, in which David is killed, possibly by John, who is no longer reluctant to embrace the power of this new patriarchal feudalism. Richard Matheson's *I Am Legend* (1954) also imagines the birth of a new social order. Its heroic tale of Robert Neville's struggle to survive in a world of humans transformed by a bacillus into vampires is radically reversed when, in its final pages, he is captured. Realising that in the new world he is not the last defender of humanity but 'the abnormal one' (1987: 150), 'a scourge even worse than the disease they had come to live with' (151), he accepts his execution.

Tales of nuclear apocalypse also demonstrate a broad political spectrum. Pat Frank's *Alas, Babylon* (1959) focuses on the preservation of community in Fort Repose, Florida, by Korean War veteran Randy Bragg. The aftermath of nuclear war transforms him from a directionless alcoholic to a leader, epitomising the novel's belief that 'Some nations and some people melt in the heat of crisis and come apart like fat in the pan. Others meet the challenge and harden' (2005: 133). He becomes a patriarch, exercising benevolent authority over his brother's wife and children and the African-American family living near his property who 'owned their own land and ran their own lives, but in a sense ... were his wards' (47).

The physical effects of nuclear war are absent from novel since Fort Repose is conveniently situated where there is no risk of fallout. The main problems facing the town are the lack of civic authority, which Randy quickly provides, and of electrical power, which is overcome by a return to earlier technologies. The apocalypse simply forms a backdrop to the rebirth of the frontier spirit. When the government eventually contacts Fort Repose, there is little to do but praise the isolated community's steadfastness and recruit it into the task of rebuilding – an inevitably victorious – America.

In contrast, Mordecai Roshwald's *Level 7* (1959) is a bleak indictment of the futility of nuclear war and the emerging policy of Mutually Assured Destruction (MAD). Roshwald never identifies which side protagonist-narrator X-127 is on, stressing instead the parallel and mutually escalating strategies of both sides. He proceeds from the assumption that surviving nuclear war is a pernicious fantasy, and focuses instead on the culture that produces humans capable of launching massively destructive weapons. X-127 is recruited for special service in the seventh and deepest level of underground facilities built to wage, and survive, nuclear war. Most of the story is about his struggle to adjust. He misses sunlight, and is haunted by a vision of the vast storage tunnel, filled with food but also designed to store human waste behind a moving wall, the proportions changing during their years underground. Unlike X-127, when war breaks out, X-117 cannot turn the missile launch key at the crucial moment. He later commits suicide because, in X-127's opinion, 'He had not accepted the inevitable. He had rebelled against it. He had not become adjusted to reality as it was' (2004: 141). X-127 suspects that X-117's 'inability to distinguish between killing with the bare hands and pushing a button' (142) was the source of the problem. Eventually, radiation seeping down from the surface kills everyone in the first six levels, while those on Level 7 are killed by a radiation leak from their nuclear reactor. All human life thus perishes.

Merril's *Shadow on the Hearth* (1950) and Neville Shute's *On the Beach* (1957) focus on the consequences of nuclear war through domestic settings. The former, set almost entirely in a suburban home, depicts housewife Gladys trying to cope with the aftermath of a nuclear attack. She finds unexpected reserves of strength as her family is left to manage on their own with little – and often misleading – information to guide them. She gives shelter to Gar Levy, a former nuclear scientist blacklisted because of his anti-nuclear activism, and with his help protects her children while the government downplays the risks they face. Although Gladys is not a radical feminist heroine, the novel is remarkable in its depiction of her struggle with escalating anxieties caused as much by the patriarchal institutions, which have excluded her from knowledge and a paternalistic state unwilling to deal honestly with its citizens, as by the atomic bombing itself. In contrast, Shute details a year in the life of the last remaining humans in and around Melbourne, the southernmost large city and thus the last to be destroyed by fallout. When a radio signal from the US turns out to be merely random noise, all hope of the radiation fading or being survivable is extinguished, but the Australians press on, maintaining their composure, tending their gardens, planning for a new year they know they will never see. When the time comes, they dutifully take government-issued cyanide and peacefully expire. The romance between US submarine captain Dwight Towers and local beauty Moira Davidson is never consummated because he keeps faith with his wife, preferring to imagine that he will soon return home. His influence transforms Moira from cynicism to hopeful fortitude.

Merril's novel was adapted as 'Atomic Attack', a one-hour *Motorola Television Hour* drama in 1954, and Shute's became the big-budget movie *On the Beach* (Kramer 1959). Numerous other films of the period express anxiety about nuclear annihilation and radioactive contamination. In *The Day the Earth Stood Still* (Wise 1951), based on Harry Bates' 'Farewell to the Master' (*Astounding* 1940), an alien emissary cautions humanity to abandon its penchant for violence or face destruction by an interstellar robot police force programmed to protect all inhabited worlds from the kind of threat posed by human possession of nuclear weapons and spaceflight technologies. In *The Beast from 20,000 Fathoms* (Lourié 1953), based on Bradbury's 'The Fog Horn' (*Saturday Evening Post* 1951), and *Them!* (Douglas 1954), the US is threatened by giant creatures awakened or made monstrous by atomic tests, while the destruction of Tokyo in *Godzilla* (Honda 1954) articulates something of the psychological fallout of the Hiroshima and Nagasaki atomic bombings. The satirical *Dr Strangelove, or, How I Learned to Stop Worrying and Love the Bomb* (Kubrick 1964), based on Peter George's *Red Alert* (1958), incisively connects nuclear proliferation to masculine performance anxiety, mocks the mythology of heroic service found in 'patriotic' Cold War films such as *Strategic Air Command* (Mann 1955) and links Wernher von Braun's development of Nazi rocket weapons at Peenemunde, using concentration camp slave labour, with his later work on US nuclear missile programmes.

Walter M. Miller, Jr's *A Canticle for Lebowitz* (1959) describes a post-holocaust world in which most of civilisation has been destroyed, and the surviving culture is deeply resistant to science and technology. In the novel's first part, the monks of St Lebowitz abbey copy and preserve any texts that survived the Destruction, but treat them as holy relics in a religion that mixes Christian mythology with new stories of the demon Fallout. In the second part, set many years later, a secular scientist visits their archives, planning to use the knowledge therein to create a new age of science, re-establishing the 'mastery of Man over the Earth' (1988: 197). The abbot cautions him against accepting that violence *must* accompany the struggles to control such technology, since this is merely a way to 'evade his own conscience and disavow his responsibility' (198). In the final part, even further in the future, a nuclear war breaks out, the cycle of destruction repeating. This era's abbot rails against the Radiation Disaster Act's provision of euthanasia facilities:

> Better for whom? The street cleaners? Better to have your living corpses walk to a central disposal station while they can still walk? Less public spectacle? Less horror lying around? Less disorder? A few million corpses lying around might start a rebellion against those responsible.
>
> (271)

What little hope Miller can muster is symbolised by a mutant creature awakened during the climactic bombings. Rejecting both the abbot's baptism and the political order, it perhaps represents the birth of a new moral sensibility.

The conflict between religion and science also shapes Leigh Brackett's *The Long Tomorrow* (1955). A century after a nuclear war, the US has reverted to pre-industrial agrarianism, adopting Mennonite values since 'only those who had lived without all the luxuries, and done for themselves with their own hands' (1975: 30) were equipped to survive in a world without cities or complex infrastructure. Young cousins Len and Esau Colter feel trapped by the constraints on knowledge this involves, and long for the lost technological wonders hinted at by Len's grandmother who remembers pre-war life as being not evil but 'All easy, and bright, and comfortable' (30). Rather than face a public birching over possession of a contraband radio, Len and Esau flee, eventually making their way to Bartorstown. Descended from a scientific project belatedly created by the pre-war government to discover a defence against nuclear weapons, this community has kept its nuclear reactor and supercomputer and, believing that a new industrial society will emerge and inevitably reinvent nuclear weapons, has continued its scientific endeavours. Over time, Len becomes disillusioned with their lack of progress, worrying that 'all they [will] get is the mathematical proof that what they're looking for doesn't exist' (199), but ultimately concludes that even if 'it was the Devil let loose on the world a hundred years ago ... it makes better sense to try and chain the devil up than to try keeping the whole land tied down in the hopes he won't notice it again' (222).

John Wyndham's *The Chrysalids* (1955), set in post-apocalyptic Labrador, also imagines a religious government, a puritanical tyranny committed to the eradication of any mutation or variation beyond what they believe to be the normal, God-ordained shape of things. Mutants born into this world are persecuted and destroyed. When a group of telepathic children is discovered, they are zealously pursued, even by members of their own families. As one of the children notes, 'what's got them so agitated about us is that nothing shows. We've been living among them for nearly twenty years and they didn't suspect it' (1987: 131). Petra, the child with the strongest powers, makes contact with others of their kind in New Zealand, who believe that the Labradorians' maniacal pursuit of an elusive stability condemns them to 'a place among the fossils' (182). The novel is rather ambivalent about the New Zealanders: the telepathic powers that enable them 'to think-together and understand one another as' non-telepathic humans 'never could' (196) suggest that they will not repeat the mistakes of the past, but their willingness to embrace their mutation as an evolutionary leap beyond the merely human reeks of social Darwinism.

Cybernetics

Cybernetics, which is concerned with the structure of regulatory systems and the operation of feedback systems, enjoyed great visibility as a new science in the post-war period, particularly through the work of Norbert Wiener, whose

The Human Use of Human Beings (1950) did much to popularise its tenets. Central to the development of robotics and other automated systems, cybernetics was also believed to be applicable to human social organisation, leading many authors to view the possibility of cybernetic social control with trepidation.

In Dick's 'Minority Report' (*Fantastic Universe* 1956), the director of the Precrime Agency, which uses precognition to prevent crimes before they can occur, is himself accused of murder. His subsequent actions exemplify feedback effects as new information is introduced, and although he escapes his apparent fate the story nonetheless reinforces the sense of an inescapable deterministic system. A more optimistic conclusion is found in C.L. Moore's *Doomsday Morning* (1957). Comus (Communications of the United States) has established a stable society, utilising polling techniques to detect dissatisfactions and manipulating the media to assuage them. In this tightly managed society,

> Comus is everybody. It's the newspapers, the schools, the entertainment. It's the communications-theory boys who quantify language, the public-relations people, the psychologists, the artists in all media who take the prescriptions the computers feed them and build sugar-coated truths that will cure any social bellyache before society knows it had one.
>
> (1987: 29)

The Secretary of State recruits Howard Rohan, a washed-up, alcoholic actor, to conduct surveillance on rebel-held territory under the guise of a travelling theatre troupe. Rohan is unaware that their portable auditorium contains psychological polling technology that can determine whether audience members are part of the resistance and have knowledge of a secret weapon that poses a threat to Comus. Obsessed with memories of his wife, who died with her lover in a car crash, Rohan eventually realises that he is living a contradiction, always thinking of her in terms of 'love and loyalty and brilliance and beauty' (173) even though she was having an affair; and just as she 'had been lovely and corrupt', he now recognises that Comus is 'beautiful and strong and corrupt' (181) and must be destroyed. The novel ends with the task of creating a post-Comus world that 'would be a harsh world, full of sweat and bloodshed and uncertainty. But a real world, breathing and alive' (236).

Wiener is directly invoked in Kurt Vonnegut's *Player Piano* (1952), a novel set after the Second Industrial Revolution that has automated routine mental as well as manual labour, leaving the majority of the population unemployed. (EPICAC, the computer that calculates 'how many everything America and her customers could have and how much they would cost' (1988: 102), controlling access to meaningful labour and thus to material well-being, is a homonym for a common emetic.) No one is safe from redundancy. When a brilliant engineer invents a machine capable of replacing him, he loses his position and is unable to obtain a design job because 'the test says no ... the machines say no' (64). Paul Proteus, despite his privileged position, is increasingly disillusioned, thanks to the aura of helplessness surrounding those whose only options are service in the Army or in the Reconstruction and Reclamation Corps. He begins to question the social costs of more efficient production through automation, arguing that 'you people have engineered them out of their part in the economy, in the market place, and they're finding out – most of them – that what's left is just about zero' (78). He becomes involved with a group of rebels who model themselves on the nineteenth-century Native American Ghost Shirt Rebellion, an ill-fated uprising which likewise represented a population marginalised by a new social order. Just as their only options were to 'become second-rate White men or wards of the white men' or to 'make one last fight for the old values' (250), so Paul's contemporaries 'have no choice but to become second-rate machines themselves, or wards of the machines' (251). At his trial, Paul testifies that 'machines and organization and pursuit of efficiency have robbed the American people of liberty and the pursuit of happiness' (272).

Bernard Wolfe's *Limbo* (1952) combines anxiety about nuclear war with fears of cybernetic domination. The novel moves between two time periods: 1972, when Dr Martine flees to an African island rather than continue to participate in WWIII; and 1990, when, under the name Lazarus, he returns from exile to America to discover that his abandoned, satirical journal has become the basis for a new social order, Immob. His final journal entries were written in rage and despair at the futility of repairing soldiers such as Teddy Gorman, a heroic bomber pilot who has killed millions, merely to enable their return to violent conflict. Reflecting on William James' *The Moral Equivalent of War* (1906), which argues that warfare will continue until an alternative method is found for establishing prestige and notions of honour and service, Martine mused about a society in which voluntary amputation fulfilled this role and wished that Gorman would bomb the EMSIAC supercomputer into oblivion rather than follow its orders. The US, now called the Strip because only the central portion remains habitable, has successfully made voluntary amputation serve the function of war, since it is the mobility of limbs, the instinct to form a fist, that produces the psychological need for war (common slogans include 'ARMS OR THE MAN', 'PACIFISM MEANS PASSIVITY' and 'NO DEMOBILIZATION WITHOUT IMMOBILIZATION'). White patriarchy remains intact – 'Those who did the menial jobs – tossing flapjacks in restaurant windows, clerking behind store counters, running elevators, driving buses and taxis – were non-amps; most of them, in fact, were women, and more than a few were Negroes' (1963: 114) – and the major political issue of the day is whether or not the use of prosthetics violates the spirit of Immob.

Martine is horrified by this literalisation of his satirical comments, but his rejection of vol-amp culture is complexly entwined with his own psychological limitations. He has sex with a woman from the East Union – the remnants of the former USSR – but deeply resents her forthright embrace of her own sexual pleasure and her expectation that he will remain passive beneath her. He later rapes her, arguing 'it's my turn now' (233), a reversal he calls 'equal rights' because 'rape was a pretty difficult business without a bit of ambivalence in the woman' (233). It is only when Martine sees his own son infantalised through the amputation of all four limbs that he begins to work through the unconscious fear of dependency on female nurture that shaped him and thus Immob. He realises that 'what he really had against his mother was not this or that real hurt but – her very existence. Her mere existence as Other, her "refusal" to be co-opted and absorbed by him. The gap between his skin and hers' (274). Thus, both his rape and Immob culture are nothing more than childish longings for wholeness and complete dependency transformed by an accompanying fear of rejection that has become hate filled. He concludes that, despite his flaws, he is morally superior to those who embrace Immob because he can accept his ambivalent and contradictory self instead of insisting upon the absolutes and purifications that lead to insane tyranny.

Paranoia

Anxieties about cybernetic systems of social control were matched by a political and cultural paranoia about difference, most obviously manifested in red scares and communist witchhunts. Dominant American ideology simultaneously emphasised individual freedom and the patriotic consumption of mass-produced commodities, a contradiction that meant any non-conformity might be construed as subversive. Katherine MacLean's 'Feedback' (*Astounding* 1951) critiques the tyranny of a democracy that forces individuals to conform to the majority opinion. 'All basic progress must start with the discovery of a truth not yet known and believed', William Dunner tells his school class, and 'Unless those who have new ideas and different thoughts be permitted to speak and are protected carefully by law, they will be attacked, for in all times men have confused difference with criminality' (1973b: 140). Inspired by this, young Johnny experiments with individuality, wearing his cap backwards despite his classmates' taunting. His mother, who remembers a period of massacres during which science and innovation where blamed for war, is terrified by such deviancy and organises the neighbourhood to take action against Dunner. He is tortured for the names of others who promote innovation, before being rescued by a fellow agitator who notes the interrelatedness of conformism and consumer culture:

> Twenty years trading in my good 'copter every year for the same condemned 'copter with different trimmings. Every year trade in my comfortable suit for some crazy fashion and my good shoes for something that doesn't fit my feet, so that I can look like everyone else.
>
> (155).

Dick's 'The Hanging Stranger' (*Science Fiction Adventures* 1953) also demonstrates the risks of being, or merely appearing, different. After a day spent working in his basement, Ed Loyce emerges to see a man hanging from a telephone pole. No one else seems to notice the corpse, or care. The police assure him that it is there for a reason, and he is relieved that it is not 'something like the Ku Klux Klan. Some kind of violence. Communists or Fascists taking over' (1990d: 32). However, he soon works out that aliens have infiltrated the town, reducing its citizens to shadows of themselves, 'their minds dead. Controlled, filmed over with the mask of an alien being that had appeared and taken possession of them, their town, their lives' (35). Loyce flees to a neighbouring town to alert the authorities, realising too late that the aliens left the body as a lure to draw out unconverted humans – and that he is to become the next piece of bait. *Invasion of the Body Snatchers* (Siegel 1956), based on Jack Finney's *The Body Snatchers* (1955), articulates similar anxieties. Doctor Miles Bennell discovers that the inhabitants of his small home-town are being replaced by emotionless facsimiles grown from alien seedpods. Repeated allusions to consumerist suburban lifestyles and technologies of mechanical reproduction – even the band at the local nightspot has been replaced by a jukebox – suggest a culture that is already transforming humans into automata. Miles' involvement with Becky Driscoll, a former girlfriend who, like him, is now divorced, and the determination with which the pod-people pursue this unmarried but presumably sexually active couple are also suggestive of the period's moralistic persecution of sexual nonconformity (as in the moral panic about homosexuals in government and education) and a determination to constrain individual freedom through the channelling of desire ('going steady' became the teenage norm and the average age at which people married dropped significantly).

Anxieties about alien modes of reproduction, interspecies miscegenation and 'appropriate' gender roles recur in such films as *Them!*, *Forbidden Planet*, *The Thing from Another World* (Nyby 1951), based on Campbell's 'Who Goes There?', *The Creature from the Black Lagoon* (Arnold 1954), *Attack of the 50 Foot Woman* (Juran 1958) and *I Married a Monster from Outer Space* (Fowler Jr 1958). In Wyndham's *The Midwich Cuckoos* (1957), filmed as *Village of the Damned* (Rilla 1960), a mysterious event leaves all the women in a small English town pregnant. They give birth to 30 pairs of golden-haired, psychic boys and girls who, as they grow up, separate themselves from the community and violently turn against anyone who hurts any of them. One of several alien colonies transplanted onto Earth, the children are really just two organisms, psychically linked but physically divided among multiple bodies. Despite his sympathy for the children, their teacher realises that he must destroy them because their dangerous otherness poses a fatal threat to humankind. Theodore Sturgeon's *More Than Human* (1953) takes the side of the 'alien' other in depicting the struggles of a community of children to negotiate their relationship with humanity. Individually, they are handicapped but when united as a *Homo Gestalt* they possess tremendous powers. Gerry, their leader, must kill the woman who has been caring for them because under her influence they deny their complementary, collective self and are becoming 'normal' atomised individuals. He regrets this necessity, and recognises the need to establish an ethics for interacting with *Homo sapiens*.

Race

Such sympathetic engagements with otherness can also be found in a number of texts that critique the racist attitudes and institutions being challenged by the Civil Rights movement and such legislative interventions as *Brown v. Board of Education* (1954), the supreme court decision that required the desegregation of schools, prompting hysteria and violence in many Southern communities. Leigh Brackett's 'All the Colors of the Rainbow' (*Venture Science Fiction* 1957) sees gentle green aliens, touring through the South, being jostled, harangued, assaulted and raped by whites who, because only one in 10,000 aliens is white, are terrified of being 'tramped under with color – all the colors of the rainbow!' (1963: 233). They insist that the aliens need to learn three basic rules: 'Niggers always keep to their own side of the road'; 'When a white man takes a mind to a female nigger, she ain't supposed to get uppity about it'; and '*You never lay a hand on a white man*' (237). Fredric Brown and Mack Reynolds' 'Dark Interlude' (*Galaxy* 1951) tells of Lou Allenby's murder of a man from the future whose discussion of ubiquitous future miscegenation convinced him that his sister had married a '*nigger*' (1963: 22). The sheriff to whom Lou confesses reassures him that he did the right thing. In Al Feldstein and Joe Orlando's 'Judgment Day' (*Weird Fantasy* 1953), a human astronaut is sent to evaluate whether or not a colony of self-reproducing robots are ready to join civilisation. An orange robot proudly shows him their faithful imitation of human democracy, assembly lines and social planning, all of which meet with approval. The astronaut insists on touring the blue robot part of town, where he finds that everything is underfunded and less well maintained. The production system for blue robots is identical to that for orange robots, except for the colour of the final carapace, a difference that is used to restrict blue robots to menial jobs, substandard education and segregated facilities. Only in the final panel of the comic does the astronaut remove his helmet, revealing that he is a black man.

Judith Merril's 'Barrier of Dread' (*Future combined with Science Fiction Stories* 1950) critiques the assumptions underpinning SF tales of interplanetary colonialism. In the far future, human civilisation 'is based on expansion – indefinite, unlimited expansion' (2005a: 38) across multiple galaxies. However, the head of government is troubled by a piece of his wife's art, prompting him to investigate the viability of expansion. He concludes that the universe is finite and that humans must therefore 'find a new form of society' that does 'not rely on the laws of dynamics' but is 'static' (40). Dick's 'Tony and the Beetles' (*Orbit* 1953) is told from the point of view of a child born in a human colony near Betelgeuse, established after nuclear war and overcrowding rendered much of Earth uninhabitable. Displaced aliens fight an ongoing war of resistance against human imperialism. Tony's father is aggressively racist about the 'beetles', but Tony has friends among the aliens and insists on calling them by their own name, Pas-udeti. When the war turns to the Pas-udeti's advantage, making abandonment of the colony inevitable, Tony, who identifies as a citizen of the only planet he has ever known, is profoundly confused. A sympathetic Pas-udeti explains that, even though Tony is his friend, the human occupation of his planet is unwelcome: 'You said you have a right here. But you don't,' he gently tells Tony, 'You said it isn't your fault. I guess not. But it's not my fault, either. Maybe it's nobody's fault' (1990e: 170).

Ray Bradbury's *The Martian Chronicles* (1950) was one of the first books produced from within the magazine tradition to find a substantial audience outside of that tradition's readership. It collected new stories with others published since

1946 in *Planet Stories, Thrilling Wonder Stories, Weird Tales* and *Collier's*, some of which critiqued contemporary race relations and the historical expansion of the US as mythologised in westerns. Bradbury's Martians are killed off by chicken pox carried by an early expedition. '–And the Moon Be Still as Bright' (*Thrilling Wonder Stories* 1948) explicitly invokes the genocide of Native Americans as an astronaut condemns human colonialism; the story, however, seems resigned to its inevitability. In 'Way in the Middle of the Air' (*Other Worlds* 1950), segregated and marginalised African Americans leave the South for Mars. While some whites lament the departure of almost-family members, the curmudgeonly Teece takes their departure as a personal insult: 'every day they got more rights.... Here's the poll tax gone, and more and more states passin' anti-lynchin' bills, and all kinds of equal rights. What *more* they want? They make almost as good money as a white man, but there they go' (1963: 70). A departing African American suggests that Teece is really bemoaning the loss of his nocturnal fun, terrorising and lynching poor blacks. In 'The Other Foot' (*New Story Magazine* 1951), not collected in the *Chronicles*, the imminent arrival of a lone white astronaut provokes an embittered Willie to agitate for the production of segregated, whites-only facilities in the 20-year-old black Martian settlement. The astronaut explains that a nuclear war has destroyed Earth, and that he has come to beg them to rescue the white survivors, offering to work their fields in exchange. As the astronaut details the extent of the destruction, including crucially the tree from which Willie's father was lynched, Willie relents and the community agrees to a fresh start for everyone on Mars. As with many liberal reformist texts of the period, the story requires African Americans to demonstrate excessive virtue and effectively exculpates white supremacism.

From UFOs to Dianetics

Despite the exchanges during the 1950s between SF and contemporary culture outlined above, there is one phenomenon that the magazine tradition adamantly refused to enrol: UFOs. The major exception was *Amazing*'s editor Raymond A. Palmer, already notorious for promoting the Shaver mysteries. In Spring 1948, he launched *Fate*, a magazine about paranormal phenomena whose first cover story was Kenneth Arnold's 'The Truth About Flying Saucers'; three years later, it carried George Adamski's account of his UFO sightings. After leaving *Amazing* in 1949, Palmer launched his own SF magazine, *Other Worlds*, which abandoned SF in the late 1950s to become the ufological *Flying Saucers, the Magazine of Space Conquest*.

Ufological narratives frequently articulate anxiety about an increasingly corporatised culture in which government has moved away from notions of democratic transparency and towards engineering expertise and doctrines of national security. Adamski's account of meeting a Venusian, which makes up the second part of *Flying Saucers Have Landed* (1953), emphasises his lack of formal education but valorises the practical and the intuitive that rationalised, corporate culture typically suppresses and excludes. However, unlike an *Astounding* protagonist, he prefers esoteric to experimental knowledge. Desmond Leslie, author of the first part of the book, is even more committed to the esoteric, linking UFOs to ancient myths. He also claims that a conspiratorial Pentagon and politicians anxious to preserve their positions are covering up the existence of benevolent visitors from Venus who are descended from refugees from Atlantis. Eschewing such 'ancient knowledge', Donald Keyhoe's *The Flying Saucers Are Real* (1950) argues that contradictions in official statements indicate the shifting policies of a secretive government preparing its citizens for the revelation that UFOs were visitors from other worlds, a position echoed in EC's *Weird Science-Fantasy* 4 (1954), a special 'Flying Saucer Report' issue that challenged the US Air Force to tell the people the truth.

The magazine tradition also refused to enrol Immanuel Velikovsky's bestselling *Worlds in Collision* (1950) and its sequels, which claimed that numerous myths, gathered from around the world, were descriptions of real, astronomical events. This peculiar exercise in comparative mythology required a complex history of the solar system in which Venus was actually a comet ejected from Jupiter in the fifteenth century BC, whose wandering to its current position also caused Mars to pass near the Earth in the eighth and seventh centuries BC. Despite the scientific community's dismissal of his ideas, they circulated so widely that in 1974 the American Association for the Advancement of Science organised a public debate on them, in which Carl Sagan demonstrated Velikovsky's ignorance of physics once more. However, some examples of unorthodox science did find a home, albeit briefly and uncomfortably, in *Astounding*. During the 1950s, Campbell's interest in parapsychology or psionics, the Dean Drive (which supposedly sidestepped Newton's Third Law of Motion) and the Hieronymous Machine (which, utilising psionic energies, could apparently function even if it only contained a diagram of its circuitry) became increasingly prominent in *Astounding*, valorising the endeavours of amateur scientists over their blinkered, professional counterparts. In May 1950, *Astounding* carried Hubbard's 'Dianetics: A New Science of the Mind', heralding the publication of his *Dianetics: The Modern Science of Mental Health* (1950). The first of several related articles, it outlines aspects of a psychotherapeutic scheme that bypassed professional psychoanalysis. Eschewing scientific, academic and corporate validation, Hubbard's system appeals to the engineering sensibilities of the practical, common man, contending that the normal human brain – the optimum computing machine – is prevented from functioning properly by traumas accumulated since the individual's conception. These traumas establish 'demon circuits' (2007: 28), causing the individual to be 'aberrated' and 'less able to survive' (35). Dianetics promises to reverse these aberrations, purify the individual from intruding exterior forces and thus overcome dangerous psychological feedback loops. Hubbard attracted coverage from *Time* and *Newsweek*, and drew various fans and writers – including, briefly, A.E. van Vogt – into Dianetics. Campbell's initial support for this unorthodox science, which Hubbard transformed into a religion, Scientology, in 1953, is indicative of, and perhaps partially a reason for, his decreasing influence on magazine SF.

Conclusion

- In the 1950s, the Cold War (including nuclear anxiety, anticommunism and celebratory consumerism) dominated American culture and the magazine and paperback tradition of SF.
- Magazine and paperback SF demonstrated an ambivalence about cybernetics, nuclear war, consumerism, corporations and governance, and a growing concern with issues of social organisation, including configurations of race, gender and sexuality.
- Significant changes in the market place and in entertainment technologies began to decentre the magazines as the site of SF production and to render exchanges between producers and fans more diffuse.
- Many actants excluded popular manifestations of the SF imagination, such as ufology, from enrolment into the genre, and Campbell's promotion of unorthodox science in *Astounding* frequently alienated readers.

6 New realities, new fictions: the 1960s and 1970s

Overview

This was a period of fierce debate among actants over the nature of SF. Writers and editors began to experiment with prose style and formal textual features and to situate SF within contemporary innovations in literature, visual arts and popular culture. Welcomed by some as evidence of a new maturity, this was lamented by others as the demise of SF. Alongside these developments, traditions of scientific extrapolation and adventure fiction continued. A number of major writers associated with both tendencies began their careers in this period. American and Soviet achievements in space, most crucially the *Apollo* Moon landings, were both celebrated and satirised. The sense of division within SF was indicative of, and frequently commented on, other cultural splits of the time, as the presumed post-war consensus was shattered by Civil Rights, Women's Liberation and Gay Pride movements, among others, and by protests over the American invasion and occupation of Vietnam. New actants in the development and definition of SF included academic journals and professional organisations for writers and critics.

Changing times

The 1960s and 1970s should have been a glorious age for SF as many of its earlier dreams and visions became realities. In 1961, Yuri Gagarin's *Vostok 1*, followed within weeks by Alan Shepard's *Freedom 7*, saw humans travel into space for the first time. Other achievements included the US *Apollo* programme, which put the first humans on the Moon (1969), the Soviet *Salyut* long-term space station programme (1971–1982) and the creation of NASA's re-useable space shuttle, as well as the launch of numerous satellites and unmanned exploration craft. Simultaneously, developments in communication and entertainment technologies led not only to portable, personal cassette players and home VCRs but also to ARPANET (1969), the computer network that would later become the Internet.

The fervour and energy around notions of a high-tech future were reflected in contemporary design, fashion and popular music, such as Eero Aarnio's chairs, Rudi Gernreich's clothing, Matti Suuronen's prefabricated, portable Futuro homes, David Bowie's extraterrestrial Ziggy Stardust persona, Hawkwind's psychedelic space-rock and Kraftwerk's electronica. Psychedelic culture embraced new forms of consciousness, frequently linked to a vaguely leftish politics of love. The unorthodox science and history of Erich von Däniken's *Chariots of the Gods* (1968) contended that the ancient monumental architecture of Africa, Asia and Latin America could not have been produced by human technologies, and therefore the Earth must have been visited by technologically advanced aliens in ancient times. His ideas were taken up in a range of SF texts, including Jack Kirby's *The Eternals* comic (1976–1978), *Battlestar Galactica* (1978–1979), *Stargate* (Emmerich 1994) and the *HALO* games franchise (2001–). In contrast, African-American jazz musician Sun Ra, who claimed to be from Saturn, incorporated the ancient wisdom and achievements of Egypt and other African civilisations into a liberatory astroblack mythology.

This period also saw the formation of professional organisations and associations and critical publications that continue to play an active part in SF's enrolment processes. In 1965, Damon Knight founded the Science Fiction Writers of America, an author advocacy group that also presents the annual Nebula Awards to outstanding works as voted for by its members (the equally prestigious Hugos, founded in 1955, are voted for by Worldcon members). In response to demands for more 'relevant' curricula, and to SF's newfound emphasis on literary techniques and its critical relationship to contemporary realities, academic attention began to mushroom. The first SF journal, *Extrapolation*, appeared in 1959. The Science Fiction Research Association and the Science Fiction Foundation were founded in 1970, the latter publishing *Foundation* since 1972. In 1973, Darko Suvin and R.D. Mullen launched *Science-Fiction Studies*. The first annual International Conference on the Fantastic in the Arts took place in 1979, leading to the formation of the International Association for the Fantastic in the Arts in 1982. This period also witnessed a growing interest in non-Anglophone SF, with many translations of European and Soviet writers, most significantly Stanisław Lem and Boris and Arkady Strugatsky.

The social world was in upheaval. While the Cold War threatened to heat up over the Berlin Wall (1961), the Cuban Missile Crisis (1962) and numerous anticolonial struggles, including the war in Vietnam (1955–1975), the counterculture challenged the imperatives of traditional authority and consumerism. Political unrest and hopeful protests took many forms – Civil Rights, Black Power, Brown Power, Native American Rights, second wave feminism, the New Left, student uprisings, anti-war movements, the Stonewall riots and the first Gay Pride marches, anti-nuclear and environmentalist movements – but always faced repression and violence. President Kennedy, Malcolm X, Martin Luther King, Jr, Robert Kennedy, Harvey Milk and John Lennon were murdered. The FBI surveilled, disrupted, defamed and suppressed dissident organisations, often illegally. The CIA had a hand in the 1961 murder of Congo's Prime Minister Patrice Lumumba and in the 1973 Chilean coup that overthrew Salvador Allende's democratically elected socialist government and established General Pinochet's murderous regime. The 1968 Soviet invasion of Czechoslovakia terminated Alexander Dubček's democratising reforms. Anti-apartheid leader Nelson Mandela was imprisoned in 1964 and

Steve Biko died in custody in 1977. The Chinese Cultural Revolution (1966–1976) saw brutal purges of purportedly pro-capitalist elements, resulting in hundreds of thousands of deaths and the displacement and impoverishment of millions.

The Vietnam War had its roots in French colonisation of South-East Asia. During WWII, French colonial forces were displaced by Japanese invaders, and after the war, the return of the French was strongly resisted. This conflict turned into a civil war between the North, supported by Soviets and later the Chinese, and the South, aided by American troops who began to arrive as 'advisors' under President Eisenhower, their number dramatically increasing under President Kennedy. President Johnson, who perceived the conflict as resistance to the global spread of communism, further expanded American participation. In 1964, it was claimed that the North Vietnamese had twice attacked American ships in the Gulf of Tonkin. These fabricated events provided a pretext for an escalation of the conflict and the deployment of regular US troops. President Nixon began to withdraw them in 1973, and the war ended in 1975. The brutality of the war, and failures by the US military to distinguish between civilians and combatants, radically changed many Americans' perception of their armed forces. One of the most infamous incidents, the My Lai massacre, involved the slaughter of 400–500 unarmed civilians, mostly women, children and the elderly, by US troops on March 16, 1968.

In 1961, the US entered the second longest period of economic growth in its history, lasting until the 1973–1975 recession. However, all was not well in America. In 1964, the rape and murder of Catherine Genovese, allegedly witnessed by 40 people who failed to intervene, created a moral panic about the lack of social responsibility among the inhabitants of large cities. Such incidents, along with the 'long, hot summer' of 1967, which saw 159 race riots in the US, accelerated the already significant white flight to the suburbs. This reduced the urban tax base and, in conjunction with reduced federal funding for social services, sped the decline of inner city conditions. In New York, for example, 'slum clearances' forced the relocation of 170,000 working-class people in the 1960s and 1970s, destroying communities and dislocating kinship networks. The recession was exacerbated by the 1973 oil embargo by Arab members of OPEC (Organization of the Petroleum Exporting Countries) in protest over the US resupplying the Israeli Army during the 1973 Yom Kippur War; by OPEC doubling the price of crude oil so as to stabilise its members' domestic economies; and by the 1973–1974 stock market crash. At the same time, the US had to come to terms with the 1973 resignation of Vice-President Spiro Agnew over corruption charges, and the 1974 resignation

of President Richard Nixon to avoid impeachment over criminal activities connected to the Watergate scandal. The counterculture had already found its dark
reflection in the months after the 1969 Woodstock Festival, with the deaths of four
people at the Altamont Free Concert and the multiple murders committed by
Charles Manson's 'family'. But even as the 1970s were ending with the Three Mile
Island nuclear leak, the Soviet invasion of Afghanistan, the Iranian hostage crisis
and the election of Ronald Reagan, abandoned black and Hispanic communities
were giving birth to hip-hop culture.

Metafictional SF

Fiction of all kinds struggled to address these new political and social realities.
Sensing that old narrative forms were incapable of meeting this challenge,
American literature in particular turned to metafiction, irony, pastiche, fragmentation and allegory. John Barth's 'The Literature of Exhaustion' (1967) argued that
'the used-upness of certain forms or the felt exhaustion of certain possibilities' in
contemporary fiction indicated that the project of literature as previously conceived
was over, but that this was 'by no means necessarily a cause for despair' (1984:
64), since a new synthesis of literature and life, more suited to the present age, was
possible. This new literature, as practiced by Barth, Donald Barthelme, William
Burroughs, Robert Coover, Joyce Carol Oates, Thomas Pynchon and Ishmael
Reed, among others, was later called postmodernist. It frequently drew on techno-
cultural imagery to articulate the social effects of the cybernetic merging of
humans with machines and other systems of control. In the *Nova Police* trilogy
(1961–1964), Burroughs' experimental 'cut-up' method of non-linear narrative
fragments created a paranoid, space-age mythology around recurring images of
chemical addiction and repressive social controls. Pynchon's *Gravity's Rainbow*
(1973) is a historical fantasia on the design, production and use of V2 rockets.
Digressive and irreverent, it involves over 400 characters and shifts in tone from
passages that channel the experience of psychedelic drugs to sober dialogues on
philosophical concepts and terse recitations of technical detail. Reed's *Mumbo
Jumbo* (1972) tells of the Jes Grew virus of black cultural emancipation and the
Wallflower Order's attempts to repress it through a black android who will
renounce African-American in favour of European culture. Such novels are characterised by a hyperreal blurring of fantasy, naturalism, SF and surrealism which
make it difficult to separate reality from its representation. This is literalised in
Angela Carter's *The Infernal Desire Machines of Doctor Hoffman* (1972), in which
war is waged through the deployment of reality-distorting machines.

In this context, distinctions between SF and other contemporary fiction became
increasingly difficult to maintain, or increasingly irrelevant. Nonetheless, while
some argued that SF should focus on new themes and techniques, embracing its
role as *the* literature of the contemporary age, others fought to retain a specific
genre identity consistent with their understanding of the magazine and paperback
tradition. However, texts published outside traditional SF venues were unevenly
enrolled into the field. Even writers such as Michael Moorcock and J.G. Ballard,

who celebrated Burroughs, championed neither Carter nor Reed; and although *Gravity's Rainbow* was a Nebula finalist, the award went to Arthur C. Clarke's *Rendezvous with Rama* (1973). *Astounding*, renamed *Analog* in 1960, remained the home of hard SF when Ben Bova took over as editor following Campbell's death in 1971; and hard-SF writers continued to emerge, including Greg Bear, Gregory Benford, Robert L. Forward, James P. Hogan, Charles Sheffield, Brian Stableford and Larry Niven, whose *Ringworld* (1970) won the Hugo, Nebula and Locus awards. Those resistant to more experimental forms of fiction often narrow down the history of the genre to a narrative that retrospectively enrols certain stories as hard SF, claiming that it has always been central, even if that also means ignoring most of the magazine and paperback tradition. A much broader view of what constituted SF was taken by *Galaxy* and *Worlds of If*, both edited by Frederik Pohl during the 1960s, *New Worlds* under Moorcock's editorship (1964–1971) and such major anthology series as Judith Merril's *Year's Best SF* (1956–1968), Damon Knight's *Orbit* (1966–1980), Terry Carr's *Universe* (1971–1987) and Robert Silverberg's *New Dimensions* (1971–1981).

The tensions between these divergent tendencies are played out in Barry N. Malzberg's *Galaxies* (1975), which is not 'a novel so much as a series of notes toward one' (1975: 7). The narrator discusses at length the difficulties involved in trying to write a hard-SF novel, about a fortieth-century spaceship captain caught in 'the black galaxy of a neutron star and … lost forever' (16), while simultaneously addressing his 'familiar theme' that the 'expansion of technology will only delimit consciousness, create greater feelings of alienation, impotence, hopelessness and so on' (22) and aspiring to surpass the '*angst*' of 'Cheever, Barth, Barthelme, Oates' (48). The planned novel will be based on two 1971 *Analog* articles by Campbell about black galaxies, but the narrator struggles to reconcile literary aims with the demands of hard SF since 'science fiction is about control, not dysfunction' (22). He admits to abandoning *Analog* in the 1960s because he was 'unable' any longer 'to read or relate to the contents of the magazine' (13). The fault, he suggests, lies in the limited ambition of *Analog*-style SF; instead,

> we need writers who can show us what the machines are doing to us in terms more systematized than those of random paranoia. A writer who could combine the techniques of modern fiction with a genuine command of science could be at the top of this field in no more than a few years. He would also stand alone.
>
> (13)

The narrator outlines various scenes that he contemplates writing and the techniques that he will use. He laments SF's typically shallow characterisation – 'the neutron star comes as close to a protagonist as this novel will ever have' (116) – and declares that he will not deny the captain's sexuality, although he knows this will contravene generic norms. While pondering possible endings – will the captain escape the black galaxy? Will she die in the attempt? Will the attempt itself trigger a universal catastrophe? – he acknowledges the pressure from genre publishers to provide an emotionally satisfying, triumphant conclusion. He settles on having the spaceship emerge in contemporary Ridgefield Park, New Jersey, since it will enable him to pose the question: how, 'from all the Ridgefield Parks of our time' will we 'assemble to build the great engines which will take us to the stars' (128)? Some of those stars, he adds, in the nearest he can manage to an inspiring conclusion, 'will bring death and others will bring life and then there are those which will bring us nothing at all, but the engines will continue, they will go on forever', and so 'after a fashion, after our fashion, will we' (128).

The collision of new realities and new forms is exemplified by Joanna Russ' *The Female Man* (1975), which combines science-fictional parallel worlds with postmodern metafiction to excoriate patriarchal culture's destructive effects on women's psyches. It contrasts the lives of four versions of the same woman – Jeannine, Joanna, Jael, Janet – whose dramatically different personalities and capacities derive from their different experiences of gender ideology. Jeannine, a timid librarian in a world in which the Depression never ended, defines herself by her ability to attract a husband and clings to her boyfriend even though he makes her unhappy. Joanna, an academic from a world similar to Russ' own, struggles to balance her identity as a human being with her gender training as a woman, chastising herself for her inability gracefully to accept casual slights while at the same time documenting the oppressive ubiquity of such incidents. She notes the impossibility of escaping patriarchy:

> nothing can put you above this or below this or beyond it or outside of it, nothing, nothing, nothing at all, not your muscles or your brains, not being one of the boys or being one of the girls or writing books or writing letters or screaming or wringing your hands or cooking lettuce or being too tall or being too short or traveling or staying at home or ugliness or acne or diffidence or cowardice or perpetual shrinking and old age.
>
> (p. 134)

Because the only way to be a full person under patriarchy is to be male, Joanna describes herself as a female man. Jael, who proposes a cross-worlds revolution against all men, comes from a dystopian future in which men and women have been at war for 40 years, and in which gender roles have been preserved but are no longer linked to male or female bodies. She satisfies her sexual needs with Davy, a lobotomised, artificial man created from chimpanzee DNA, whom she treats like a non-sentient object. Janet comes from Whileaway, a future eutopia where men died out 800 years ago and women are free to develop as full persons. She is self-confident, as fully at home expressing her emotions as her physical strength, and embraces both (lesbian) marriage and a career. The ideal of female subjectivity to which the others aspire, she is appalled by Davy, suggesting that something is lost to women if militant gender discrimination is their only path to full personhood. Jael, however, hints that such militants, not a plague, were responsible for the eradication of men that made Whileaway possible.

Modernist techniques were adapted by various New Wave authors. John Brunner's *Stand on Zanzibar* (1968) reworks elements of John Dos Passos' *U.S.A.* trilogy (1930–1936) and Brian Aldiss' *Report on Probability A* (1967) draws on Alain Robbe-Grillet's *nouveau roman*. Aldiss' *Barefoot in the Head* (1969) and Philip José Farmer's 'Riders of the Purple Wage' (1967) are both exercises in Joycean wordplay. Experimental prose was not entirely new to SF in this period. Alfred Bester's *The Demolished Man* (1953) utilises typography to represent conversations among telepathic characters, and *The Stars My Destination* (1957) is at its most innovative when it depicts the protagonist's experience of synaesthesia.

The novel moves towards some kind of synthesis, in which fulfilment need not be premised on a gender war, a single-gendered society or the adoption of the role of the female man. In a metafictional conclusion, all four women are identified as an 'I' by the narrator as she says goodbye to them and the themes they embody. The final paragraphs, addressed directly to the book itself, encourage it to go out into the world and not to 'scream when you are ignored' or 'complain when at last you become quaint and old-fashioned' (213) for the day when the book can no longer be understood by readers is the day 'we will be free' (214).

Philip K. Dick wrote his most important novels in this period, emphasising the destabilisation of ontological certainty by deploying such standard SF props as Martians, robots and spaceships, along with van Vogtian plot reversals to produce a uniquely paranoid vision of shifting, and perhaps groundless, reality. In the fictional world of *The Man in the High Castle* (1962), an alternative history in which the Axis powers won WWII, there exists a suppressed alternative history novel, *The Grasshopper Lies Heavy*, in which the Allies won the war, but in a metafictional twist, it is not our world that it describes. *Flow My Tears, the Policeman Said* (1974) is set in the authoritarian state that arose after the countercultural and racial unrest of the 1960s led to a Second American Civil War. One day, the celebrity Jason Taverner wakes up to find that the world has no memory or record of his existence. After the only person to recognise him dies, things slowly return to normal as the effects of an experimental, reality-warping drug she had taken wear off. In *Ubik* (1969), survivors of a corporate assassination attempt begin to experience historical regressions and the decay of commodities into earlier forms while a mysterious entity attempts to consume their life force; the protagonist eventually realises that they did not survive the bombing at all. In *Martian Time-Slip* (*Worlds of Tomorrow* 1963; book 1964) an autistic child, believed to be able to predict the future, actually appears to be able to change reality. The novel loops back to an encounter among key characters several times, becoming more dreamlike with each repetition.

In contrast to Dick's use of familiar generic elements, some SF of the period is barely recognisable as such. For example, Pamela Zoline's 'The Holland of the Mind' (1969), published in Langdon Jones' *The New SF* anthology, intersperses into the rather mundane story of a marriage breaking down through bored routine other passages describing Dutch history, Dutch/English vocabulary lists, analyses of paintings by Dutch masters and excerpts from an instruction manual on artificial respiration. These interpolations suggest parallels between the failed marriage, the at-times misleading similarities between languages which can impede communication, the process of artificially forcing someone to keep breathing and the omnipresent threat of flood. Holland is 'the paradigm of civilization, of the attempt to make civilization; the island, bailing to keep above the sea, planted with flowers' (1971: 211), but in the end the protagonist learns 'what we know and do not believe, that he was breakable, and that the dykes made only an uneasy peace with the water and that, in the end, the water is bigger and can wait longer for victory' (214).

Swinging new visions

Three major publications defined, albeit in different ways, this New Wave of SF. Harlan Ellison's anthology *Dangerous Visions* (1967) challenged the predominantly optimistic and sexually anaemic magazine and paperback tradition by collecting original stories too 'controversial' to publish. Judith Merril's anthology *England Swings SF* (1968) introduced American readers to the literary and avant-garde SF she had encountered in the UK and was promoting in her *F&SF* column and *Year's Best* collections. Preferring the term 'speculative fiction', and stylistic innovation over shocking content, Merril reprinted stories that were less obviously engaged with science and technology or with keeping SF distinct from other fantastic forms. Many of her selections came from the third major publication, the British magazine *New Worlds*, edited by Moorcock. In his first editorial, 'A New Literature for the Space Age' (1964), Moorcock called for SF to develop new methods of mediating and addressing space-age realities. Citing William Burroughs as an example, he argued that new literary techniques are the answer to the stagnation of not only SF but of the novel itself. He published many of the key stories and novels of the period, including some that other magazines would not even contemplate, with Norman Spinrad's 'obscene' *Bug Jack Barron* (1967; book 1969) prompting newsagents W.H. Smith's financially devastating refusal to stock *New Worlds* and questions in Parliament over the magazine's Arts Council funding. Throughout Moorcock's editorship, *New Worlds* made connections to other contemporary cultural and artistic movements, and the larger format issues published between 1969 and 1971 emphasised graphic design.

Dangerous Visions favoured stories that challenged bourgeois, Christian moral sensibilities. In Robert Bloch's 'A Toy for Juliette', a time-traveller abducts people for his granddaughter, named after de Sade's Juliette, to sexually abuse, torture and kill. When he mistakenly brings her Jack the Ripper, it is Juliette who is killed. Ellison's sequel, 'The Prowler in the City at the Edge of the World', follows Jack as he learns about the future city to which he has been brought. He kills its inhabitants, only to discover that these jaded immortals allowed him to do so for their own amusement. Although Ellison's sense of the dangerous can seem rather adolescent – far from being upset by Juliette's death, her grandfather tells Jack 'I was satisfied with the way you disposed of her. In a way, I'll miss the little twit. She was such a good fuck' (2009b: 149) – his afterword describes his rather more substantial ambition to produce a story that makes the reader confront 'the Jack in all of us', 'the Jack that tells us to stand and watch as a Catherine Genovese gets knifed, the Jack that condones Vietnam because we don't care to get involved, the Jack that we need' (2009a: 169). Theodore Sturgeon's 'If All Men Were Brothers, Would You Let One Marry Your Sister?' interrogates the last remaining sexual taboo of an interstellar future in which 'you can do anything you want to or with any kind of human being, or any number or combination of them, as long as you can pay for it' (2009: 397), except incest. Sturgeon contends that the physiological consequences of inbreeding have been exaggerated, and that we need to abandon this – and, by implication, other – archaic prejudices. Poul Anderson's 'Eutopia' tells of the flight of a Parachronic Research Institute agent from Norland, one of many small feudal countries in a parallel North America, to escape execution for a sexual indiscretion. The sympathetic ruler of neighbouring Dakoty agrees that his consensual dalliance with the child of a Norland household is not sufficient to war-rant death, until he realises that the child was male. Sonya Dorman's 'Go, Go, Go, Said the Bird' challenges sentimental notions of family. In its post-apocalyptic future, food is so scarce that cannibalism is accepted practice. The story reflects the thoughts of a woman as she flees a hunting party, remembering children she has nurtured and children who were killed because of their deformities, and how her son, Neely, became tribal leader. She imagines that if she reaches the safety of home, she will live to care for her grandchildren, but at the last minute she is brought down by axe-wielding Neely, who is leading the pursuit. When she begs for her life, he replies 'we're all hungry' (2009: 452) and dismembers her.

Larry Niven's 'The Jigsaw Man' contends that the expansion of transfusion and transplant procedures will eventually defeat campaigns to abolish the death pen-alty. Lew, knowing he will be condemned to death, makes a daring escape from the jail he is sharing with organ-leggers, only to be cornered in the neighbouring hospital where legitimate transplants occur. Before he is recaptured, Lew destroys banks of preserved organs so that his death sentence will be for a substantial crime. To his dismay, however, the court does not even mention it since there is sufficient evidence to sentence him to death and organ-harvesting for his traffic offences. In his afterword, Niven asks, 'what happens when the death of one genuine criminal can save the lives of twenty taxpayers?', and replies 'Morals change. Much of the science/art of psychology has dealt with rehabilitation of criminal. These tech-niques will soon be forgotten lore, like alchemy' (2009: 252). This assessment reveals some of the limitations of social extrapolation in what was beginning to be known as the hard-SF tradition. Although the story seems to recognise the elasticity of ideological constructions, Niven's binary opposition of the 'genuine' criminal and the taxpayer indicates the developing right-wing orientation of hard SF.

A central concern of *England Swings SF* is the relationship between social criticism and art. Keith Roberts' 'Manscarer' (1966) is set in an artist's Colony established by the state to provide absurd spectacular entertainments for the workers when they emerge from the vast subterranean warrens in which they live for daytrips to the coast. Following a fatal accident, a disquieted artist, convinced that they have abdicated their social responsibility, refuses to continue producing such distractions: 'we fell off the thin edge, the tightrope between creativity and dilettantism, between free thought and aimless posturing for applause … without us, they'll forget they're living in Hell; they'll just sludge down into a sort of great doughy mass, and forget how to think, and how to eat, and one day they'll forget how to breathe' (1968: 160–161). They abandon the Colony and return underground, despite the discomfort and hardships it will involve. More obliquely, in 'The Squirrel Cage' (*New Worlds* 1967), Thomas M. Disch imagines himself confined in a featureless room, with no memory of life before his captivity and no idea of how long he has been there. Suicide and escape are impossible. He is 'free to write down anything' he feels like on a typewriter, but convinced that whatever he writes 'will make no difference' (1968: 125). He concludes that

> I might just as well be lifting weights as pounding at these keys. Or rolling stones up to the top of a hill from which they immediately roll back down. Yes, and I might as well tell lies as the truth. It makes no difference what I say.
>
> (134)

He wonders if he is being kept in a zoo by aliens, but decides that it is more likely to be run by ordinary humans. The terrifying thing, though, is not the indifference of his hypothetical keepers and spectators, but that someone might one day say, 'All right, Disch, you can go now' (139).

Merril also reprinted three stories by J.G. Ballard, perhaps the most important and controversial figure of the New Wave. 'You and Me and the Continuum' (*Impulse* 1966) begins with an 'author's note' about a break-in at the Tomb of the Unknown Soldier and the various traces of a possible perpetrator found on the record labels of pop singer known as The Him, in a paper on schizophrenia and in an unpurchased TV pilot. He might be 'a returning astronaut suffering from amnesia, the figment of an ill-organised advertising campaign or, as some have suggested, the second coming of Christ' (1968: 95). This note is followed by 26 paragraphs organised alphabetically by heading, from Ambivalent to Zodiac, which juxtapose images from contemporary consumer culture with scientific prose and visions from the sexual imagination of the protagonist, who recurs in a various guises across the stories Ballard later collected in *The Atrocity Exhibition* (1970). These stories are primarily concerned with the fictional elements of everyday reality, which he attempts to map across the world of public events, the immediate personal environment and the inner world of the psyche: 'where these planes intersect, images are born' (Merril and Ballard 1968: 104). Reality is now so mediated, so infused with consumerist images, that – as in Freudian dream analysis – it has become necessary to consider both its manifest and latent content. Consequently, Ballard organises the content of fiction so as to indicate its deeply divergent latent meaning, with surreal results that in turn indicate the peculiarity of a world constructed and experienced through powerful public discourses and one's own psychological flux. In 'The Assassination of John Fitzgerald Kennedy Considered as a Downhill Motor Race' (*Ambit* 1967) and 'Plan for the Assassination of Jacqueline Kennedy' (*Ambit* 1967), Ballard obliquely relates recurring popular cultural images – the Zapruder footage of Kennedy's assassination; glamorous film stars, celebrities and politician's wives – to subjective experience and psychosexual desire. The infiltration of politics by advertising techniques and image management is a common theme in New Wave, but nowhere is it more powerfully stated than in Ballard's 'Why I Want to Fuck Ronald Reagan' (*International Times* 1968). Not selected for *England Swings SF*, it deploys scientific and psychoanalytic prose to dissect the psychosexual appeal of Ronald Reagan, then governor of California, and its manipulation in political advertising. Ballard reduces Reagan to 'a series of posture concepts, basic equations which reformulate the roles of aggression and anality' (1990: 106) so as to tease out the disturbing basis of Reagan's political success: his ability to convey a reassuring image.

Moorcock's *New Worlds* often elaborated the connections among technophilia, masculinity, imperialism, managerialism and space-age hyperbole in an ironic light, and made manifest the latent content of genre conventions. For example, the protagonist of Harvey Jacobs' 'Gravity' (1968) passionately believes in the US space programme. Dismissing any suggestion that its resources be redirected to addressing social problems, he autoerotically embraces the phallic, ejaculatory imagery of rocket launches. He has sex with an astronaut's disenchanted wife while watching news coverage of her husband's mission. Hiding in a broom cupboard when the press come to interview her, he dreams pulp dreams of '*The elimination of disease and hunger. ... The construction of alabaster cities. Conquest of the galaxy. The liberation of love through vigorously applied Technology*' (2004: 11). Barrington Bayley's 'The Four-Colour Problem' (1971) interrogates the mathematical formulas for producing coloured maps of political boundaries, interweaving dense 'Technical Sections' with social commentary to demonstrate the ways in which science can become a metaphor for social life. A succession of discursive modes and narrative fragments – from references to Burroughs' fiction and Kennedy's assassination to a tale about a racist's testicular transplant resulting in him fathering black and Chinese children – satirise the militarisation of science, the dehumanisation of the subject within corporate and political thinking and the unacknowledged sexual fantasies informing much SF. Charles Platt's 'The Disaster Story' (1966) lays bare the appeal of apocalyptic fiction: the last individual is able to roam as he pleases, with the entire store of Western civilisation as his personal fiefdom and without the complications of other people: 'the last woman on Earth ... will be young and physically attractive and she will love me and serve me unquestioningly. She will be the last symbol I need' but 'I will still remain the only person existing, for I shall certainly not treat her like one' (2004: 282). In such a world, 'the feeling of *lacking* I used to feel – or used to imagine I felt – in the old time, will be satisfied' (282). Ironically, many New Wave authors, including Ballard, Moorock and M. John Harrison, would continue to treat women as symbols in their fiction, however self-consciously.

Ballard was a frequent contributor to *New Worlds*, where other authors took up his concern with an increasingly mediated, consumer culture that blurs distinctions between fantasy and reality. Moorcock's stories about Jerry Cornelius – a hip, bisexual, sometimes black, sort-of secret agent and occasional hermaphrodite-messiah – reiterate material familiar from the British globe-trotting adventure and espionage fiction of John Buchan, Sax Rohmer, Leslie Charteris and Ian Fleming and from such television adventure series as *Danger Man* (1960–1961, 1964–1966), *The Avengers* (1961–1969) and *The Saint* (1962–1969), so as to reveal the gulf between fantasies of a benevolent empire and the realities of the Cold War. 'The Tank Trapeze' (1969), for example, arranges Jerry and other characters in a series of encounters in Orientalist settings, interspersing these tableaux with a timeline of events taken from *The Guardian*'s reporting of the Soviet invasion of Czechoslovakia.

The Cornelius stories also contributed to *New Worlds*' metaphorical exploration of the notion of entropy. In thermodynamics, the amount of energy in a closed system remains constant; but since no use of energy is completely efficient, the amount available in the system for work will reduce, or the system's entropy will increase, until heat death – the point at which no energy differentials remain in the system and thus no energy is available for work. While thermodynamic entropy came to be understood as the amount of disorder in a system, information theory took it to mean the amount of information in a system, which increases with disorder. Out of this complex and apparently paradoxical set of ideas, a powerful metaphor for the passing of the imperial world order and the proliferation of media and information was fashioned. In 1969, *New Worlds* reprinted Thomas Pynchon's 'Entropy' (*Kenyon Review* 1960), which contrasts a hermetically-sealed hothouse (thermodynamic entropy) with a raucous party (informational entropy) in a neighbouring apartment. Pamela Zoline's 'The Heat Death of the Universe' (1967) uses entropy to express the never-ending drudgery of childcare and domestic labour. Sarah longs for a life in which 'there are things to be hoped for, accomplishments to be desired beyond the mere reproductions, mirror reproduction of one's kind' (2004: 138) but is condemned to the closed system of suburbia, reduced to 'filling the great spaces of Space with a marvellous sweet smelling, deep cleansing foam' (142). Although she is 'vivacious … witty … happy and busy … and only occasionally given to obsessions concerning Time/Entropy/Chaos and Death' (137–138), she eventually snaps, furiously smashing things in the kitchen she has just cleaned.

New Worlds also satirised the absurd, dehumanising routines of corporate life. In John T. Sladek's 'Masterson and the Clerks' (1967), Henry C. Henry's clerical post with the Masterson Engineering Company involves the pointless, circular but meticulously performed production, distribution, processing and filing of paperwork whose only function seems to be the production of further paperwork. The narrative becomes increasingly surreal as boredom sets in and the clerks' battle against entropy loses ground. Masterson, who has started eating health food and lifting weights in his office, seems to grow younger every day, while his clerks are laid off one by one. Art, the man who prepares their pink slips, turns out to be Masterson's father. The founder of the company, he has become so alienated that he enthusiastically prepares his own pink slip, and responds with genuine surprise and grief on finding it in his pay packet. Fear and paranoia pervade the office as the staff dwindles. A group emerges that blames Jews, peoples of colour and communists for standing in the way of efficiency, progress and civilisation. Trite motivational posters encourage 'ACCURASY' (2004: 215), and as Henry ruminates on an axiom offered to him when he was hired – 'If you work good, we'll do good by you' (193) – it mutates into increasingly bizarre, nonsensical iterations – 'If few work good, we'll do good by you', 'If few were good weal, do good by you' (223). This entropic decline continues until a crew arrives to demolish the apparently abandoned building.

Language, communication and power

New Worlds' writers also reflected on language itself as a constructed, contingent human system of meaning that does more than merely reflect the world. For example, David Harvey's article, 'The Languages of Science' (1967), draws attention to the repercussions of the degree to which the language of science – which claims to be objective and tends to reduce social processes to natural, and therefore unchangeable, ones – has come to dominate contemporary life. An unreflective attitude towards language, he warns, blinds us to the degree to which the language we use shapes our perception of the world and the opportunities for social action within it. For example, the language of economics implies that economies tend towards equilibrium, whereas in reality 'the rich regions grow rich while the poor regions grow relatively poorer' (2004: 386).

Sensitivity to the culturally specific, contingent dimensions of language enriched much of this period's SF, such as Samuel R. Delany's *Babel-17* (1966) and Ian Watson's *The Embedding* (1973), novels of human/alien communication that engage with the idea that language can change consciousness. Delany's best selling *Dhalgren* (1975) offers a potent image of life in America's decaying inner cities. It recounts the adventures of a young man who cannot remember his name but becomes known as Kidd or Kid. In the virtually-deserted, lawless city of Bellona, almost completely cut off from the rest of the world, he mixes with countercultural youths, street gangs and a middle-class family clinging to the remnants of a bourgeois lifestyle in an abandoned apartment building. Delany's racially diverse characters comment overtly on the politics of colour in America: one recurring story involves the alleged rape of June, a 'little blond-headed seventeen-year-old' girl, by George Harrison, the 'biggest, blackest buck in the world' (2001: 71). The novel, which continually stresses the gap between experience and its representation, shows how this inflammatory image is the product of a certain kind of discourse, and those who know the pair talk about June's sexual pursuit of George, noting the degree to which her own desire was formed by the notion of the 'biggest, blackest buck'. (The fluidity of sexual desire is a recurrent theme, with Kidd participating in graphically described straight, gay and group sex.)

Dhalgren begins in the middle of a sentence, 'to wound the autumnal city' (1), and ends with another fragment, 'I have come to' (801), thereby forming a circle of endless reading. When Kidd arrives in Bellona, he finds a journal that also starts with this sentence, and begins to write poetry on its blank pages. The last sixth of the novel transcribes pages from his own journal of life in Bellona, including crossings-out, corrections, his retrospective commentary on some passages, indicators of the manuscript's materiality (references to staples, missing pages and illegible words) and interpolations by two different editors. He notes the gulf between things as written and things as he remembers experiencing them, and concludes that the journal is false because there is never time to write/think/reflect at the moment an event is happening, making it a 'chronicle of incidents with a potential for wholeness they did not have when they occurred' (734).

Following the success of his book of poems, *Brass Orchid*, Kidd is asked by a reporter whether the group with whom he lives 'believes' in violence, to which he replies, 'that isn't something you believe in. That's something that happens' (Delany 2001: 638). Pressed as to whether he thinks, 'objectively', that his lifestyle is 'a good way' to live, he replies, 'it depends on what you think of the way the rest of the world is living' (639). *Dhalgren* is, thus, concerned not only with the alienation of many young people from dominant American values, the racial and class polarisations of modern urban life and the heteronormative oppression of sexual diversity, but also with the political relevance of language itself.

The mediation of reality is also central to Norman Spinrad's *Bug Jack Barron*. Jack Barron's eponymous television show investigates and resolves issues that bother his viewers, but despite his apparent outrage he is too reliant on corporate sponsorship to challenge the status quo. A founder of the Social Justice Coalition, he later exchanged countercultural politics for economic security, losing his wife, Sara, in the process of selling out. He becomes involved in the machinations around a Congressional Bill that will make the Immortality Foundation the only organisation permitted to freeze terminally ill people for resuscitation when cures have been found. When Jack's investigation of alleged racial discrimination draws unwanted attention to the Bill, Benedict Howards tries to buy his public support, even revealing that the Foundation has discovered how to make people immortal. Meanwhile, in an attempt to dislodge the long-incumbent Democrats from the White House, Jack is jointly proposed by the Republicans and S.J.C as their Presidential candidate not because of his politics (he no longer seems to have any), but because he is 'a marketable commodity ... like a nice ripe Limburger, an image behind which [Republicans] can unite with the S.J.C. to win the Presidency' (1972: 72). Jack and Sara are reunited and accept Howards' bribe – the immortality treatment – so that they can be together forever. Too late, Jack discovers that the treatment involves implanting endocrine glands from lethally irradiated black children. Sara commits suicide, freeing Jack to use his show to reveal the truth. The immortal, but now deranged, Howards is institutionalised. The novel ends anticipating the presidential race against the disgraced Democrats' new candidate,

Malcolm Shabazz (i.e. Malcolm X). No one suspects that Jack intends, if elected, to resign in favour of his own black vice-president.

Thomas M. Disch's *Camp Concentration* (*New Worlds* 1967; book 1972) also reflects on language and power, its title punning on campness, the mental activity of concentrating and on concentrating something, whether through a chemical process or in a concentration camp. Sacchetti, imprisoned as a conscientious objector, keeps a journal that begins on May 11. On June 2, he announces that he has been kidnapped to another prison, run by a private corporation. He fears that he is now beyond the law, subject to an interminable sentence, although the conditions at Camp Archimedes are an improvement. The warden, Haast, welcomes him and explains that they wish him to keep a journal of his experiences. His fellow inmates are subjects of an experiment using a drug derived from syphilis, which scientists believe will enable 'the bringing together of two hitherto distinct spheres of reference, or matrices' – 'literally, the mind disintegrates, and the old distinct categories are for a little while fluid and capable of re-formation' (1980: 53) – and thus produce original, genius thought. However, it also causes neural damage, leading to insanity and, after 90 days, death. Written during the Vietnam war, the novel connects such experimentation to the other processes of waging war, both legal and illegal, undertaken by the US.

Although Sacchetti believes that he is merely there to document events, it soon becomes clear from his increasingly manic diary entries that he too has been infected. He eventually discovers that the inmates' obsession with alchemy as a repressed science was merely a cover for their escape plans. They have secretly developed a method of transferring consciousness between bodies, and use it to change places with the guards. The ending, however, remains pessimistic: looking at the diseased body he has left behind through his new eyes, Saccheti writes: 'the mind *is* destitute and bare. Finally it is reduced to the supreme poverty of being a force without an object. I exist without instincts, almost without images; and I no longer have an aim' (164).

Robert Silverberg's *Dying Inside* (*Galaxy* 1972; book 1972) is also concerned with the isolation and alienation that arise from the experience of difference, re-imagining the telepathic mutant not as a triumphant superman or a martyred harbinger of posthuman evolution, but as the fallible, often weak and lonely David Selig, who merely happens to be able to read minds. Now 41, balding and with deteriorating eyesight, he feels his power failing, his access to the thoughts of others becoming blurred. As he narrates his daily life, explaining how he came to be single and supporting himself by ghost-writing term papers for Columbia students, he comments on events, such as the My Lai massacre, that coincided with watersheds in his own life. Ironically, being able to bypass the shortcomings of language and thus fully to know the mind of another has never enabled him to be close to anyone. His sister resents the sense of always being spied upon. His first love, whose thoughts he could not read, left him for another, more predatory telepath who appeared to have an 'instinctive, intuitive grasp of [her] emotional needs' (1972: 168). His one other serious relationship ended when his partner took acid: while he was overwhelmed by her telepathic projections, his self-loathing infiltrated her experience, changing how she saw him. As the novel ends, David and his sister are fragilely reconciled. Although he grieves when his power disappears completely, he senses that the difficult work of human communication among equals will lead to a more fulfilling life.

Lifestyle SF

Sexually liberated lifestyles and recreational drug use recur in this period's SF, and some texts, such as Robert A. Heinlein's *Stranger in a Strange Land* (1961), were embraced by large countercultural readerships. Michael Valentine Smith, the surviving son of two members of the failed *Envoy* mission to Mars, is raised by Martians, learning their culture and psychic abilities (telepathy, teleportation, telekinesis and the ability to 'discorporate' things). A later expedition brings him to Earth, and because he has inherited the enormous wealth of the *Envoy*'s crew and, according to Earth law, might be the owner of Mars, an anxious government detains him. Liberated by a sympathetic nurse and protected by Jubal Harshaw, 'LL.B, M.D., Sc.D., bon vivant, gourmet, sybarite, popular author extraordinary, and neo-pessimist philosopher' (1971: 80), he fosters a countercultural movement based on Martian wisdom.

Jubal is an anti-intellectual demagogue, preferring the innate good sense of the common man to, for example, pretention in art, declaring

> it's up to the artist to use language that can be understood. Most of these jokers don't *want* to use language you and I can learn; they would rather sneer because we 'fail' to see what they are driving at. If anything. Obscurity is the refuge of incompetence.
>
> (309)

Impassioned, he defends his own work as art even though 'most of [it] is worth reading only once' (310) and elevates commercial success over critical acclaim. Jubal is a right-wing libertarian, embracing an individualist style of American democracy. A particular target of his contempt and the book's satire is the Fosterite Church of the New Revelation, which – with its emphasis on consumerism, profitability and access to greater knowledge through more substantial donations – parodies both Scientology and the megachurches of the post-war Protestant revival. Michael eventually starts his own religion, 'the Church of All Worlds, Inc.' (305), which teaches members the Martian language and, through it, to 'grok' the universe as it really is: god is in everything and all are god. To 'grok' means to

> understand so thoroughly that the observer becomes part of the observed – to merge, blend, intermarry, lose identity in group experience. It means almost everything we mean by religion, philosophy, and science – and it means as little to us as color means to a blind man.
>
> (206)

The assumptions of human culture prevent most people from being able to grok, but sexual dimorphism allows humans access, through heterosexual sex, to a state of consciousness that exceeds what Martians can achieve: 'The joining of bodies with merging of souls shared in ecstasy, giving, receiving, delighting in each other – well, there's nothing on Mars to touch it, and it's the source, I grok in fullness, of all that makes this planet so rich and wonderful' (397). This vaguely spiritual sense of an altered state of consciousness, of fusion between self and other, appealed – along with the novel's celebration of sexual promiscuity – to the emerging counterculture (it inspired elements of the neopagan movement and, more notoriously but with little actual evidence, Charles Manson). Despite on some level recognising the social construction of heterosexual norms and gender roles, the novel's sexism and homophobia have caused its reputation to wane.

Frank Herbert's *Dune* (*Analog* 1963–1964, 1965; book 1965) also achieved a cult readership, becoming one of the best-selling SF novels of all time, spawning sequels, prequels, games, a film adaptation (Lynch 1984) and a television mini-

Countercultural and anti-authoritarian SF films

La Jetée (Marker 1962)

Alphaville (Godard 1965)

Sins of the Fleshapoids (Kuchar 1965)

Diabolik (Bava 1968)

Night of the Living Dead (Romero 1968)

Watermelon Man (Van Peebles 1970)

THX 1138 (Lucas 1971)

Punishment Park (Watkins 1971)

Conquest of the Planet of the Apes (Thompson 1972)

Zardoz (Boorman 1974)

Dark Star (Carpenter 1974)

The Terminal Man (Hodges 1974)

A Boy and His Dog (Jones 1975)

Rollerball (Jewison 1975)

God Told Me To (Cohen 1976)

The Man Who Fell to Earth (Roeg 1976)

Coma (Crichton 1978)

Invasion of the Body Snatchers (Kaufman 1978)

Alien (Scott 1979)

Born in Flames (Borden 1983)

series (2000). It recounts the political struggles between the aristocratic Atreides and Harkonnen over the desert planet Arrakis, the source of melange, the psychotropic spice needed to navigate space. Paul, the son of Duke Leto Atreides by his concubine Jessica, a member of the elite and mysterious Bene Gesserit order, is at the centre of this conflict. When the Harkonnens invade Arrakis, Paul and Jessica flee to the desert and take refuge with the indigenous Fremen. Paul learns about Arrakis' complex ecosystem and the Fremen's secret long-term plan to make the deserts bloom. He teaches them the Bene Gesserit 'weirding way' and leads them in the struggle to overthrow the Harkonnens, which eventually sees him replacing the Emperor. The novel's wide appeal can be attributed to three qualities. First, it mixes SF premises with narrative conventions and a style that, after the spectacular American success of J.R.R. Tolkien's *The Lord of the Rings* (1954–1955) in the mid-1960s, had come to be associated with heroic fantasy. Its court intrigues, dynastic successions, feuds, exotic settings and peoples, fabulous beasts, secret martial arts, swords and daggers helped to attract a wider audience than that usually identified with SF. Second, its depiction of the Arrakis ecosystem and the technologies and techniques necessary for human life in such an extreme environment addressed both a hard-SF audience desirous of technical detail *and* the emerging environmentalist movement. Finally, its interest in alternative religions, meditation and transformed consciousness held a countercultural appeal similar to that of *Stranger in a Stranger Land*. In contrast to Heinlein, Herbert includes a number of strong female characters who find ways to work within and around the limitations of gendered, hierarchical social structures, perhaps attracting a feminist readership, too. However, Herbert's vision is as relentlessly heterosexist – and homophobic – as Heinlein's, indicating a greater conservatism than much of the New Wave and feminist SF of the period.

Philip K. Dick's afterword to *A Scanner Darkly* (1977) describes it as a lament for named friends destroyed by drug use, whether through death, physical impairment (he includes himself in the list) or permanent psychotic break; the novel also critiques the criminalisation of drug users and the prioritisation of punishment over treatment. Unknown to his housemates, Bob Arctor is an undercover narcotics agent for the Orange County Sheriff's Department. Moreover, law enforcement agencies are so riddled with corruption that his identity must be kept secret from his employers, too. As Agent Fred, he wears a scramble suit, which projects fragmented samples of hundreds of faces over his own features, appearing to his colleagues and handlers as nothing more than a 'vague blur' (1991: 22). When Fred is ordered to spy on Bob, his sense of his own identity starts to fall apart. When Fred watches surveillance recordings of Bob, he is surprised by some of Bob's actions; and when posing as Bob, he increasingly identifies with drug users and feels no commitment to his mission. This is exacerbated by his growing addiction to the psychoactive Substance D, which causes the two hemispheres of his brain to dissociate from and compete with each other. He finally experiences a psychotic break, which unknown to him was a Federal agency's plan all along, so that he can be infiltrated into one of the recovery centres believed to be the source of Substance D. By the end of the novel, Fred/Bob, whose real name is never revealed but who is now called Bruce, has lost all trace of identity, becoming nothing more than a vague blur.

Optimistic, liberal SF continued to be popular, most obviously on television. In the UK, *Doctor Who* (1963–1989), conceived as a children's programme, often reflected New Wave ambivalence about imperialism, albeit in more conventional narrative forms, and interrogated automation and authoritarianism through recurring Dalek and Cybermen antagonists. *The Prisoner* (1967–1968), depicted the Cold War as an absurd game, condemning automation and bureaucracy without ever quite managing to embrace countercultural values, while the grim space opera *Blakes 7* (1978–1981) was oddly prescient of Margaret Thatcher's 1980s. In the US, *The Twilight Zone* (1959–1964) consisted of one-off SF, fantasy and horror dramas, many of them cautionary tales about intolerance, conformity and political complacency; imitators included *The Outer Limits* (1963–1965) and *Night Gallery* (1970–1973). *Star Trek* (1966–1969) attempted to revise the colonialist vision of much space opera and to imagine a post-scarcity future in which sexism and racism have disappeared and Earth is united under a single, peaceful government. Its eventual impact could not have been foreseen. It was almost cancelled after season two, but a fan-organised campaign played a role in prompting its renewal for a further season. While it is impossible to ascertain how much weight this campaign carried with network executives, the belief that their intervention saved the show gave fandom a new confidence and energy and was a watershed in the transformation of fandom away from privileging print SF. The series' popularity in syndication helped to launch an ongoing film franchise and four spin-off series, beginning with *Star Trek: The Motion Picture* (Wise 1979) and *Star Trek: The Next Generation* (1987–1994), respectively.

Like *Dune*, *2001: A Space Odyssey* (Kubrick 1968) addressed both a hard-SF audience, with its painstaking depiction of space travel and technologies, and a countercultural one, with its arthouse tendencies, corporate satire and lengthy, psychedelic effects sequences. Building on Kubrick's audio-visual spectacle, *Star Wars* (Lucas 1977) returned SF to its colourful space opera roots, inflected by post-Tolkien fantasy. Despite Lucas' conscious indebtedness to Edgar Rice Burroughs and *Flash Gordon*, his tale of a beautiful princess, beleaguered rebels, the mysterious Force and a farmboy's role in saving the galaxy from an evil empire had little in common with contemporary innovations in print SF except, perhaps, its omnivorous intertextuality. However, it can be credited with the revival of SF cinema – often with big budgets – that continues to the present day, even if it might also be blamed for reducing SF film to cross-marketed, heavily merchandised, action-driven spectacular blockbusters. Nonetheless, it too had countercultural appeal. Beyond the film's reworking of the mythic journey of the hero and its vague mysticism, the Empire could be imagined as the oppressive Amerika against whom the counterculture was struggling; part of its wide success, however, lies in the fact that it did not demand to be understood in this way. *Close Encounters of the Third Kind* (Spielberg 1977) also mapped out a retreat from countercultural commitment as protagonist Roy Neary flees the problems posed for him by lower middle-class life, strong women and responsibility, to be whisked away from it all by benevolent, child-like aliens. Spielberg's subsequent SF films, from *E.T.: The Extra-Terrestrial* (1982) to *Indiana Jones and the Kingdom of the Crystal Skull* (2008), demonstrated a growing conservatism in their focus on the insular worlds of suburban families and hard-won reconciliations between fathers and sons.

Anti-war SF

Star Trek's emphasis on exploration and communication rather than conquest also resonated with anti-war protestors (although the series frequently violated its own principle of non-interference, and imposed the Federation's 'superior' morality on other planets and species). Alluding explicitly to *Star Trek*, James Tiptree, Jr's 'Beam Us Home' (1969) considers the attraction of such liberal humanist futures while also indicting the flight from reality that they might involve. Hobie is unable to cope with the contemporary world,

> which was then quite prosperous and peaceful. That is to say, about seventy million people were starving to death, a number of advanced nations were maintaining themselves on police terror tactics, four or five borders were being fought over, Hobie's family's maid had just been cut up by the suburban peacekeeper squad, and the school had added a charged wire and two dogs to its patrol. But none of the big nations were waving fissionables, and the U.S.-Sino-Soviet détente was a twenty-year reality.
>
> (1978: 359)

He fantasises that he is merely a visitor to this world, which will eventually evolve beyond its 'primitive stage' (360). He joins the Air Force to become an astronaut, but the space programme is temporarily suspended so that the US can fight a brutal war against Guévarrista revolutionaries in Latin America. Reassigned to active duty, he is horrified by what he witnesses and, delirious from the effects of a bacteriological weapon, flies his plane straight up into the sky. Rescued by an alien spacecraft, he returns to his real 'HOME!' (374); or he hallucinates all this just before dying.

Ursula K. Le Guin's *The Word for World Is Forest* (1976) deconstructs narratives of interplanetary colonisation and criticises US imperialism. The terrestrial military forces on New Tahiti have displaced and enslaved the indigenous Athsheans and are aggressively deforesting the planet. The Athshean word for 'world' is 'forest', not 'earth', so this is a profound violation of their way of life. Despite deriving from the same genetic stock, the humans refuse to consider the green-skinned natives as humans, but their frequent (and unpunished) rape of female Athsheans indicates a simultaneous recognition and disavowal of this relationship. The authorities do not listen to the anthropologist Lyubov when he tries to explain that

> for four years [the Athsheans have] behaved to us as they do to one another. Despite the physical differences, they recognised us as members of their

species, as men. However, we have not responded as members of their species should respond. We have ignored the responses, the rights and obligations of non-violence. We have killed, raped, dispersed, and enslaved the native humans, destroyed their communities, and cut down their forests. It wouldn't be surprising if they'd decided that we are not human.

(1982: 62)

SF responds to the conflict in Vietnam

The June 1968 *Galaxy* carried two paid advertisements on facing pages showing SF writers' positions on US involvement in Vietnam. The left-hand one was signed by 72 people and 82 signed the right-hand one, including the following:

We the undersigned believe the United States must remain in Vietnam to fulfill its responsibilities to the people of that country.	*We oppose the participation of the United States in the war in Vietnam.*
Poul Anderson	Forrest J. Ackerman
Leigh Brackett	Isaac Asimov
Marion Zimmer Bradley	Ray Bradbury
John W. Campbell	Samuel R. Delany
Hal Clement	Lester del Rey
L. Sprague de Camp	Philip K. Dick
Edmond Hamilton	Thomas M. Disch
Robert A. Heinlein	Harlan Ellison
Dean C. Ing	Carol Emshwiller
P. Schuyler Miller	Damon Knight
Sam Moskowitz	Ursula K. Le Guin
Larry Niven	Katherine MacLean
Jerry E. Pournelle	Barry Malzberg
George O. Smith	Judith Merril
Jack Vance	Mack Reynolds
Jack Williamson	Gene Roddenberry
	Joanna Russ
	Norman Spinrad
	Kate Wilhelm
	Donald A. Wollheim

A spaceship arrives with a device that will replace the 50-year 12-month communication delay between Earth and this outpost with instantaneous communications, making the colonists 'answerable' (108) for their actions. One faction, believing this is a trick, destroys an Athshean village in an attack that evokes the My Lai massacre, provoking a rebellion that forces humans from the planet. This retreat is not depicted as a defeat, as many viewed the analogous situation in Vietnam, but as an appropriate and respectful, if belated, action that leaves open the possibility of future communication should the Athsheans desire it.

Vietnam veteran Joe Haldeman's *The Forever War* (1974) recounts the experiences of Private Mandella, drafted in the 1990s, who becomes Major Mandella by the war's end 1000 years later. The Taurans, a previously unknown alien species, are suspected of attacking human ships when they emerge from collapsars (which enable movement between remote parts of the galaxy). In response, the United Nations Exploratory Force provides armed escort vessels and occupies planets near the collapsars. The time-dilation effects of such space travel mean that although the war lasts for a millennium, Mandella's subjective experience of it is around five years. Much of the novel is a bitter satire on the stupidity of the army's training and tactics, its willingness to casually waste lives and the inadequate preparation of troops for armed combat. When his first tour of duty is completed, Mandella returns to an overcrowded Earth that has no space for him, so he reluctantly reenlists and is immediately assigned to combat duty. Hypnotically primed to see the Taurans as fiends who rape women and slaughter babies, 'a hundred grisly details as sharply remembered as the events of a minute ago, ridiculously overdone and logically absurd' (1976: 62), his first close-quarters engagement with the enemy is not a battle but a massacre of disoriented beings who offer no resistance. When he later tries to talk about this experience, his critical comments are transformed into praise for the military. When the war is over, Mandella discovers that – in an echo of the Gulf of Tonkin incident – it was provoked by the twentieth century's military elite in order to stimulate an ailing economy. He concludes that 'you couldn't blame it all on the military, though. The evidence they presented for the Taurans' having been responsible for the earlier casualties was laughably thin. The few people who pointed this out were ignored' (232).

Conclusion

- SF's relationship to science and engineering became increasingly critical as the genre responded to new social movements and drew on the energy and techniques of postmodernist fiction. Although Campbellian SF remained important, it could no longer be claimed as the core of the genre, so the retrospective construction of a hard-SF tradition, often associated with more conservative politics, began in earnest.
- The professionalisation of SF writers and the rise of SF studies added new voices to ongoing enrolment processes.
- SF's presence in book form and with a distinct marketing label was solidified by a number of bestsellers. However, following Tolkien's *The*

Lord of the Rings, heroic fantasy begins to emerge as a serious competitor. Even as SF drew on fantasy forms, there was a popular and theoretical drive to distinguish between them.

- While some SF films partook of the experimental styles of contemporary art cinema, towards the end of this period SF cinema became increasingly associated with spectacular blockbusters.

7 New voices, new concerns: the 1960s and 1970s

Overview

Among the political movements of the period, three in particular found SF images and techniques useful for exploring their concerns: anti-racism, feminism and environmentalism. Works critiquing gender and sexuality, including explicitly feminist texts, were the most successful at being enrolled into literary SF, partly because of the active participation of feminist writers, editors and fans as actants in this process. Environmental issues were more prominent in SF film. Politically radical and formally experimental texts tended to be less fully enrolled than more conventional narratives, repeating the tension between aesthetic and commercial priorities in the New Wave controversy. This turn to social and political themes tended to de-emphasise the hard sciences, drawing instead on such 'soft' sciences as anthropology, economics and sociology.

Race

In the US, Civil Rights struggles became increasingly heated in the 1960s. The desegregation of Southern institutions often led to violent clashes. In 1957, Arkansas' governor instructed the National Guard to prevent black students from attending a Little Rock high school, provoking President Eisenhower to dismiss the Guard and despatch the 101st Airborne division to protect the students; and in 1962, James Meredith successfully sued the University of Mississippi to gain admission, but had to be accompanied by US Marshalls. Passive protests such as the Montgomery Bus Boycott (1955–1956) and lunch counter sit-ins (starting in Greensboro in 1960) gave way to more overt confrontations. Freedom riders, testing the 1960 Supreme Court decision that interstate buses could not be segregated, faced harassment and violence in Southern states, including from police. During the 1964 Mississippi Freedom Summer, three civil rights workers aiding in black voter registration were murdered. In 1966, during his March Against Fear from Memphis to Jackson, James Meredith was injured by a sniper and the rapidly growing march was later attacked by state police. Many activists moved towards a demand for revolution, and Martin Luther King, Jr began to be overshadowed by such leaders as Malcolm X of the Nation of Islam and Bobby Seale,

Stokely Carmichael and Huey P. Newton of the Black Panther Party for Self-Defense. Simultaneously, many African nations were winning independence from European colonial powers, including Cameroon, Senegal, Togo, Madagascar and Nigeria in 1960, Sierra Leone, Tanzania and Rwanda in 1961 and Algeria and Uganda in 1962. Some African-American activists began to articulate a Pan-Africanist vision, emphasising the links between the heritage of slavery in the US and the colonial occupation of Africa. Arguments for Black Power and Black Pride saw the development of a Black Arts Movement that sought to recover and adapt traditional African forms. Popular music was given a distinctly science-fictional aspect by such performers as Jimi Hendrix, Sun Ra, Parliament-Funkadelic and Earth, Wind & Fire.

It was not just the New Wave that was sceptical of space age triumphs. Following the *Apollo 11* Moon landing, Emory Douglas' cartoon for the *Black Panther* newspaper (July 26, 1969), headed 'Whatever is good for the oppressor has to be bad for us', depicts pig-police unloading slaves onto the Moon, one of whom mutters, 'I knew we should have stop [sic] this shit before it got off the ground'; a second cartoon (August 23, 1969) depicts a space-suited pig hammering a 'Whites Only' sign onto the Moon (Durant 2007: 40–41). Gil Scott-Heron's 'Whitey on the Moon', from the album *Small Talk at 125th and Lenox* (1970), counterpoints its account of the everyday misery of ghetto life with the refrain 'but whitey's on the moon'. This sense of disenfranchisement is central to African-American SF of the period, and is frequently used by white writers to add some measure of complexity to otherwise one-dimensional, more-or-less incidental, black characters, such as the black astronauts in *UFO* (1970–1973) and Ben Bova's *Millennium* (1976) and *Kinsman* (1979).

Marvel Comics' white-authored superhero Luke Cage, who debuted in 1972, indicates how such limited characterisation could nonetheless resonate with African-American experience. In a reworking of Captain America's origin story and the Tuskegee experiments, Carl Lucas, imprisoned for a crime he did not commit, undergoes an experimental scientific procedure in order to sway his parole board. He becomes hypermuscular, his skin as hard as steel. Escaping to New York to clear his name, he becomes a hero for hire, self-consciously passing as a super-hero, because it is 'one line [of] work where powers like [his] seem natural' (Goodwin 1972: 7). *Luke Cage, Hero for Hire* linked differential access to technology, wealth and prestige to skin colour, and articulated the alienated black identity that W.E.B. Du Bois and Frantz Fanon had described in terms of double consciousness and colonised subjectivity. His adopted name alludes to an imprisonment he feels even though no longer incarcerated. He has no conventional off-duty secret identity, no mask to put on and take off. He is always Luke Cage, visible in the role he must play in order to survive, and since his superpowers consist of hitting things really hard and withstanding being hit really hard, he embraces this stereotype, performing black male rage so convincingly that opponents rarely notice that he also outsmarts them.

Since the 1940s, liberal SF writers tended either to presume a colour-blind future in which race goes unmentioned because it is no longer an issue (but typically

In the 1960s, American comic books entered 'the Silver Age', generally identified with Marvel Comics' writer Stan Lee and artist Jack Kirby's creation of new, more realistic superheroes. Beginning with the Fantastic Four (1961) and the Incredible Hulk (1962), these new heroes were flawed individuals with personal lives and problems, as well as superpowers. Probably the most influential was Spider-Man (1962), created by Lee and Steve Ditko, who articulated the struggles of young people growing up, their values diverging from those of their parents' generation. These new Marvel heroes, accompanied and aided by other changes in the industry, enabled comic books to begin to address more mature themes and offer social critique. Marvel also introduced a number of African-American superheroes, including Black Panther (1966), The Falcon (1969), Luke Cage (1972), Blade (1973), Brother Voodoo (1973), Black Goliath (1975) and Storm (1975). In this period, DC Comics, lagging behind Marvel's Silver Age innovations, did introduce Black Lightning (1977).

failed to include characters of colour) or to use aliens and robots as metaphorical figures of otherness (but typically failed to address contemporary racial politics very specifically). In this period, some continued unthinkingly to reproduce racist assumptions, while others attempted to be provocative about racial issues, the most egregious examples being Robert A. Heinlein's *Farnham's Freehold* (1964) and Richard W. Brown's 'Two of a Kind' (*Amazing* 1977). However, a growing number of writers began to use SF frameworks to explore the consequences of colonialism and systemic racism. Robert Bateman's *When the Whites Went* (1963), Alan Seymour's *The Coming Self-Destruction of the U.S.A.* (1969) and Christopher Priest's *Fugue for a Darkening Island* (1972) build on the tradition of catastrophe fiction, and John Hersey's *White Lotus* (1965) reworks a yellow peril scenario so as to subject white Americans to the experience of slavery. John Brunner's *The Jagged Orbit* (1969) and Peter Dickinson's *The Green Gene* (1973) depict segregated dystopias. In Barry Norman's thriller *End Product* (1975), set several generations after a genocidal war has eradicated all peoples of African origin and diseases have depleted livestock populations, governments conspire with corporations in the mass farming of 'afrohominids' or 'ediblacks' – purportedly a species of tailless, hairless, black-skinned primate – as a replacement meat source. Warren Miller's *The Siege of Harlem* (1964) and Edwin Corley's *Siege* (1969) depict black secessionists seizing Manhattan, while John Jakes' time-travel romp *Black in Time* (1970) features white supremacists and black revolutionaries attempting to 'improve' the world by assassinating historical figures. Samuel R. Delany, one of the few black writers working in the magazine and paperback tradition, deploys space-opera conventions to critique colonial ideology in *Empire Star* (1966), and Michael Moorcock's *Oswald Bastable* trilogy (1971–1981) draws on Edwardian future war fiction to construct alternative histories of the twentieth century that expose the brutalities and legacies of European and American imperialism.

A.M. Lightner's *The Day of the Drones* (1969) and Mack Reynolds' *North Africa* trilogy (1961–1978) demonstrate the possibilities and the problems of working with and against the historical inertia of specific forms. Lightner depicts a world 500 years after a devastating nuclear war, in which an African society dispatches an expedition to Europe in search of white survivors. In this role-reversed colonial adventure, future Africans retain a tribal structure (albeit under a centralised civic-political authority), are institutionally prejudiced against lighter skin tones, have placed advanced science and technology under taboo and are dependent on old white technology to transport the expedition. Inevitably, the female protagonist, Amhara, falls in love with a member of the civilisation they discover, and returns to Africa with an invaluable treasure that again suggests the superiority of the vanished whites: the complete works of Shakespeare. However, the conclusion is more conciliatory than is usual in colonial adventure fiction. Rather than destroying the lost civilisation or making a return to it impossible, Amhara insists that they must not merely loot its ancient treasures: 'We cannot benefit from their heritage unless we reach out in friendship to our white brothers.... The way is open if we want to take it' (1969: 213).

Reynolds' trilogy, the first two volumes of which were serialised in *Analog* (1961–1962), attempts to present Africa as a rich tapestry of peoples, places, cultures and languages, but ultimately treats the continent as series of physical and social engineering projects and a site for the military-political strategies and tactics of renegade African-American aid workers attempting to unify and modernise a primitive, tribal population. The trilogy can be seen as extrapolating Du Bois' notion of the 'talented tenth', the educated African Americans who can become leaders of the struggle, and – courtesy of the Campbell/Heinlein SF tradition of which it is a part – as an eminently *reasonable* revision of Schuyler's *Black Empire* (*Pittsburg Courier* 1936–1938), stripped of terroristic revenge fantasy but still requiring charismatic authoritarianism. Homer Crawford and other aid workers have found it useful in their attempts to change African behaviours and traditions to ascribe their propaganda to a mythical leader, El Hassan, a role Crawford eventually must adopt in order to lead the North African revolution. Reynolds critiques the ideology of 'development', with several passages explaining how First World nations use aid to subsidise their own industries and to tie Third World 'beneficiaries' into their political and economic structures and goals. The novel also mocks the Soviet orthodoxy that pre-capitalist societies cannot transform themselves directly to socialist societies, which leads to the USSR covertly supporting the anti-communist El Hassan because his revolution will prepare Africa for a socialist revolution, while the US opposes him, despite his anti-communism, in order to protect its economic interests. Nonetheless, Reynolds does replicate the ideology of progress and deny agency to Africans, who must be tricked into following its dictates; and despite repeated references to the Afrodiasporic heritage of El Hassan and his First World colleagues, they often seem indistinguishable from white characters.

Wilson Tucker's *The Year of the Quiet Sun* (1970) strikes a more elegiac note. Futurologist Brian Chaney is a reluctant participant in a government time-travel project intended to determine the accuracy of his forecasts and thus shape future policy. His blackness, only hinted at in the first half of the novel, becomes increasingly relevant when the President orders a mission to discover whether he will be re-elected. Arriving in 1980, Chaney discovers that Chicago is under siege and divided by a makeshift wall; initially a barrier built by rioters to prevent 'the passage of police and fire vehicles' and completed by 'both blacks and belligerent whites' (1972: 99), it is now a permanent fixture, 'built of cement and cinder blocks; of wrecked or stolen automobiles, burned-out shells of city buses, sabotaged police cars, looted and stripped semi-trailer trucks; of upended furniture, broken concrete, bricks, debris, garbage, excretion … corpses' (98). Trips further into the future reveal that race war quickly tore the US apart. Chaney, stranded in the post-apocalyptic future, meets a colleague who lived through it all. She suggests that if a family that he had spotted in the distance

> were healthy, they were eating well and living in some degree of safety. If the man carried no weapons, he thought none was needed. If they had a child and were together, family life has been re-established. And if that child survived his birth and was thriving, it suggests a quiet normalcy has returned to the world, a measure of sanity.
>
> (187)

It is unclear whether Chaney shares this dying woman's 'hope for the future' (187).

African-American authors produced a cycle of militant near-future fiction that has not traditionally been enrolled into SF. In Sam Greenlee's *The Spook Who Sat By the Door* (1969), Freeman spends years playing two roles – a subservient, grateful negro around white people, an upwardly mobile playboy around the black middle class – so that he can train as a CIA agent and then organise ghetto gangs into an army. The novel ends as revolution begins to spread from city to city. (Ivan Dixon's 1973 film adaptation was allegedly suppressed by the FBI). In Nivi-kofi A. Easley's *The Militants* (1974), COON (Coordinated Organization of Nationalists), 'a black organization dedicated to the overthrow of the government, Capitalism, and Honkyism in general' (1974: 53), conducts a brief reign of terror in New York, before the novel loses track of these political goals and instead begins to figure a eutopian future in terms of a sexually explicit, inter-racial *ménage à trois* in a swanky new apartment building. The novel's misogyny indicates some of the difficulties that arose from a Black politics that described generations of oppression in terms of the social, political, economic and cultural emasculation of African-American men, sometimes leading to discourses and practices which furthered the marginalisation and oppression of African-American women. Equally problematic treatments of black male sexuality, especially in relation to white women, are common in white-authored fiction, even when the overall tenor of the work is anti-racist. As Delany's *Dhalgren* suggests, such stereotypes and anxieties about miscegenation have a dangerous, but complex, persistence.

In Julian Moreau's *The Black Commandos* (1967), Denis Jackson, who has dedicated himself to bringing 'his body to a peak of physical perfection no other man in all history had attained!' (1967: 23) and raising his IQ until it was 'well beyond the power of any known test of intelligence to measure!' (24), leads an army of black superscience warriors – 'they weren't ordinary niggers … almost like from the future' (128) – in a campaign to 'execute key members of the racist power structure' (72) so as to speed its total collapse. Blyden Jackson's *Operation Burning Candle* (1973) attempts a similar semiotic warfare, based on a more overtly science-fictional premise. Aaron Rodgers, believing that the 'thread that ties' black people together in a kind of 'collective consciousness' has somehow been augmented by 'technological progress in communications' (1973: 174), reasons that he can trigger revolutionary change by staging an event so traumatic that it shocks African Americans out of the 'acceptance and resignation' (93) that this shared consciousness reinforces. Serving in Vietnam, he recruits black US troops into a guerrilla force to perform the 'final symbolic act' (104), a 'trauma from which even the white folks couldn't escape because the accomplished fact of it would necessarily shatter their own self-concept and all the myths, complacency, and the concept of black people as passive, accepting and afraid' (93). The novel

Black fabulations

Many Afrodiasporic authors produced fiction containing elements that might equally be associated with SF, fantasy, fable, folklore, horror, myth, magic realism, naturalism and metafiction. Examples include:

Ralph Ellison, *Invisible Man* (1952)

Ishmael Reed, *Flight to Canada* (1972)

Barry Beckham, *Runner Mack* (1972)

Gayl Jones, *Corregidora* (1975)

Chester B. Himes, *Plan B* (1983)

A.R. Flowers, *De Mojo Blues* (1983)

Toni Morrison, *Beloved* (1987)

Charles Johnson, *Middle Passage* (1990)

Jewelle Gomez, *The Gilda Stories* (1991)

Phyllis Alesia Perry, *Stigmata* (1998)

Colson Whitehead, *The Intuitionist* (1999)

Tananarive Due, *The Living Blood* (2001)

Nalo Hopkinson, *The Salt Roads* (2003)

Anthony Joseph, *The African Origins of UFOs* (2006)

ends ambiguously, with a wounded Rodgers bleeding to death, but it is hinted that the assassination of prominent racists at the Democratic Convention might actually 'break the chain so that the next generation of black children will start out with a whole new psychological framework' (174).

This cycle's most important writer is John A. Williams, whose career started with semi-autobiographical novels mapping the systematic, day-to-day operations of the intertwined systems of capital and race, before turning to SF and thrillers better to analyse these structures. For much of its length, *The Man Who Cried I Am* (1967) appears to be a more ambitious version of his earlier work, alternating between Max Reddick's life in May 1964 and the preceding 25 years of his career as a novelist and journalist. This historical and social background serves, however, to anchor the two terrible conspiracies he discovers: in 1958, Britain, France, Belgium, Portugal, Australia, Spain, Brazil, South Africa and the US formed the Alliance Blanc to prevent newly independent African nations forming a Pan-African federation; and the US, 'sitting on a bubbling black cauldron' (1971: 349), also developed the genocidal KING ALFRED plan, which in 'the event of widespread and continuing [domestic] racial disturbances' (354) will 'terminate, once and for all, the … threat to the whole of American society, and, indeed, the Free World' posed by '22 million members of the Minority, men, women and children' (355). The novel ends in a hesitation between possible futures: if Max disseminates this information, it might provoke widespread disturbances; if he does nothing, KING ALFRED provisions will remain in place should black resistance grow sufficiently to be deemed a threat anyway. The *best* imaginable future is the barely possible prevention of genocide. *Sons of Darkness, Sons of Light* (1969), which features a plan to hold Manhattan hostage in exchange for reparations and reforms, is a little more optimistic about forming a genuine alliance with disenfranchised and sympathetic whites. *Captain Blackman* (1972) switches between the present moment, in which Captain Abraham Blackman, serving in Vietnam, is wounded trying to save his men from ambush, and the suppressed history of African-American soldiers since the War of Independence. The latter strand takes up most of the novel, as Blackman is apparently projected back to – or, delirious, imagines – Lexington in 1775 and then the Battle of Charleston, the Indian Wars, the Spanish-American War, both World Wars, the Spanish Civil War and the Korean War. This account not only demonstrates how consistently black soldiers were mistreated by their own army but also historicises Blackman's situation, enabling him to perceive what he must do. The final chapter, set 30 years later, begins with high-ranking officials planning the resegregation of US armed forces so that they can be relied upon to suppress black domestic insurgency. However, Blackman has been building a secret army in Africa, infiltrating its light-skinned members into every part of the high-tech military so as to seize the US nuclear capability and global communications and control systems.

None of these African-American SF novels are able to imagine moving beyond the need for urgent and radical change into a differently constituted future. Octavia E. Butler's *Kindred* (1979) turns to the constraints that history continues to exercise on daily life, combining a time-travel narrative with a specifically

African-American literary form, the slave narrative. In 1976, the year of the American bicentennial, African-American Dana is on several occasions thrown back in time to the antebellum Maryland plantation on which her ancestors were slaves. This SF conceit enables Butler to flesh out Dana's learned knowledge of the past with a realistically-depicted, subjective experience of slavery, and to indicate the extent to which systemic racism perpetuates this past into the present and, if it continues, any potential future.

Feminism

In this period, a more overtly activist 'second-wave' feminism emerged. Although certain legal equalities – enfranchisement and the rights to education, employment and property ownership – had been achieved in many countries, structural discriminations against women continued everywhere. In Western nations, feminists began to draw attention to reproductive rights, domestic and sexual violence and the division of labour perpetuated by the nuclear family. Birth control pills were becoming available even as Helen Gurley Brown's *Sex and the Single Girl* (1961) argued that women should be able to enjoy sexual, as well as financial, independence. Betty Friedan's *The Feminine Mystique* (1963) details the alienated experience of middle-class suburban housewives; three years later she became the first president of the National Organization for Women (NOW). Consciousness-raising groups that helped women to explore their identities beyond the strictures of patriarchal systems spread across America, and feminist scholarship made inroads into academia. In 1967, Shulamith Firestone and other left-wing feminists formed New York Radical Women, which was involved in the protests outside the 1968 Miss America pageant during which a sheep was crowned and items of conventional femininity – high heels, cosmetics, false eyelashes, girdles, bras – were dumped in a 'Freedom Trash Can'. Firestone's *The Dialectic of Sex* (1970) argues that the patriarchal family was part of a class system preventing women and children from being fully human, and urges the creative use of technology to free women from the repressive social structures erected on women's role in reproduction. The Equal Rights Amendment to the US Constitution passed Congress in 1972 (although it has never been ratified), and the 1973 *Roe v. Wade* and *Doe v. Bolton* Supreme Court Decisions upheld a woman's right to make her own choices about pregnancy.

Many female SF fans, editors, authors and academics embraced feminism and sought to transform SF through its insights, the most prominent being Joanna Russ, who moved fluidly among these communities. Her essay 'The Image of Women in SF' (1970) provoked controversy by arguing that SF should do more than merely reproduce limited cultural roles for women and should use its extrapolative and speculative potential for political praxis. Although *Extrapolation* and *Science-Fiction Studies* published articles that subjected SF to feminist analysis in the 1970s, more substantial interventions took place in convention programming and in such fanzines as *WatCh* and *Janus*. In 1975, the fanzine *Khatru* published an exchange that captured aspects of these debates about gender, whose participants included Russ, Ursula Le Guin, James T. Tiptree (not yet known to be Alice Sheldon) and Samuel R. Delany. Pamela Sargent's *Women of Wonder* (1974), *More Women of Wonder* (1976) and *The New Women of Wonder* (1978) anthologies highlighted women's contributions to SF, publishing fiction by Le Guin, Russ, Tiptree, Eleanor Arnason, Leigh Brackett, Marion Zimmer Bradley, Suzy McKee Charnas, Sonya Dorman, Carol Emshwiller, Anne McCaffrey, Vonda McIntyre, Katherine MacLean, Judith Merril, C.L. Moore, Kit Reed, Josephine Saxton, Joan D. Vinge, Kate Wilhelm, Chelsea Quinn Yarbro and Pamela Zoline. Sargent's introductions helped to recover the history of women's SF, drawing attention to such writers as Pauline Ashwell, Rhoda Broughton, Mildred Clingerman, Ann Warren Griffith, Zenna Henderson, E. Mayne Hull, Alice Eleanor Jones, Andre Norton, Wilmar Shiras, Francis Stevens and Margaret St Clair. Sargent also offered critical commentary on contemporary SF concerned with gender, and argued that feminist sensibilities had transformed the genre, stating that 'If one is going to write about a future patriarchal world, one at least [now] has to explain why it is that way instead of taking it for granted' (1978: xxvi). The number of award-winning stories in these anthologies – Russ' 'When It Changed' (1972), McIntyre's 'Of Mist, and Grass, and Sand' (1973), Le Guin's 'The Day before the Revolution' (1974) – is just one indicator of the success of feminist SF in this period.

Critical assessments that describe this period as the one in which feminism 'discovered' SF, and vice versa, overlook women's earlier contributions to the genre. However, authors such as Russ and Tiptree did use SF explicitly to articulate feminist politics. Russ also published a number of important essays, later collected in *To Write Like a Woman* (1995) and *The Country You Never Have Seen* (2007), which highlighted limitations in the ways in which SF writers and critics addressed gender. Sarah Lefanu's *In the Chinks of the World Machine* (1988), whose title comes from Tiptree's 'The Women Men Don't See' (1973), provided feminist critical readings of Charnas, Le Guin, Russ and Tiptree. Building on Russ' *How to Suppress Women's Writing* (1983), which satirically outlined the conscious and unconscious strategies by which women are excluded from the literary canon, Lefanu identified the selective erasure of female authors and stories about family, sex and gender from contemporary critical debates. She sought to enrol women's gothic fiction – largely ignored, apart from *Frankenstein* – into SF. She argued for the innate affinity of SF and feminism, since the genre enabled explorations of alternative realities in which, for example, the presumed naturalness of patriarchal structures might be questioned. Such visions, she contends, are inseparable from real-world political struggle, providing 'a rehearsal in the imagination for what might be in the world' (1988: 50).

The most passionately political works of this period imagine all-female societies or depict male–female relations as war between absolutely different entities, an idea further explored in important feminist work of the 1980s such as Margaret Atwood's *The Handmaid's Tale* (1985) and Sheri S. Tepper's *The Gate to Women's Country* (1988). In *Walk to the End of the World* (1974), Suzy McKee Charnas depicts a misogynist post-holocaust future, ruled entirely by men, who treat subservient Fems as domestic animals and blame them for humanity's faults.

20 works of feminist SF

Rosel George Brown, *Galactic Sibyl Sue Blue* (1968)

Monique Wittig, *The Guérillères* (1969)

Doris Lessing, *Memoirs of a Survivor* (1974)

Kit Reed, *The Killer Mice* (1976; collects short fiction 1959–1976)

Vonda N. McIntyre, *Dreamsnake* (1978)

Joanna Russ, *The Two of Them* (1978)

Suzette Haden Elgin, *Native Tongue* (1984)

Jody Scott, *I, Vampire* (1984)

Ursula K. Le Guin, *Always Coming Home* (1985)

Connie Willis, *Fire Watch* (1985; collects short fiction 1978–1985)

Pamela Sargent, *The Shore of Women* (1986)

Carol Emshwiller, *Carmen Dog* (1988)

Pat Murphy, *Points of Departure* (1990; collects short fiction 1980–1990)

James Tiptree, Jr, *Her Smoke Rose Up Forever* (1990; collects short fiction 1969–1981)

Katharine Burdekin, *The End of This Day's Business* (1990; written 1935)

Rebecca Ore, *The Illegal Rebirth of Billy the Kid* (1991)

Marge Piercy, *He, She and It* (1991)

Melissa Scott, *Shadow Man* (1995)

Candas Jane Dorsey, *Black Wine* (1997)

Tricia Sullivan, *Maul* (2004)

The first sequel, *Motherlines* (1978), contrasts this with two female communities: the first, established by escaped Fems and thus shaped by extremist sexual segregation, remains dystopian, merely reversing the hierarchy between men and women; the other, constituted by women who reproduce asexually, represents a eutopian alternative. Two later sequels, *The Furies* (1994) and *The Conqueror's Child* (1999), recount the war between men and women and their eventual reconciliation into a plural and inclusive society. In James Tiptree's 'Houston, Houston, Do You Read?' (1976), temporally displaced astronauts discover an all-female society in Earth's future. Their domineering attitudes cause the women to conclude that, although they might usefully contribute to the gene pool, they are too dangerous to live. Joanna Russ' 'When It Changed' (1972) presents *The Female Man*'s Whileaway not as an alternative future but as an isolated colony planet populated entirely by women (a virus killed all the men in the first generation). When a spaceship arrives from Earth, one of the (male) crew keeps asking 'where are all the people?' until the narrator realises 'he did not mean people, he meant *men*, and he was giving the word the meaning it had not had on Whileaway for six centuries' (1978: 232). The men insist that the women's lives are unnatural, that 'there is only half a species here' and that 'men must come back' (236). The story ends with the narrator contemplating their arrival, acknowledging that 'when one culture has the big guns and the other has none, there is a certain predictability about the outcome' (237). An equally uncompromising vision is found in Tiptree's 'The Women Men Don't See'. Following a plane crash, the narrator, Don Fenton, vacillates between dismissal and lust as he describes his fellow passengers, Ruth and Althea Parsons. He is troubled and annoyed by their failure to respond to the crash in the manner he expects of women. Ruth rejects his implication that her calm competence and unmarried status stem from her being 'a professional man-hater' or 'lesbian' (1995: 324), or that she is a champion of 'women's lib', contending that

> Women have no rights, Don, except what men allow us. Men are more aggressive and powerful, and they run the world. When the next real crisis upsets them, our so-called rights will vanish … We'll be back where we always were: property. And whatever has gone wrong will be blamed on our freedom, like the fall of Rome was.
>
> (1995: 325)

When aliens arrive, Ruth and Althea beg to go with them into the unknown rather than remain on Earth.

Jody Scott's satirical *Passing for Human* (1977) wittily critiques both sexism and speciesism in its tale of dolphin-like alien anthropologists who visit Earth in manufactured human bodies modelled on popular culture. The female protagonist, Benaroya, is variously incarnated as Brenda Starr, Emma Peel and Virginia Woolf as she conducts her field work, part of which is intended to discover if women 'really were second-class citizens as they claimed' (1977: 33). In her Mrs Peel body, she is 'mugged five times … raped twice … pick-pocketed eleven times … kicked and slapped often … given 837 religious tracts; groped 159 times, and propositioned repeatedly' (116). The ultimate target of the satire, however, is the suffering of the many animals killed, abused and otherwise exploited by a culture whose 'mad superstition teaches … they are valuable and sacred, but animals can be slaughtered wholesale' (167). Angela Carter also uses the idea of transformed bodies in *The Passion of New Eve* (1977). Playboy Evelyn, lured by an attractive woman to the headquarters of feminist radical Mother, is transformed into 'the object of all the unfocused desires that had ever existed in my own head. I had become my own masturbatory fantasy' (2005: 75). As a woman, Evelyn experiences sexual abuse and humiliation, and is forced to have sex with Tristessa, the beautiful actress he idealised, who is actually a transvestite, an empty screen for the projection of male fantasies of female identity. Ultimately, Evelyn regresses to infancy and a new entity is born whose combined experience of male and female embodiment and socialisation might find a way through the morass of gender differentiation.

The degree to which gender differences are socially rather than biologically produced – one of the axioms of second-wave feminism – became a significant theme in 1960s SF. Theodore Sturgeon's *Venus Plus X* (1960) alternates between two narratives. In one, Herb and Jeannette struggle to negotiate the sex roles of mid-twentieth-century suburbia as they raise two children, Karen and Davey. Herb never challenges the sexist humour of his friend Smitty, but as the father of a young daughter he grows uncomfortable with its aggressive implications. He spoils Karen, treating her with a gentleness he denies to Davey, who must behave like a man, and thus unwittingly cultivates Davey's resentment of Karen, thereby perpetuating gendered identities and antagonisms. In the other narrative strand, Charlie wakes up in a place called Ledom and, unable to determine the sex or gender of any of its inhabitants, struggles to understand its customs and mores. He eventually begins to accept that if he 'did not come from a culture which so exhaustively concentrated on differences which were in themselves not drastic, [he] would be able to see how small the differences actually were' (1998: 78). Both Charlie and Herb find themselves increasingly persuaded that gender is socially constructed – markers of sexual difference 'are nothing in themselves, for any of them, in another time and place, might belong to both sexes, the other sex, or neither. In other words, a skirt does not make the social entity woman. It takes a skirt plus a social attitude to do it' (164) – but neither is able fully to transform his attitudes and actions. In a surprise ending, Charlie discovers that Ledomians are hermaphroditic by choice, not through genetic mutation, and thus rejects them as unnatural. It is then revealed that he is a Ledomian upon whom the personality of an outsider has been imprinted to test whether the world is ready to accept their more egalitarian culture. Ledom, they conclude, must continue to watch and wait.

Ursula Le Guin's *The Left Hand of Darkness* (1969) imagines a society without permanent sexes. Gethenians periodically enter 'kemmer', a phase in which one lover takes on either male or female secondary sexual characteristics in response to the changes being undergone by the other lover (maintaining a compulsory heterosexuality for which the novel has been criticised). The protagonist, Genly Ai, is an emissary from a world of fixed sexual dimorphism, with distinct gender roles and expectations. Le Guin's tale of political intrigue and negotiation emphasises the extent to which notions of sexual and gender difference unconsciously permeate assumptions and behaviour. Ai repeatedly misperceives people and events, leading to mistakes that put his life at risk, before learning the irrelevance of gender when interacting with Gethenians, warning that 'unless he is very self-assured, or senile, his [successor's] pride will suffer. A man wants his virility regarded, a woman wants her femininity appreciated, however indirect and subtle the indications of regard and appreciation. On [Gethen] they will not exist. One is respected and judged only as a human being. It is an appalling experience' (2003: 95). As with this hypothetical successor, Le Guin uses the masculine pronoun for the ungendered Gethenians, drawing criticism for reproducing the patriarchal assumptions of English grammar and inspiring the use of gender-neutral pronouns in later SF.

SF also begins to imagine a future in which one can alter one's body at will, thus detaching subjectivity from embodiment and notions of gender identity, an idea explored critically in Samuel R. Delany's *Triton* (1976). The novel depicts a eutopia in which one can (consensually) gratify any sexual desire or fetish and modify one's embodiment and psychological orientation as one wishes. Bron Helstrom is profoundly unhappy because his own sexual orientation – logical sadism – epitomises the all-but-eradicated patriarchal ideal of male dominance and female subservience. A woman with whom he is obsessed finds his proposal – 'Become one with me. *Be* mine. Let me possess you wholly' (1976: 209) – oppressive rather than romantic. In despair, he transforms himself into the kind of woman he thinks men like him deserve but who rarely actually exist. He celebrates masculinity and denigrates femininity in terms one might find in the most stereotyped pulp SF:

> I just guess women, or people with large female components to their personalities, are too social to have that necessary aloneness to act outside society. But as long as we have social crisis – whether they're man-made ones like this war, or even natural ones like an ice-quake – despite what it says in the ice-operas, we need that particularly *male* aloneness, if only for the ingenuity it breeds, so that the rest of the species can survive.
>
> (257)

Bron's perspective is repeatedly challenged. He is reminded that this aloof masculinity is responsible for more deaths and threats to human survival than it ever prevented, and told that because 'women have only really been treated ... as human beings for the last ... sixty-five years ... whereas men have had the luxury of such treatment for the last four thousand', they 'are just a little less willing' than men 'to put up with certain kinds of shit', such as the subservient role he desires of them (252–253). Bron ends the novel equally unfulfilled in either gender.

Echoing Shulamith Firestone's arguments that '*pregnancy is barbaric*' (1988: 188), John Varley's 'Manikins' (1976) is premised on the notion that women are the only true humans and that men are women who have been taken over by alien parasites. Men inject a 'white ... waste product' into women during intercourse, polluting the womb and causing foetuses 'to grow too large for the birth canal' (1983: 144) and childbirth thus to be painful and sometimes fatal. 'They've trained you to believe in their values, their system', Barbara explains, 'What you begin to realize is that they are imperfect women, not the other way around' (138). Reproduction is one of the targets of Joanna Russ' *We Who Are About To ...* (1975), which satirically refutes the heroic ideal of restarting civilisation when a handful of spaceship passengers are stranded on a harsh but viable world. The narrator rejects such proposals, and their requirement that the women be subordinated to their reproductive capacity so as to populate the planet, pointing instead to such matters as their lack of technology and uncertainties about local diseases and foodstuffs. She lampoons the assertion that 'Civilization must be preserved', telling her fellow survivors that 'Civilization's doing fine' but they 'just don't happen to be where it is' (1977: 31). Zöe Fairbairns' *Benefits* (1979) extrapolates a dystopian future from neoliberal discourses about social welfare and conservative social policies that privilege supposedly traditional family structures. It was prompted by the Wages for Housework Campaign in the UK, and by debates about whether the newly introduced Child Benefit should be paid to the mother rather than the father, allowing her some small measure of financial independence but simultaneously reinforcing gender roles. In the novel, measures are introduced to keep men, who 'should' be working, from receiving welfare payments, and to modify the child welfare benefits system in ways which channel women out of the workplace and into maternal roles. As the state becomes increasingly fascist, a cult of mother-hood develops. The emerging women's movement is criminalised, and the language of 'family values' is used to further repress women. Sexism, 'defined as hatred of women in their natural role' (1979: 145), becomes an offence. Alongside eugenic policies, technoscientific advances are deployed to intervene in pregnancy and birth. However, this has unanticipated consequences when the combined effect of prophylactic chemicals in the water supply, the antidote given to women deemed fit to be mothers, and the regime of dietary supplements forced upon them result in the birth of monstrous and short-lived children. In the final pages, this tragedy makes possible a future in which women's insights and priorities will shape future social and technological policy.

Contemporary television series such as *The Bionic Woman* (1976–1978) offered images of femininity combined with technological power. However, while Jaime Sommers' bionic abilities enabled her to undertake dangerous government assignments, this was a supplement to her more traditional feminine occupation as a teacher, and she was repeatedly shown performing domestic labour at bionic speeds. *The Stepford Wives* (Forbes 1975), based on Ira Levin's 1972 novel, offered a more sinister image of wives being replaced by compliant robot doubles uninterested in the feminism disrupting suburban norms. Yet, technology need not be seen as oppressive to women. Firestone's contention that 'artificial reproduction is not inherently dehumanizing' (1988: 189) offered space for thinking about the ways in which technology might be used to free women from the reproductive labour through which patriarchy justifies women's inferior social role. New reproductive technologies might enable women and men to share equally in the production of social life as well as the reproduction of human life. Marge Piercy's *Woman on the Edge of Time* (1976) incorporates this ideal into its eutopian future. Connie Ramos struggles against racism, sexism and domestic violence, and is institutionalised in a psychiatric hospital after violently defending her niece from assault. There, she discovers that she is able to visit a potential future whose inhab-itants live in harmony with the environment: 'we have limited resources. We plan cooperatively. We can afford to waste ... nothing. You might say our – you'd say religion? – ideas make us see ourselves as partners with water, air, birds, fish, trees' (1991: 125). Children are born from artificial wombs and raised by multiple par-ents, and neither parenting nor any other kind of labour is divided along gender lines. Belief in this future world fuels Connie's resistance to the patriarchal forces oppressing her in the present, and a brief glimpse of an exploitative and polluted alternative future makes her even more determined to fight for its realisation despite overwhelming odds.

Environmentalism

Environmental activism, focusing particularly on pollution and overpopulation, also increased during this period. The Club of Rome think-tank commissioned *The Limits to Growth* (1972), a report on world population, industrialisation, pollution, food production and resource depletion, which envisioned likely economic and social collapse in the twenty-first century. A decade earlier, Rachel Carson's *Silent Spring* (1962) forcefully captured the destructive consequences of the growing dependence on chemicals for agriculture and pest control – techniques exported to the Third World as 'Green Revolution' aid. Concern for other species led to the founding of the World Wildlife Fund (now Worldwide Fund for Nature) in 1966 and, in 1972, Greenpeace, which developed from anti-nuclear activism against US missile tests in Alaska. The first Earth Day was celebrated in 1970, the first UN conference on the environment held in 1972. Green parties began to become a significant political presence, although much less so in the US than Europe. In the US, Ralph Nader supervised projects investigating air and water pollution and the Food and Drug Administration's (FDA) approval of food additives; he also lectured widely on the environment, especially the destruction of water resources. By the end of the decade, environmental activism became increasingly radical, with groups such as Earth First! embracing direct action.

SF responded to these developments in various ways. Some depicted polluted and overpopulated dystopias, some ecological eutopias, while others insisted that the only sensible solution was to expand beyond Earth's ecosystem into space. *Ruins of Earth* (1973), edited by Thomas M. Disch, organised 16 stories – addressing themes such as ubiquitous automation, nature's disappearance from daily experience, gridlock, pollution and human extinction – under four headings that indicate ecologically-informed SF's dystopian tendencies: 'The Way It Is', 'Why It Is the Way It Is', 'How It Could Get Worse' and 'Unfortunate Solutions'. Pollution and overpopulation are also common in SF films of the period: *Silent Running* (Trumbull 1972) depicts the one man's vain attempts to save a space ark housing the last examples of terrestrial plants and animals; in *Z.P.G.* (Campus 1972), a policy of Zero Population Growth makes childbirth illegal for a generation; *It's Alive* (Cohen 1974) sees an outbreak of mutant births as humans begin to evolve to fit a polluted world; and the hedonistic future of *Logan's Run* (Anderson 1976), based on William F. Nolan's 1967 novel, is predicated on the resource-saving euthanasia of everyone over thirty.

Ernest Callenbach's *Ecotopia* (1975) offers a more positive vision. In 1980, Northern California, Washington and Oregon seceded and established an alternative, ecologically sound economy and lifestyle. In 1999, William Weston is the first US journalist allowed into this breakaway state. Initially sceptical, he is gradually won over by the community he finds there. The novel alternates between his journalistic despatches and his private journal, in which he reflects upon his observations and experiences. He notes strategic uses of technology to reduce pollution and waste (books are print-on-demand, teleconferencing reduces travel) and the transformed social conditions arising from changed attitudes towards production and the natural world. Workers are empowered within an economic system that does not prioritise profit over other concerns (reduced profitability and lower wages, which enable better working environments and shorter workdays, are often preferred) and free healthcare is universal. Petroleum-based products have been virtually eliminated, and the cost of consuming resources includes their replenishment (before making a large lumber purchase, one must first spend several months planting new trees and caring for the forest) so as to 'achieve the stable-state life systems which are our fundamental ecological and political goal' (1977: 23). Women hold positions of power in equal proportion to men and relationships are conducted without all the baggage of the patriarchal gender hierarchy – indeed, Weston's eventual defection is largely motivated by the opportunity for a different kind of partnership with a woman. Overtly polemical, *Ecotopia* extrapolates new technologies and social relationships so as to propose a realistic, attractive alternative to environmentally destructive, patriarchal capitalism.

John Brunner's *The Sheep Look Up* (1972) is much bleaker. Taking its title from a line in John Milton's 'Lycidas' (1638) about a corrupt church failing to feed its hungry flock, the novel critiques a capitalism that simultaneously destroys the environment *and* sells products to filter the air and water it has polluted and to supplement the food it has robbed of nutrition. Interweaving scenes from the lives of people from different socio-economic backgrounds in a polluted future, the plot concerns a foodstuff, Nutripon, sent as part of an aid package to Third World countries. A contaminated shipment causes hallucinations and murderous violence, which some believe is part of a genocidal plot against peoples of colour, provoking an international crisis. A UN investigation eventually discovers that the shipment was contaminated by toxic waste in the Nutripon factory's water supply, implying that a profit-driven system is sufficient, without conspiracy, to produce such disastrous consequences. Meanwhile, the poor and middle classes in America face the devastating effects of pollution and industrialised food production. An entire growing season is lost when, to avoid financial losses, agricultural suppliers include a harmful variety of pesticide-immune worms in batches of regular worms imported into the US to process the soil. Water supplies are often dangerous if unfiltered, and the new water filters quickly clog with bacterial waste. Activists discover that the expensive, supposedly organic, Puritan foods contain as many chemicals as the cheaper brands eaten by the poor – who are resigned to fleas, lice, polluted air and ubiquitous eye, skin and throat infections. Former activist Austin Train returns to prominence when his name is used by kidnappers trying to force the wealthy Bamberley to provide water filters for the poor. Train uses his trial to make one final plea: 'at all costs, to me, to anyone, *at all costs* if the human race is to survive, the forcible exportation of the way of life invented by these stupid men must ... be ... *stopped*' (2003: 353, original ellipses). The novel concludes that 'We can just about restore the balance of the ecology, the biosphere, and so on – in other words, we can live within our means instead of on an unrepayable overdraft, as we've been doing for the past half century – if we exterminate the two hundred million most extravagant and wasteful of our species' (363).

Brunner's *Stand on Zanzibar* (1969) focuses on overpopulation. Its vision of an overcrowded near future centres on Chad C. Mulligan, Donald Hogan and Norman House. Mulligan was 'a sociologist', but 'gave it up' (1978: 21) when he found everyone read his iconoclastic books but failed to act on them. At one point, he rationalises taking the decision to embrace whatever pleasures can be found on the Earth's sinking ship because it is now too late to change anything. Hogan, who was recruited by the government when in college, is suddenly activated and sent to investigate and, if necessary, assassinate Sugaiguntung, a geneticist who believes he can optimise human embryos *in utero*, since the US government does not want this technology to be possessed by a Third World country. Hogan rooms with Norman House, an Afram who works for a huge corporation, General Technics, that wants to take over the economy of an independent African nation, Beninia, so as to ensure a market for ocean-bed raw materials that would otherwise be too expensive to extract; in exchange, the corporation will enable and ensure the country's rapid development. Through its various plots and conspiracies, *Stand on Zanzibar* provides a tour of an overcrowded world, linking increased social fragmentation and violence to overcrowded conditions and drawing attention to the exacerbation of global inequities as more and more people compete for fewer and fewer resources. At one point, a lunar colonist notes that life on the Moon is not so alienating as on this dismal Earth.

Harry Harrison's *Make Room! Make Room!* (1966) also portrays an over-crowded and resource-depleted future. It critiques religious prejudices against birth control, and the expanding gap between rich and poor as greater demand for resources permits fewer and fewer to continue to enjoy the lifestyle of post-war, middle-class America. A tale of the impossibility of human community and love in overcrowded and impoverished circumstances, it follows a police officer, Andy, his roommate, Sol and a high-class prostitute, Shirl, with whom Andy falls in love. Shirl tells Andy, 'I don't want anything in this world except to be happy, and I've been happier these weeks with you than I ever was at any time in my life before' (2008: 147), but after a few months of living on rationed water, without adequate electricity or space, she is drawn back into her previous life. When Sol dies of complications related to untreated pneumonia, a family of ten moves into the apart-ment, ensuring Shirl's departure. The novel ends in despair. As in *The Sheep Look Up*, the most disenfranchised are able to strike out only at each other, not the well-insulated architects of their poverty. *Soylent Green* (Fleischer 1972), adapted from Harrison's novel, introduces a conspiracy to use human corpses in a suppos-edly soy-based foodstuff but discards much of the wider social context and critical engagement with population and resource management.

A number of SF texts highlight species relations as part of a shifting attitude towards nature and otherness. Philip K. Dick's *Do Androids Dream of Electric Sheep?* (1969) combines anxiety about dehumanisation with an emphasis on human connections to other beings. All but extinct, animals have become so cher-ished that if people are unable to obtain a live pet they are expected to lavish care on a robot animal instead. This is contrasted with the brutal treatment of artificial humans created for off-world labour. Androids who escape their enslavement and come to Earth are hunted and killed without compunction by bounty hunters such as Rick Deckard. Deckard, who is supposed to love even artificial animals but treats artificial humans as faulty machines to be eradicated, struggles to find and retain his humanity. Cordwainer Smith's *Instrumentality* stories (1950–1993), published in various magazines but predominantly *Galaxy*, elaborate a future history in which animals genetically engineered to approximate humans serve as an underclass. They explore human alienation from ourselves and from non-human subjects that we view only in terms of their utility as resources. 'The Ballad of the Lost C'Mell' (*Galaxy* 1962), 'The Dead Lady of Clown Town' (*Galaxy* 1964) and *Nostrilia* (1971) present the underpeople's revolutionary uprising, which is simultaneously about transforming relations with a labour underclass and with a non-human species. Naomi Mitchison's *Memoirs of a Spacewoman* (1962) de-emphasises colonial ambitions and pays greater attention to alien species as fellow subjects and to alien locations as environments rather than merely backdrops for adventure. It focuses not on resource acquisition but on communication and what might be learned about the self through embracing the perspective of alien others: 'The earliest expeditions had wasted their energies and equipment on "exploration", whereas present tendencies are all towards acclimatisation and the kind of detailed knowledge of a locus which makes it "home"' (1985: 94). Although most of the species the protagonist encounters look more like caterpillars, starfish or jellyfish than humans, she makes no such distinction when seeking to communicate with them.

Margaret St Clair's *The Dolphins of Altair* (1967) imagines select humans as partners in the dolphins' revolt against human encroachments on their habitat and enslavement of their kind for research and entertainment purposes. Both species are descended from aliens who settled on Earth hundreds of thousands of years previously. Amphibious on their own world, they had to choose between living on the land or in the sea, eventually dividing into two peoples, bound by a covenant. The dolphins use a kind of telepathy, to which some humans are sensitive, to enlist the aid of Madelaine, Sven and Dr Lawrence in liberating captive dolphins. Pursued by the military, the dolphins eventually decide to recover an ancient technology that can be used to melt the polar ice caps, intending simultaneously to dilute the pollution in the oceans and distract their human adversaries. However, this will cause tidal waves and floods so harmful to humans that the dolphins abandon the plan, only for Lawrence to steal the technology and use it on his own initiative. The sea people are once again safe, and although the loss of life is regrettable, 'some demographers have called the floods a blessing in disguise, since they brought the world population down to a point where it was more compatible with world resources' (1967: 185). Ian Watson's *The Jonah Kit* (1972) also explores human–cetacean cooperation and communication but comes to a more pessimistic conclusion: cetaceans decide to kill themselves rather than continue to live in the world as shaped by humanity. Many contemporary films, such as *Frogs* (McCowan 1972), *Phase IV* (Bass 1974), *Jaws* (Spielberg 1975), *Day of the*

Animals (Girdler 1977), *Piranha* (Dante 1978), *Long Weekend* (Eggleston 1978) and *The Swarm* (Allen 1978) depict nature remorselessly striking back at human-kind, often through mutations resulting from environmental pollution or other disruptions to species habitat.

Technophilic SF's rather different response to the *Limits to Growth* thesis and environmental concerns – urging human expansion into space – is epitomised by Ben Bova's *Kinsman* novels. In *Kinsman*, which reworks several stories published between 1965 and 1978 in various magazines and anthologies, Chet Kinsman wants nothing more than to be an astronaut. Alienated from his Quaker father, who condemns him for enlisting in the airforce so as to become eligible for the space programme, the youthful Kinsman insists that his aspirations will not be polluted by military agendas. He refuses to participate in an anti-war demonstration, telling its organiser 'Somebody's got to make sure that the Nation's defended while you're out there demonstrating for your rights' (1981: 18). He does fly wartime missions, but somehow manages to avoid combat. Later, though, he kills a cosmo-naut defending a Soviet satellite from his espionage. He is wracked by guilt, mainly because his victim turned out to be female, but retains his conviction that an expanded space programme is the only way to solve America's problems:

> Without a strong space effort you won't have the energy, the raw materials, the new wealth that you need to rebuild the cities. Space gives us a chance, a hope – space factories and space power satellites will create new jobs, increase the Gross National Product, bring new wealth into the economy.
>
> (184)

Despite this rhetoric about service to humanity, his main motivation is to escape from a world he despises into space, '*where you can start over, new fresh, clean*' (186): 'The most important thing we'll ever do is to set up permanent colonies in space. It's time for the human race to expand its ecological niche' because 'this whole planet's becoming an overcrowded slum' (279). The novel concludes with Kinsman's machinations to be appointed the head of the new lunar colony, believ-ing that although he will command a military base he can ensure the Moon will not house any weapons. *Millennium* follows Kinsman's heroic efforts to preserve his vision, taking over – with the Russian moonbase leader's cooperation – the lunar installations and American and Soviet anti-ICBM satellites. Declaring lunar inde-pendence, Kinsman uses these missile defence systems to impose global peace and a magical new weather control technology to 'optimize crop yields, improve health, make fortunes for resorts, divert storms, improve fish populations, maybe even save the dolphins before they go the way of the whales' (1977: 206), bringing space-based prosperity and renewal to an otherwise doomed planet.

Conclusion

- There has been an uneven enrolment of texts from this period con-cerned with race, gender and environmentalism. Feminist SF was most successful at being enrolled, winning a number of major awards, while fiction by peoples of colour from outside the magazine and paperback tradition is only now being recovered.

- SF engaged with these issues from a wide range of political positions. This is perhaps most obvious in texts concerning pollution, overpopulation and resource depletion, which range from dystopian warnings and ecocatastrophes to optimistic renewals of the frontier that sidestep these problems by refusing to see Earth as a finite system.
- There was a decreasing emphasis on science as the defining feature of the genre, and the influence of the magazines waned as paperback markets expanded and other media turned to the genre. Those seeking to enrol SF into projects such as feminism or environmental activism were less concerned with Campbellian extrapolation than with the capacity of SF images, ideas and techniques to articulate urgent political concerns.

8 New politics, new technologies: the 1980s and 1990s

Overview

In this period, dramatic political, social and cultural changes accompanied the rise of neoliberalism. The renewal of Cold War tensions and the threat of nuclear annihilation gave way in the 1990s to new political and economic configurations. Important innovations in information technology nurtured the growing sense of an increasingly globalised world. There was a renewed interest in hard SF, associated at first with mainly conservative authors. The emergence of cyberpunk, which caught the popular and academic imagination in contexts that were not necessarily concerned with SF more generally, catalysed speculative treatments of subjectivity and embodiment in relation to virtuality and genetic engineering. Hard SF turned to address these issues, too.

Changing times

The 1980s were dominated by the political agendas associated with Ronald Reagan and Margaret Thatcher. Both embraced neoliberal economic theories, emphasising the importance of profit and a supposedly healthy economy above other considerations (e.g. quality of life, environmental impact, maximum employment, poverty reduction) and minimising state controls on the flow of capital while simultaneously reinforcing restrictions against international flows of labour. Both leaders dismantled welfare state provision, reducing government responsibility for pensions, healthcare and unemployment assistance, and launched savage attacks on organised labour. While direct taxation on individuals was reduced, indirect taxation climbed, with disproportionate consequences for the poor. Corporations and the wealthy benefitted from massive tax cuts, while much of the public sector, including public utilities, was privatised. The resulting revitalisation of parts of the economy came at the cost of the welfare of the poorest citizens and of poorer nations, accelerating the rate at which the gap between rich and poor had been growing since the mid-1970s. Access to loans from the International Monetary Fund (IMF) and World Bank were increasingly subject to requirements to sell public utilities – such as water and power – to private, foreign capital and to reduce spending on social programmes so as to guarantee interest repayments.

One of the economic drivers of the US recovery in the 1980s was state investment in high-tech military and aerospace industries, including the space programme, a strategy intimately tied to Cold War goals. A new generation of manned space vehicles was inaugurated by the 1982 *Columbia* space shuttle launch. However, plans for a space-based missile defence programme, dependent on a relatively cheap, reusable transport system, further heightened fears of nuclear war, especially as Reagan cast superpower rivalry in terms of opposing an evil empire. This Cold War came to an end with the fall of the Berlin Wall in 1989, a wave of popular uprisings across Eastern Europe that removed communist parties from power and the dissolution of the USSR in 1993. Among the many armed conflicts of the period, those in the Middle East, particularly the first Palestinian intifada (1987–1993) and the first US-led invasion of Iraq (1991), produced a major discursive shift that replaced Cold War binaries with the more amorphous threat of 'terrorists', typically characterised as ethnic or religious others who are simultaneously invisible and ubiquitous, irrational and well organised.

The period also saw many new technologies become part of daily life. The CD began to replace vinyl records and audio cassettes in 1980, the Walkman was launched in 1981 and domestic VCRs were common by the end of the decade – all of which have already been superseded by newer, digital technologies. The first personal computers, the Commodore PET and the Apple II, were released in 1977. Seven years later, the Apple Macintosh was introduced with a now legendary advert, directed by Ridley Scott and aired during the Super Bowl, which deployed the imagery of George Orwell's *Nineteen Eighty-four* to imply the liberatory potential of the 'portable' personal computer. The first Internet browser was introduced in 1991. The degree to which Western culture became reliant on computers is indicated by the Y2K panic over potential computer malfunctions as the date changed from 1999 to 2000. The period was also characterised by genetic research and biological panics. AIDS was first identified in 1981, and its cause, HIV, in 1983. Because gay men constituted one of the at-risk populations, HIV–AIDS became the focus of intense homophobia. DNA fingerprinting became possible from 1984, and the project to map the human genome, launched in 1990, was concluded in 2003. Research into genetically modified organisms, particularly food crops, began, with the first GM consumer product, the Flavr Savr tomato, being approved by the FDA in 1994. Dolly, the first cloned mammal, was born in 1997.

Fast-paced social and technological change, particularly in relation to information technology and genetics, empowered and challenged the genre. SF proliferated into popular culture, providing iconography and imagery for various cultural forms engaged with the current moment, from advertising to cultural theory; at the same time, the present appeared to catch up with and overtake SF, making the genre sometimes seem merely descriptive of quotidian reality or quaintly old-fashioned. Several new magazines – *Isaac Asimov's Science Fiction Magazine* (1977–), *Omni* (1978–1995) and *Interzone* (1982–) – achieved prominence, but magazine sales overall continued to decline. The marketplace for novels also became increasingly competitive. Partially driven by the demands of large bookstore chains utilising new computer technologies to monitor stock levels and sales, publishers focused on promoting big name authors and bestsellers, with a catastrophic effect on the 'mid-list' of relatively productive, modestly successful authors. Further pressures on SF arose from the continued expansion of fantasy fiction, often shelved with SF, and from fiction franchises based on successful films, television series, games and comics. The development of digital games, a new generation of comics writers and artists, many of whom were associated at some point with the British comic *2000 A.D.* (1977–), and the increased availability in translation of Japanese manga and anime saw major new sites of SF production and definition proliferate outside the older community of writers, editors and fans associated with the magazine and paperback tradition.

Hard SF and the new right

Perhaps the exemplary hard-SF novel of the 1980s is Gregory Benford's *Timescape* (1980), which negotiates between this supposed generic core and a critical understanding of science not as a set of abstract rules waiting to be discovered but as the product of human history. It alternates between the 1960s and the environmental crisis of 1998. In the latter period, physicists attempt to use tachyons – particles that travel faster than light, and thus backwards in time – to send a signal into the past to warn about the devastating consequences of certain pollutants and thus prevent their own hopeless situation arising. However, the only way for this message to be received is as interference in readings taken from an experiment being conducted by Gordon Bernstein 35 years earlier. In both timeframes, Benford shows not merely the processes by which experiments are set up and hypotheses tested but also the whole contingent world of human experience that, often unacknowledged, shapes scientific practice. Personalities and interpersonal relationships influence the funding, conduct and reception of research. Bernstein's superiors encourage him to attribute the 'noise' to any cause other than intentional communication, and because of this struggle over scientific paradigms they initially fail his PhD student's comprehensive examination. The category 'noise' itself encourages the labelling of anomalous phenomenon as irrelevant, and it is only Bernstein's willingness to be unconventional that enables receipt of the message, although its actual impact comes in unexpected ways.

A note left in a safety deposit box rented in the 1960s informs the 1998 protagonists 'MESSAGE RECEIVED' (1980: 133), but they have no way of knowing how effective their intervention has been, and their own situation continues to deteriorate. It is only in the final pages that we realise there is hope for the future. The 1960s narrative refers to such events as the Vietnam War, Martin Luther King, Jr's March on Washington and the *failed* assassination of President Kennedy. In 1974, the President is not Ford but Scranton, and it is not Nixon but Robert Kennedy who has been compelled to resign over a wiretapping scandal. Bernstein meets Gregory Markham – one of the most important scientists in the 1990s sections, who died before being able to share a vital insight – and this alternative 1974 erases the future tragic death the reader has already witnessed, a figuration of the different future that might unfold.

Timescape includes detailed reflections on quantum entanglement and descriptions of the consequences of chemical pollution. Its depiction of forewarned scientists preventing ecological catastrophe resonates with a tendency within hard SF to imagine that technology can always solve the problems we create for ourselves, thus avoiding systemic analysis of these problems and the need to advocate social change. However, *Timescape* is distinguished from such fiction by its insistence on contingency, relationality and complex determinism in the practice of science, and by the nature of the message sent back in time, warning the past to avoid the path taken rather than beaming it a miraculous, technological solution.

The use of the term 'hard SF' sometimes reflects an actant's desire to exclude from the genre not only more overtly fantastical texts but also those felt to be drifting away from some purported core relationship to science and towards leftist and/ or feminist political critique, not least of capitalist, patriarchal technoscience. Benford, whose subsequent novels are less nuanced, was a member of the Citizens Advisory Council on National Space Policy, one of the more extraordinary manifestations of the rise of the new right in American politics. This group consisted of scientists, engineers, former astronauts, retired military personnel and SF writers, including Greg Bear, Robert A. Heinlein, Dean Ing, Larry Niven, Jerry Pournelle and G. Harry Stine, as well as SF publisher Jim Baen and Bjo Trimble, the fan who played a major role in the campaigns to renew *Star Trek* and to name an actual space shuttle *Enterprise*. Their report advocating the development of high-tech defences against nuclear weapons was well received by President Reagan (his letter of commendation adorns the back of *Mutual Assured Survival* (1984), Pournelle and Ing's popularised version of the report published by Baen) and informed the development of his Strategic Defense Initiative or 'Star Wars' programme.

Mutual Assured Survival insists that disarmament is a fool's dream, inevitably undermined by a USSR it characterises as inherently duplicitous and frighteningly ahead of US weapons development. It argues that the cornerstone of global peace is increased funding for a space programme, supported by private industry, which would soon reap enormous profits. A lunar base would not only provide a secure location for early warning systems, but also enable profitable mining of lunar resources. Space is presented as a new frontier that Americans must conquer with military force, because although 'purely scientific exploration of the high frontier' (1984: 118) is desirable, it is unrealistic. The Council's commitment to neoliberal economics and right-wing libertarian politics is evident in its characterisation of NASA as a top-heavy, moribund bureaucracy and in its frequent invocation of the benefits that private industry will bring to – and take from – a profit-driven space programme. One appendix proclaims that 'the **rediscovery of progress** is a reasonable goal for the United States in the 1980s. Progress is possible. We do not have to accept limits to growth' (185); another claims that

> we have witnessed a progressive erosion of our ability to act in the best interests of our nation by more than twenty years of accommodation to international pressures and 'world opinion,' as these have been described to

us by politicians and the public media, yearning to accommodate in order to avoid confrontation with our enemies, the enemies of our kind of free society.

(205)

This is a deeply science-fictional moment in US history, in which a text straight from the Campbell–Bova tradition influenced national policy with global consequences. Although SDI was set in motion in 1984, and aspects of it continue in the Missile Defense Agency, SF writers did not have the president's ear for long and their more ambitious dreams have not been realised.

The presumption that space will be militarised, however, persists. Orson Scott Card's Hugo and Nebula award-winning *Ender's Game* (1985) presents the brutalisation of a child into an unthinking killing machine who can genocide an alien species as a succession of rites of passage (the sequels are more measured in tone). The 12-volume *Man-Kzin Wars* series (1988–2009), containing stories by Bear, Benford, Ing, Niven, Pournelle, Poul Anderson, Donald Kingsbury, S.M. Stirling and others, depicts a series of human victories over an alien species. This interstellar conflict is part of a secret experiment, conducted by another species, to breed aggression out of Kzin by eradicating, in each of five successive wars, the most violent proportion of their population. This period also saw the emergence of best-selling technothrillers, such as Craig Thomas' *Firefox* (1977), Tom Clancy's *The Hunt for Red October* (1984) and Dale Brown's *Silver Tower* (1988), of survivalist fiction, such as Jerry Ahern's *Survivalist* (1981–1993) and William W. Johnstone's *Ashes* (1983–2003) series and of military SF as a distinct subgenre, largely driven by Baen Books. Alternate history, a subgenre that also expanded in this period, frequently followed the example of Ward Moore's *Bring the Jubilee* (1953) in taking a battle as the point of historical divergence. For example, in Harry Turtledove's *The Guns of the South* (1992), the course of the American Civil War is changed when time-travelling Afrikaners supply General Lee with AK-47s; more modestly, in Eric Flint's *The Rivers of War* (2005), Sam Houston suffers a less serious injury at the Battle of Horseshoe Bend than he did in reality but this leads to the emergence of a radically different US. The period also witnessed the underground success of William Luther Pierce's *The Turner Diaries* (1978), selling over 500,000 copies. It depicts the near future destruction of a dictatorial, Jewish-controlled federal government that dared to impose strict gun control laws; the rebels then oversee the ethnic cleansing of the US and the global genocide of peoples of colour.

While many of these examples might be considered marginal or extreme, depictions of high-tech conflict constitute a basic appeal of much of the period's SF, including the *Star Wars* and *Star Trek* franchises, such films as *Stargate* (Emmerich 1994) and *Starship Troopers* (Verhoeven 1997) and television series such as *Babylon 5* (1994–1998) and *Stargate SG-1* (1997–2007). Obviously, this wide range of texts cannot be said equally to reflect the new right's perspective. For example, David Drake's *Hammer's Slammers* stories (1974–2006) demonstrate the sympathy for combat soldiers, distrust of officers and scepticism about politicians one might expect of a Vietnam veteran, while Lucius Shepard's *Life During Wartime* (1987) and Lewis Shiner's *Deserted Cities of the Heart* (1988) overtly critique US imperialism in Latin America. However, the very prevalence of military scenarios indicates a normalisation of militarised space exploration, colonisation and conflict resolution within contemporary SF.

New right values are celebrated in Niven and Pournelle's *Footfall* (1985), which fantasises about a think-tank of SF writers being called in to advise the President on how to defeat an alien invasion, and *Oath of Fealty* (1981), set in the self-contained, high-tech city of Todos Santos. The latter explores two ethical questions about this 'arcology'. First, to what extent is the defensive use of force against antagonistic outsiders justifiable? And, second, what obligations does it owe to neighbouring Los Angeles, upon which it relies for material goods and consumers? Critics call Todos Santos 'the nest' or 'the hive', insect metaphors that emphasise its caste system, its citizens' apparent lack of individuality and its parasitic relationship on the nearby city. When some teenagers penetrate Todos Santos' security systems, Preston Sanders, who has no way of knowing that they are merely pretending to be bomb-carrying terrorists, makes the difficult decision, when all other options have failed, to stop them with lethal gas. His trial becomes the focal point of tensions between the two cities. Todos Santos' main opposition comes from an environmental activist group, FROMATES (Friends of Man and The Earth Society), who contend that the arcology consumes far more than its share of resources and constitutes a mode of living unsustainable if extended to the wider population. The novel's response to this argument is to depict the FROMATES as irrational Luddites and to focus instead on the heroic strength of character displayed by the upper echelons of Todos Santos' management.

Consistent with *Mutual Assured Survival*, the novel blurs capitalism with freedom and insists that technological advances mean that there need be no limits to economic growth. Todos Santos' economic success is attributed to the brilliant Barbara Churchward, who specialises in neoliberal takeovers. Contemplating the purchase of a factory, she concludes that the people working there will not long continue to generate revenue, but that it is worth stripping of its other assets. This is possible because Todos Santos is relatively autonomous, unconstrained by 'most of the stupid regulations that businesses outside had to live with' (1981: 92). Although such restraints had, in reality, preserved many aspects of social life from being dominated by the profit motive until neoliberal deregulation became the norm, Todos Santos is not presented as a late capitalist dystopia, as it might have been in novels such as Marge Piercy's *He, She and It* or Octavia Butler's *Parable* series (1993–1998). Rather, it is a corporate-feudal eutopia, in which 'there is not even a pretense of equality – or rights, nor of duties and responsibilities' but there is 'loyalty, and it runs both ways' (170). Although Todos Santos requires substantial technological innovation (building techniques, transportation systems and waldos so that residents can work in remote locations, including the Moon, without leaving the city), the novel is unconcerned with their invention or social consequences. They exist merely to the extent they can be used to prop up an argument about how best to organise human society.

Reporter Thomas Lunan, a disillusioned former countercultural, is invited to make a documentary about Todos Santos. He is inevitably seduced by its shared vision of a community in which surveillance and security forces are benign protectors rather than arbitrary oppressors. The superiority of corporate feudalism over (alienating, bureaucratic, impersonal, corrupt) liberal democracy – THINK OF IT AS EVOLUTION IN ACTION is a recurring slogan – prompts Art Bonner, Todos Santos' CEO, to defy the legal authority of the US to try Sanders over the teenage intruders' deaths, breaking him out of jail and smuggling him out of the country to become the CEO of a new African arcology. When an LA detective accuses Todos Santos of putting itself 'completely above the law … judge and jury and executioner', Lunan claims that their decision not to execute the FROMATES members who kidnapped and raped Barbara demonstrates that 'they've chosen to stay part of the human race', protesting 'your brand of justice' (322) but remaining within the bounds of human community.

Apocalyptic fiction

The period's ambivalence about technological developments and new right fantasies of American hegemony is evident in the resurgence of nuclear anxieties. Despite the disastrous 1986 Chernobyl reactor meltdown, these were focused almost exclusively on the possibility of nuclear war. For decades, the MAD doctrine that automated retaliatory systems and the capacity for overkill made winning a nuclear war impossible had brought a degree of stability to superpower relationships. However, SDI publicity and propaganda – and Reagan's belligerence towards the USSR – contributed to a growing sense of insecurity in a world containing enough atomic weapons to destroy it many times over.

Non-print SF contributed most to the public imagination of the coming apocalypse. The *Mad Max* trilogy (Miller 1979–1985) presumed a devastated future of feudal tribes, limited resources and rule by violence. *Hardware* (Stanley 1990) combined nuclear apocalypse with a fear of machines turning on humans. The remains of a Mark XIII military robot accesses a power supply and assembles a new body to fulfil its primary mission of killing humans, a cynical government's solution to there being too many people and too few resources. In *The Terminator* (Cameron 1984) and *Terminator 2: Judgment Day* (Cameron 1991) cyborgs from the future return to the present, first to kill Sarah Connor, mother of a future resistance leader, and later to kill her teenage son, John. Kyle Reese, the soldier sent back to protect Sarah, tells her the history of her future, in which the nuclear defence computer network achieved self-awareness, perceived all humans, not just the enemy, as a threat and triggered a global nuclear war; it then began to build machines to root out and destroy the remaining human population. The first film ends with Sarah, pregnant by Kyle, intent on raising John to fulfil his destiny; the second moves further away from the idea of the future being fixed, suggesting that it might be changed and nuclear holocaust avoided. *WarGames* (Badham 1983) also addresses these dual fears of nuclear war and automated systems. A teenage computer hacker who unwittingly engages a military computer in a game of Global Thermonuclear War must find a way to stop it treating this simulation as real and launching an attack. However, the film's overt message is not about the dangers of ceding authority to automated decision-making processes but about what the computer learns from simulating all possible nuclear war scenarios: once the first missile is fired, no matter by whom, there can be no winner.

The television movies *The Day After* (1983) and *Threads* (1984) depict the experience of living through a nuclear attack. Both represent the consequences as devastating, but the former, made in the US, is far more optimistic than the latter, made in the UK. *The Day After* shows the suffering, but also the triumph, of a group of Kansans who band together to help one another and to ensure the provision of uncontaminated food and water. Although civilisation does persist, the images of flattened landscapes, dead and decaying livestock, charred bodies and victims of radiation sickness shocked many of its initial audience. *Threads* takes it title from the flexible but fragile fabric of interconnections that holds society together, and charts its erosion as Sheffield residents survive a nearby nuclear strike to live through fallout and nuclear winter. Borrowing a technique from Peter Watkins' anti-nuclear docudrama *The War Game* (1965), commissioned by the BBC but banned from broadcast until 1985, *Threads* intersperses its narrative with statistics about the number of deaths from the blast, from radiation and later from starvation, hypothermia, cholera and dysentery. It includes the kind of bleak scenes found in *The Day After*, but also shows rats feeding on decaying corpses abandoned in streets and homes, and people turning on one another, fighting for scraps of food and being shot by the few who try to maintain law and order. Much more relentless than *The Day After*, it shows the impossibility of quickly restoring agriculture in the absence of adequate sunlight, fertilisers and fuel; and it depicts a post-nuclear future in which, after 15 years, technology is at medieval levels, life expectancy is in the thirties and the generation raised since the disaster speaks a pale imitation of human language.

Russell Hoban's *Riddley Walker* (1980) is similarly bleak. Written in thickly accented phonetic prose laden with puns that form a complex web of associations, it requires the reader not only to work out the meaning of individual sentences but also to keep multiple possible interpretations in mind so as to grasp the meaning of the whole. This innovative approach models the breakdown of language as, two millennia after a nuclear war, writing has more or less disappeared and humanity has returned to pre-industrial levels of technology. The novel tells of the political struggle between Pry Mincer (Prime Minister) and Wes Mincer (Westminster), focusing on the puppet show of Eusa, loosely connected to the medieval legend of Saint Eustace, used to explain the nuclear disaster that produced their world. The story of Eusa involves his temptation by Mr Clevver, represented by the Satan puppet, and the Littl Shynin Man the Addom, who is split apart when Eusa finds 'the NO. uv the 1 Big 1' (1998: 31), and who, in the conflation of various legends, becomes confused with Christ. One faction tries to rediscover the power of explosive energy, dreaming of a return to a world in which humans 'set the air boats out beyond the sarvering gallack seas' (110), but they succeed only in blowing themselves up. There is no heroic nurturing of civilisation through a dark period, no rebuilding of the past. Only human folly persists.

The pessimism of the 1980s and 1990s is reflected in other kinds of apocalyptic narratives. Tim LaHaye and Jerry B. Jenkin's *Left Behind* novels (1995–2007) and their spin-offs blend SF with dispensationalist interpretations of biblical prophecy about the Rapture and the End Times suffering of the remaining sinners. The television series *V* (1984–1985) featured apparently benevolent but actually predatory aliens, while *The X-Files* (1993–2002) combined stories of strange phenomena with a conspiratorial narrative arc about a government that is not only concealing evidence of alien invaders but actively collaborating with them. *Strange Days* (Bigelow 1995), set on New Year's Eve 1999 in Los Angeles, captures something of this millennial anxiety and paranoia. Former cop Lenny Nero uncovers, through a technology that allows one to relive the digitally recorded experience of another, a racist conspiracy. In a narrative that consciously echoes the events leading up to the 1992 LA uprising, which followed the acquittal of four white police officers despite their brutal and unwarranted assault on African American Rodney King being caught on video, Lenny's investigation of an illegal recording of a prostitute's rape and murder eventually reveals that the LAPD murdered an influential and politically engaged rapper. The new millennium is welcomed with an acknowledgement that social advances have not kept pace with technological progress.

Cyberpunk and postmodernism

Cyberpunk has done more than any author, subgenre or movement to fashion connections between SF and academic scholarship. Although it represents only a small fraction of SF, its impact on the genre has been considerable and its high profile both within and without traditional SF readerships – cyberpunk author William Gibson even appeared as himself in the television miniseries *Wild Palms* (1993) – means that it tends to dominate perceptions of the period. Like the New Wave, cyberpunk represented itself as a radical break with existing SF, turning to an imaginative examination of new, intimate technologies, both digital and genetic, and the possibilities of networked identities. The paradigmatic cyberpunk novel is William Gibson's *Neuromancer* (1984), a caper narrative in which an artificial intelligence secretly hires a group of misfits to liberate it, including Case, a down-and-out hacker stripped of his ability to jack into cyberspace; Molly, a street-samurai with surgically implanted mirrorshades and retractable scalpel blades beneath her fingernails, who purchased her modifications by working as a meat puppet prostitute; Armitage, an artificial personality constructed on the shattered remains of a former special forces officer; Riviera, a drug addict and thief whose implants can project holograms; and the Dixie Flatline, the recorded personality and skills of a dead hacker. The frequently frenetic action introduces a shabby dystopia of ubiquitous information and communications technologies and biotechnological body modifications, of multinational capital and corporate globalisation, of social and ecological collapse. The natural world has all but disappeared, simulations abound and marginalised characters find ways to survive in the post-industrial detritus. Along with 'Burning Chrome' (*Omni* 1982), *Neuromancer* also introduced Gibson's influential vision of cyberspace as a virtual realm of abstract geometries, colours, shapes, trajectories and velocities, its depiction of information circulation a potent metaphor for the global circulation of capital.

Cyberpunk's most polemical advocate was Bruce Sterling. His preface to the 1986 *Mirrorshades* anthology contends that 'cyberpunks are perhaps the first SF generation to grow up not only within the literary tradition of science fiction but in a truly science-fictional world' (1986: xi) and links them to the oppositional culture of punk rock. This heady fusion of 'high tech and the modern pop underground' (xi) differs from other SF in two key ways: first, for cyberpunks 'technology is visceral ... Not outside us but next to us. Under our skin; often, inside our minds' (xiii); second, cyberpunk is politically engaged with a globalised world. However, beyond announcing cyberpunk's subversiveness, Sterling has little to say about its politics, and much of the ensuing critical debate has focused on its political shortcomings. Many also questioned the newness of cyberpunk – pointing to such earlier writers as J.G. Ballard, Alfred Bester, William Burroughs, Philip K. Dick, Samuel R. Delany and John Varley – and Sterling's preface recruits numerous major American and British authors into cyberpunk's family tree (but neglects such significant female authors as James Tiptree, Jr and Joanna Russ).

At cyberpunk's core was the work of Gibson, Sterling, Pat Cadigan, Rudy Rucker, Lewis Shiner and John Shirley, all of whom were distancing themselves from the label and declaring cyberpunk dead by the time it came to wide public attention. Shiner's 'Confessions of an Ex-Cyberpunk' (1991) complained that derivative writers had reduced the 'form into formula' (A17), substituting a check-list of clichés for any critical engagement with the realities of global capitalism. These widely reproduced images and ideas include direct human interface with computer systems and information networks; a world dominated by multinational corporations rather than national governments; AIs or other networked, sentient systems that rival human hegemony; and young, hip, semi-criminal, outsider heroes who regard the body as mere 'meat'. However, alongside opportunistic imitators, authors such as Misha, Laura Mixon and Melissa Scott deployed cyberpunk material to interrogate and critique its premises, and rather than dying out cyberpunk has arguably undergone a 'sea change into a more generalized cultural formation' (Foster 2005: xiv). Cyberpunk images and ideas certainly proliferated through other media – from *Blade Runner* (Scott 1982) and *Videodrome* (Cronenberg 1983) to *eXistenZ* (Cronenberg 1999) and *The Matrix* (Wachowski brothers 1999), from *Max Headroom* (UK 1985; US 1987–1988) to *VR.5* (1995), and from Howard Chaykin's *American Flagg!* (1983–1986) to Warren Ellis and Darick Robertson's *Transmetropolitan* (1997–2002) comics. It also had a strong impact on Japanese popular culture, including live-action films such as *Tetsuo* (Tsukamoto 1989) and *Gunhed* (Harada 1989), but more obviously in such manga and anime as Katsuhiro Otomo's 1988 cinematic adaptation of his then-uncompleted

Akira (1982–1990) manga, and Shirow Masamune's *Ghost in the Shell* (1989) manga, whose 1995 cinematic adaptation by Mamoru Oshii prompted film and television anime sequels. Increasingly available to Western audiences through specialist publishers, domestic video, DVD, satellite and cable technologies and the internet, manga and anime have had a widespread impact on European and US culture in general, and SF in particular, reflecting in reality aspects of *Neuromancer*'s vision of a Japanese-dominated future.

Cyberpunk took many forms. Gibson's focus on information and communications technologies explored the consequences of merging human and machine experience in simulated realities and the role of representation in shaping our experience and understanding of reality. Sterling, in contrast, was more concerned with posthumanism, which he explored through the struggle between Mechanists and Shapers in *Schismatrix* (1985), in which space-going humans have chosen alternative methods of modifying their bodies: Mechanists use digital, electronic and mechanical prostheses; Shapers, genetic engineering. While there are still 'primitive', unmodified humans, the real destiny of humans is to continue to evolve. The Shaper/Mechanist conflict over the right way to do so is ultimately a red herring; just as there is no single best form for posthumanity to adopt, so there is no best method. Diverse adaptations to the variety of ecological niches must of necessity produce equally valid 'daughter species' to *Homo sapiens*.

Neal Stephenson's *Snow Crash* (1992) concerns a virus transmittable by both computer code and biological fluids. In a near-future America balkanised into franchised gated communities or 'burbclaves', half-African-American/half-Korean Hiro Protagonist lives in a U-Stor-It locker near LAX. His hacker skills in the virtual Metaverse compensate for his lack of agency in everyday life, and he enjoys the kind of slacker 'lifestyle that sounded romantic to him as recently as five years ago' (1992: 21) rather than trying to translate his cyber-prowess into material success. Hiro discovers that the eponymous virus is related to Sumerian, the first human language, which a priestly caste used to control a static culture. The Tower of Babel story, he surmises, is the legend of a hacker who subverted this language so that humanity could emerge as sentient individuals instead of being a nonsentient system running a code. In this way, Stephenson reverses the posthuman futurological speculations of Hans Moravec and Ray Kurzweil, who conceive of humans as disembodied minds running on a biological substrate and thus as uploadable onto other hardware systems, such as computers.

Snow Crash's engagement with economics – at one point, the narrator suggests that 'the franchise and the virus work on the same principle: what thrives in one place will thrive in another' (190), making franchises a form of social disease – continues to resonate strongly with subsequent analyses of global capital, such as Manuel Castells' three-volume *The Information Age* (1996–1998), which argues that information technology has ushered in a new and different version of capitalism that relies simultaneously on the free flow of capital across boundaries and restrictions on the mobility of labouring bodies. Castells' argument implies that the cyberpunk fantasy of disembodiment is integrally connected with capitalism's own fantasies and material operations.

Other cyberpunk novels

Rudy Rucker, *Software* (1982)

Steven Barnes, *Streetlethal* (1983)

Lewis Shiner, *Frontera* (1984)

K.W. Jeter, *The Glass Hammer* (1985)

John Shirley, *Eclipse* trilogy (1985–1990)

George Alec Effinger, *When Gravity Fails* (1987)

Michael Swanwick, *Vacuum Flowers* (1987)

Lisa Mason, *Arachne* (1990)

Misha, *Red Spider White Web* (1990)

Laura Mixon, *Glass Houses* (1992)

Melissa Scott, *Trouble and Her Friends* (1994)

Nicola Griffith, *Slow River* (1995)

Richard K. Morgan, *Altered Carbon* (2002)

Cyberpunk was widely criticised for masculinism and misogyny, for its depiction of women as malleable objects of male fantasy and its often fearful representations of the female body. Pat Cadigan, the only woman writer linked with the original cyberpunks, demonstrated greater sensitivity to issues of embodiment and agency, particularly in *Synners* (1991) and *Fools* (1992). The latter explores the idea that the self can be written, rewritten and compartmentalised like code, its narrative alternating between different person as (signalled by different typefaces) that occupy the same body but are largely unaware of each other. Marva, an actress, is struggling to control Marceline, a character she has created who keeps taking over her body and who might have sold her identity to a corporation that sells franchise identities; Marceline, a memory junkie, believes that she is real, and the subject of some conspiracy. It transpires that Marva was a fake identity implanted in Mersine, a deep-cover Brain Police officer who would emerge and retake control of her body once Marva had succeeded in infiltrating a rogue identity franchise operation. When Marva experimented with direct mind-to-mind communication with another actor, Sovay, the layered personalities were revealed prematurely, and Marva hired Marceline to eliminate Mersine, who she claimed was just a fragment of a character she had once played. When the investigation is concluded, Mersine is in what she believes is someone else's body – although the Brain Police insist that she must have had her own surgically altered when undercover – and her sense that both Marva and Marceline are present and real persists.

Mersine's next case reveals that when she went mind-to-mind with Sovay, he too discovered he had a buried Brain Cop persona, leading her ultimately to conclude that the entire population has been so modified. Everyone has become an aspect of a single, Brain Cop personality, producing a frightening homogeneity that they cannot consciously perceive. Reality and identity are no longer separate from their simulations, and in this hypermediated world the 'authentic' and the 'fake' no longer have meaning. Mersine and Marva decide to purge themselves from Marceline, leaving '*at least one other person in the world. Someone to Escort the Brain Police out of this world and leave it to* people *again*' (1992: 294). Marceline awakes with no memory of her recent past. Freed from memory addiction, her future is unwritten.

Cyberpunk's success is partly explained by the extent to which it was taken up in wider coverage of and debates about contemporary culture, including attention from a range of academic disciplines that elevated it to 'the supreme *literary* expression if not of postmodernism, then of late capitalism itself' (Jameson 1991: 419). Larry McCaffery argued that cyberpunk and other postmodern literature illuminated important aspects of a present moment in which technology was 'reshaping human interactions, perceptions and self-concepts' (Kadrey and McCaffery 1991: 18), post-industrial capitalism was eroding social security, sub-jectivity was fragmenting and any distinction between reality and its simulations was increasingly difficult to perceive. Many commentators identified a conver-gence between SF and literary fiction as SF motifs and methods became increas-ingly commonplace in the latter, and Sterling (1989) claimed that a new genre, 'slipstream', was emerging from this process. Istvan Csicsery-Ronay, Jr influen-tially treated the work of Jean Baudrillard and Donna Haraway as SF undertaken in the form of critical theory. He argued that 'SF' does not name 'a generic effects engine of literature and simulation arts (the usual sense of the phrase "science fic-tion"), so much as a mode of awareness, characterized by two linked forms of hesitation' (1991: 387): a logical hesitation regarding the feasibility of realising certain kinds of imagined futures, and an ethical hesitation regarding the consequences of doing so.

A selection from Sterling's slipstream list

William S. Burroughs, *Naked Lunch* (1959)

John Barth, *Giles Goat-Boy* (1966)

John Fowles, *The Magus* (1966)

Thomas Pynchon, *The Crying of Lot 49* (1966)

William Kotzwinkle, *Doctor Rat* (1976)

Robert Coover, *The Public Burning* (1977)

David Morrell, *The Totem* (1979)

Alasdair Gray, *Lanark* (1981)

Christopher Priest, *The Affirmation* (1981)

Salman Rushdie, *Midnight's Children* (1981)

Ted Mooney, *Easy Travel to Other Planets* (1981)

John Calvin Batchelor, *The Birth of the People's Republic of Antarctica* (1983)

Angela Carter, *Nights at the Circus* (1984)

Paul Auster, *City of Glass* (1985)

Carolyn Hill, *Amanda and the Eleven Million Mile High Dancer* (1985)

Denis Johnson, *Fiskadoro* (1985)

Patrick Süskind, *Perfume* (1985)

Iain Banks, *The Bridge* (1986)

Ian McEwan, *The Child in Time* (1987)

David Foster Wallace, *The Broom of the System* (1987)

Baudrillard outlines a historical transformation in which a previously stable understanding of semiotic signs as standing in for – and faithfully representing – reality had gradually shifted into scepticism about our ability to grasp any reality outside of systems of representation. He argues that, because semiotic signs derive their meaning from their relationship to other semiotic signs, representations refer only to themselves, producing simulations in which distinctions between representation and reality collapse and become meaningless. Simulacra and simulations have displaced the natural and the original, and powerful models of the world govern reality, effectively preceding it. He identifies this situation with postmodernism. Haraway repeatedly draws on SF images and ideas, particularly in her most influential essay, 'A Cyborg Manifesto' (1985), which used the figure of the cyborg to argue for a new socialist-feminist politics of subjectivity. Haraway's work is particularly concerned with the relationship between 'nature' and 'culture', categories that are discursively – and thus ideologically – constructed in an ever-changing binary. Her cyborg is a reaction to (gendered) assumptions about technology's inherent domination that necessarily rely on a myth of the organic and natural body as the site of resistance. Hence, her famous conclusion, 'I would rather be a cyborg than a goddess' (1991: 181). She urges socialist-feminists to shape technoculture to more progressive ends.

Like these theorists, such postmodernist authors as John Barth, Donald Barthelme, Robert Coover, Don DeLillo and Mark Leyner utilise SF's resources to interrogate contemporary reality. William T. Vollmann's *You Bright and Risen Angels* (1987) mixes SF with 'postmodernist allegory', which solicits 'an allegorical interpretation from the reader' but withholds 'any indication of *specific* allegorical content' (McHale 1989: 141), to tell the story of the war between insect revolutionaries and the reactionary inventors of electricity. Epigraphs situate this war in various contexts, including Nazi abuse of subject populations, Lenin's pronouncements on the modernisation of Soviet agriculture and industry and advertisements for guns and ammunition. The novel considers the dehumanising effects of both technology and discourses of otherness, and underscores the profit motive at the root of technological innovation to deflate satirically any rhetorical celebration of progress, the frontier or the human spirit. Kathy Acker's *Empire of the Senseless* (1988) alternates between the first-person voices of Abhor, a half-human/half-robot adolescent girl, and her boyfriend, Thivai. Beginning with a section called 'Elegy for the World of the Fathers', it explores violence against women enacted literally and symbolically in a patriarchal culture obsessed with explicit sexual representation. Acker's style involves unattributed borrowing and remixing of other literary texts, in this instance *Neuromancer*. Her recontextualisation of Gibson identifies the misogyny inherent in the equation of cyberspace with the female body, a hostile territory for hackers to penetrate and conquer. *Empire of the Senseless* contains the explicit representations of sexuality and violence typical of Acker's work but, like the fiction of Ishmael Reed and Angela Carter, it self-reflexively interrogates its own representations, elaborating the relationships between physical violence and the discursive violence that dehumanises female subjects and uses notions of romantic love to disguise political disenfranchisement.

Hard SF and embodiment

Hard-SF responses to the prospect of genetic engineering, human–machine interfaces and nanotechnology also explored the relationships among embodiment, identity and social organisation. Greg Egan's philosophical fiction frequently deployed mind-altering technologies to query fundamental ideas about identity. 'Learning to Be Me' (*Interzone* 1990) explores Moravec's claim that we will soon be able to upload human consciousness into computers, thereby achieving immortality in machine bodies. A device called the Jewel, installed in children, faithfully monitors and models the individual's brain: if the Jewel diverges from the 'real' individual's choice, it is corrected, a process that continues until the individual elects to have his or her decaying biological brain removed and the Jewel take over permanently. The narrator's Jewel fails to synchronise and thus his surgery is a kind of permanent death. It is unclear whether he is an anomaly, or whether this happens, to varying degrees, with every individual. In 'Closer' (*Eidolon* 1992), a couple who have been experimenting with transplanting their Jewels into various bodies, including each other's, allow their Jewels to be merged temporarily into a third consciousness in order to know one another as intimately as possible. For differing reasons, this experience destroys their desire for each other. 'The Moral Virologist' (*Pulphouse* 1990) responds to the moralistic hysteria that greeted the AIDS epidemic. It tells of a deranged Christian geneticist who designs a virus that will kill adulterers and homosexuals. His faith in biologically engineering God's will is shaken, but only briefly, when a prostitute points out that the ingenious logic of his lethal virus means that it will transfer to breastfeeding children. In 'Axiomatic' (*Interzone* 1990), a bereaved pacifist purchases a brain modification that will enable him to avenge his wife's death by killing her murderer.

However, in so doing, he neither overcomes his grief nor enjoys his revenge, but unexpectedly discovers a taste for the sense of certainty that accompanies the complete devaluation of human life.

Becoming posthuman was not merely a cyberpunk fantasy. The Extropians, a group founded by Max More in 1988, 'see humanity as a transitory stage in the evolutionary development of intelligence' and advocate increasing the extropy – the 'extent of a system's intelligence, information, order, vitality, and capacity for improvement' – of the human organism through modifications to mind and body using neuroscience, genetics, smart drugs, robotics, mind-uploading and nanotechnology (More). In the twenty-first century, a similar group called Transhumanists believe that in the future super-intelligent machines will merge with humans to create new, transcendent entities.

Nancy Kress' *Beggars* trilogy (1993–1996) also considers the social changes and problems that might emerge from genetic engineering. In *Beggars in Spain* (1993), a modification allows parents to give their children the advantages that come with never needing to sleep, thus creating more time for productive activity. Social resentment of the Sleepless grows, especially when it is discovered that they do not age. Tony, the founder of Sanctuary, where he and the other Sleepless might live in safety and isolation, is murdered, radicalising most of the Sleepless community. They begin to see themselves as a new species and to question what they, the strong and capable, owe to the weak, the human 'parasites' on Sleepless economic productivity. This problem is illustrated by the question of what one should do about the 'beggars in Spain' (2004: 56). The economist Kenzo Yagai argues that 'the basic tool of civilisation is the contract. Contracts are voluntary and mutually beneficial' and are the opposite of 'coercion, which is wrong' (27). Yagaists, therefore, regard any charity given to the 'beggars' as morally suspect, weakening the exploited giver and robbing the beggar of 'the chance to achieve, and to trade what he achieves with others', which is 'to rob him of his spiritual dignity' (28). As she matures, the Sleepless Leisha questions the wisdom of this quasi-philosophical justification of neoliberalism. Yagaism holds that 'competition among the most capable leads to the most beneficial trades for everyone, strong and weak' (48), but Leisha learns that this is false: the weak often suffer, and the so-called strong need the so-called weak in unanticipated and surprising ways. Leisha finds herself relying on her unaltered, Sleeper twin as they grow older, and it is only because of her charity towards an impoverished Sleeper boy, who grows up to be an artist, that the Sleepless are able to access the brainwave state of dreaming and thus their unconscious minds. Leisha doubts whether trade is a suitable norm for human interactions and rejects Yagaism's linear, contractual, one-to-one exchange model of society, arguing instead that 'it's an ecology ... each niche needed, even if they're not contractually bound' (95).

Jennifer Sharifi and Calvin Hawke function as Leisha's foils. Sharifi, whose efforts to protect the Sleepless become increasingly draconian, designs the next generation of 'Superbright' Sleepless. Their synaptic processes are so accelerated that they think in complex, multidimensional strings rather than conventional syntax. Sharifi resents Sanctuary space station having to pay taxes to support Sleeper 'beggars', and attempts to secede from the US, threatening to destroy several cities with biological weapons. However, the Superbrights, who are appalled by Sanctuary's euthanasia of those who cannot perform at hyperproductive levels, intervene to stop her. Hawke, leader of We-Sleep Industries, argues for solidarity among Sleepers who will otherwise become completely obsolete in the new economy. While his inflammatory, hate-filled methods are condemned, his fears about growing human redundancy are valid. Leisha eventually concludes that 'what the strong owe beggars is to ask each one why he is a beggar and act accordingly. Because community is the assumption, not the result, and only by giving nonproductiveness the same individuality as excellence, and acting accordingly, does one fulfil the obligation to the beggars in Spain' (221–222). She decides that '*there are no permanent beggars in Spain. Or anywhere else. The beggar you give a dollar to today might change the world tomorrow. Or become father to the man who will*' (399). In *Beggars and Choosers* (1994) and *Beggars Ride* (1996), Kress' attention turns to the necessity of direct political mobilisation and struggle to produce social change.

Joan Slonczewski's *A Door into Ocean* (1986) uses biological metaphors to explore alternative political arrangements. The all-female, ocean world of Shora faces occupation and annexation by Valedon, pitting the pacifist Sharer's life-shaping technology – a kind of non-invasive genetic engineering – and belief in ecological symbiosis against a masculinist culture of military domination. Sharers coexist with Shora's other species, eschewing agricultural technologies and the use of high-tech defences against predatory species; in contrast, the Valans have already eradicated another anthropoid race on Valedon, and there are few references to other animal species there. As tensions worsen, neither side sees the other as human: Sharers do not believe that Valans live as humans since they are so destructive to the ecosystem and other species; Valans believe that Sharers need not be treated as equals but can be exterminated like any other animal. The Sharer Merwen tells the Valan General Realgar that 'When you come to see that your survival is inseparable and indistinguishable from mine, then we both will win' (1986: 377), but he cannot transcend the winner–loser binary. Sharer non-violent resistance ultimately succeeds in forcing Realgar to abandon conquest – the common soldiers grow weary of attacking the women and children who passively occupy places from which they have been forbidden – but the Sharers also see this as a defeat since the hoped for consensus and cooperation between peoples is never achieved. Slonczewski's *Brain Plague* (1991) also explores cooperation between species in the tale of an artist who serves as host to a colony of intelligent microbes.

Greg Bear's *Blood Music* (1985) is central to both cyberpunk and hard SF. Reflecting on 'the ranks of magnitude of all creatures, small as microbes or great as humans', it observes that humans consider 'a single human death' to so far outweigh the death of trillions of microbes, 'the peasants of nature', as to be utterly incommensurate, provocatively extending this parallel to add that 'we believe this as firmly as the kings of France believed in their hierarchy' (1985: 1). Vergil Ulam is a maverick geneticist whose unrelenting self-obsession alienates his co-workers. He is fired for disregarding safety protocols and experimenting with mammalian DNA, work he kept secret from his supervisors so that he could later obtain his own patents on these advances in biochip technology. Rather than destroy his lab cultures as ordered, he injects the 'noocytes' into himself, intending to harvest them. Instead, he becomes a living research environment, a world in which the noocytes continue to evolve, eventually achieving collective consciousness and civilisation. They begin to alter the unattractive Ulam, who becomes less clumsy, loses weight and ceases to need glasses, rebuilding him 'from the inside out' (60). On one level, this is a version of Richard Dawkins' 'selfish gene' theory, which contends that larger organisms and complex biological functions are merely ways for individual genes to ensure their own reproduction. In the 1980s and 1990s, conservative social commentators adopted a crude version of this theory to explain human social behaviour, enabling them to reduce socio-economic differences and problems to the inevitable unfolding of biology and thus to claim that supporting social programmes was a futile denial of 'human nature'.

Bear, a far more nuanced thinker, calls into question human assumptions about species hierarchies. Ulam decides that rather than try to control or suppress the noocytes, he should capitulate to them because 'they are more capable' (73). The noocytes spread like a plague, dissolving living beings into their collective, conscious biomass, transforming the surface of the globe. Yet, life goes on. Untransformed individuals are treated kindly by the noocytes, who communicate with them through avatars modelled on people they once knew who are now part of the noocyte biomass. These avatars – at once reconstructions of and more than their originals – encourage the untransformed to join them, apparently sincere in their belief that life is better as part of a microbial collective intelligence. Echoing Arthur C. Clarke's *Childhood's End* (1953), the novel ends on the cusp of a final, dramatic shift whose precise nature remains unknown. The noocytes, as intelligent observers, have altered the quantum nature of reality, which is ultimately 'nothing but information' (177). Normally, events on the quantum level are beyond the observation of intelligent beings, but not for the noocytes, who create a 'kind of strain' (239) on space-time. When it is released, the universe is reorganised, giving everyone a chance to be more and better than they had been in their previous lives.

Conclusion

- Divisions between leftist and right-wing SF continued, the latter primarily associated with hard SF. However, many also criticised the conservatism of cyberpunk, particularly in its treatment of gender, sexuality, race and global inequities. Later cyberpunk articulated and answered these critiques. Simultaneously, the conservative dominance of hard SF waned.

- With its wide appeal beyond traditional readerships, cyberpunk had three important legacies: an array of images, ideas and techniques with which to depict and examine a world that continues to be shaped by global capitalism and information technology; a growing interdisciplinary interest in SF among previously uninterested academic communities; and a commercial drive to market new writers and texts as innovative subgenres and movements.
- Contemporary advances in science and technology and science-fictionalised cultural and critical theory prompted new explorations of embodiment, intelligence and the nature of human consciousness.
- With the increased sense that reality has caught up with SF and that literary fiction has of necessity become science-fictional, the tools that the genre developed could no longer be considered its sole property.

9 Empire and expansion: the 1980s and 1990s

Overview

In this period, social activism was increasingly organised around the identity politics of sexuality, race and gender, and the environmentalist and anti-corporate-globalisation movements. The SF that engaged with these issues was typically critical of discrimination and the exclusion of otherness, frequently using alien perspectives to reveal the strangeness of dominant ideologies. Space opera experienced a dramatic resurgence, often in ironic and self-reflexive forms that commented critically on the colonial underpinnings and other troubling aspects of earlier SF. Overt intertextual allusions to other texts, SF and otherwise, became commonplace. The consolidation of global entertainment industries had a significant influence on the kind of SF produced, with lucrative titles appearing across many media: novels, television series and digital games being made into films, films inspiring novels, television series and digital games and so on.

Changing times

The economic shifts of the 1980s and 1990s, combined with new information technologies, saw the consolidation of a global capitalist order under supranational, neoliberal organisations and agreements that perpetuated structural inequalities favouring Western nations, including the IMF, the World Trade Organization, the World Bank, the G7 and G20 groups of industrialised nations, the European Union and the North American Free Trade Association. Many commentators began to bemoan the declining power of nation-states, arguing that rather than representing the interests of their populations they now exist to serve the economic order itself, which was often described as an autonomous entity, inevitable and somehow natural. This economic globalisation is, however, accompanied by transnational cultural flows that bring diverse communities into increasing contact with one another. As economic globalisation produced a crisis of democratic agency, accompanied by a loss of class identity, subjects 'increasingly organize[d] their meaning not around what they do but on the basis of what they are, or believe they are' (Castells 2000: 3). Thus, people more and more understood themselves not necessarily in relation to their immediate, physical situation, but in terms of cultural and identity communities – often organised around bonds of gender, sexuality, race, ethnicity and religion – which might be geographically dispersed. Struggles around identity politics in this period utilised information technologies to (re)assert a sense of individuality and community in a digital economy that was rapidly erasing differences between places and peoples, reducing all to a flattened terrain of labour and consumption.

SF, which throughout the post-war period tended to imagine the future in terms of Cold War polarities, reflected this shifting global order. Cyberpunk and other dystopian futures emphasised economic (rather than political) divisions, typically between wealthy Northern and impoverished Southern nations, often seeing the US marginalised by East Asian economies. Resistance was to be found in the margins of society, and often consisted of learning merely to survive, as in Geoff Ryman's *The Child Garden* (1989), Karen Joy Fowler's *Sarah Canary* (1991), Jack Womack's *Random Acts of Senseless Violence* (1993) and Colson Whitehead's *The Intuitionist* (1999). SF's institutional structures increasingly acknowledged the importance of identity politics to the genre. WisCon, an explicitly feminist SF convention established in 1977, grew in importance. Since 1991, the James Tiptree, Jr. Award for speculative fiction that explores gender has been presented at WisCon; and in 1999, the Carl Brandon Society, which presents awards for speculative fiction by people of colour and for SF about race and ethnicity, was founded there. These awards are not necessarily given to SF, but to a broader category that includes SF, fantasy and horror, acknowledging resonances and convergences among these genres that earlier, more rigid categorisations denied or precluded.

In part, such convergences are the result of market pressures: heroic fantasy, building on the success of Tolkien, the 1960s re-issues of Robert E. Howard's *Conan* stories and the *Dungeons & Dragons* role-playing game, was successfully consolidated as a popular genre by Terry Brooks, Stephen Donaldson, David Eddings, Raymond Feist, Robin Hobb, Robert Jordan, Guy Gavriel Kay,

---

Science fantasy crossover series

C.J. Cherryh, *The Faded Sun* (1978–1979)

John Varley, *Gaea* (1979–1984)

Robert Silverberg, *Majipoor* (1980–2000)

Joan D. Vinge, *Snow Queen* (1980–2000)

Julian May, *Pliocene Exile* (1981–1984)

Brian Aldiss, *Helliconia* (1982–1985)

Mary Gentle, *Orthe* (1983–1987)

Storm Constantine, *Wraeththu* (1987–1989)

Brian Stableford, *David Lydyard* (1990–1994)

David Zindell, *A Requiem for Homo Sapiens* (1993–1998)

Mercedes Lackey, Tad Williams and others; simultaneously, the *Star Wars* franchise generated an audience for fantasy-like adventure fiction in science-fictional settings. One 'response to this mounting rivalry' was for SF 'to adopt textures and tones from [its] affiliated genres', producing 'works of science fantasy with crossover appeal' (Latham 2010: 37). Another was an increasing insistence on the 'hardness' of 'real' SF, closely associated in this period with Greg Bear, Gregory Benford and David Brin and reinforced by Isaac Asimov's and Arthur C. Clarke's best sellers, late works which typically revisited earlier successes. Cyberpunks likewise lambasted SF's turn to the fantastic, even as they participated in a postmodern culture concerned with sampling, hybridising and erasing boundaries between high and low culture.

Popular postmodernism

Brian Attebery argues that SF has a distinctive way of borrowing from its vast storehouse of stories, ideas and images, not merely recycling but self-consciously following *and* diverging from them. The 'oldest meanings don't go away', he argues, but 'are complicated, obscured and rendered ironic by subsequent re-imaginings' (2005: 14). For many writers in this period, SF was not a dead weight of tradition but a vast synchronic network of possibilities upon which to draw in monumental yet energetic works of recapitulation. This sense of multiplicity, of parallel worlds in which it is always possible for history to unfold differently, is evident in such films and television programmes as the *Back to the Future* trilogy (Zemeckis 1985–1990), *Quantum Leap* (1989–1993) and *Sliders* (1995–2000), in steampunk SF, which gleefully imagines marvellous Victorian technologies in dark, Dickensian settings and in Alan Moore and Dave Gibbons' *Watchmen* comic (1986–1987). Set in an alternative 1980s, in which the Watergate scandal did not happen and Nixon is still president, *Watchmen* follows a group of retired, Cold War superheroes who used their powers to ensure American hegemony. They are badly damaged, deeply flawed people. One of their number, believing only a global cataclysm can unite a fragmenting world, fakes a devastating alien attack on New York. The narrative is fleshed out with excerpts from Nite Owl's autobiography, Rorshach's psychiatric records, Silk Spectre's scrapbook, Ozymandias' interoffice memos about merchandising, an article filling in some of the history of American comic books in this alternative world and so on. Further commentary on the narrative is provided by an interpolated story from a reissued 1960s pirate comic, *Tales of the Black Freighter*, written by one minor character and read by another. Moore and Gibbons' deconstructive reflections on the relationships among superheroes, totalitarianism and eutopianism, and their metatextual and formal innovations, saw them credited – along with Neil Gaiman, Frank Miller, Grant Morrison, Warren Ellis and others – with transforming comic books into an adult medium.

The fiction of Howard Waldrop and Kim Newman exemplifies this postmodern aesthetic of ironic sampling and intertextual allusiveness, drawing on SF and other popular fictions to proliferate alternate worlds that comment on our own.

> **Steampunk**
>
> Tim Powers, *The Anubis Gates* (1983)
>
> James P. Blaylock, *Homunculus* (1986)
>
> K.W. Jeter, *Infernal Devices* (1987)
>
> William Gibson and Bruce Sterling, *The Difference Engine* (1990)
>
> *The City of Lost Children* (Jeunet and Caro 1995)
>
> Paul Di Filippo, *The Steampunk Trilogy* (1995)
>
> Alan Moore, *The League of Extraordinary Gentlemen* (2000)
>
> Thomas Pynchon, *Against the Day* (2006)

Waldrop's textual playfulness frequently emphasises the cultural biases embodied in genre tropes, displaying their evasions of contemporary realities by restoring them to a more fully rounded social world. For example, 'The Ugly Chickens' (1980) evokes histories of colonisation and slavery to establish plausibly the survival of dodos in rural Mississippi as late as the 1920s. The post-apocalyptic 'Heirs of the Perisphere' (*Playboy* 1985) depicts a trio of animatronics – a robot Mickey Mouse, Donald Duck and Goofy – intended to replace human workers in Disney theme parks, who walk from Tokyo to the site of the New York World's Fair in the hope that the time capsule buried there will reveal what has happened to the world. 'Night of the Cooters' (*Omni* 1987) imagines Wells' Martian invaders targeting Pachucho County, Texas, pitting down-to-earth Sheriff Linley against the alien threat. 'All About Strange Monsters of the Recent Past' (*Shayol* 1980) follows a deserting soldier in a world devastated by the monsters and aliens of 1950s SF movies. His journey across the American southwest – 'Not far from here, the first A-bomb went off.... This is where it started. This is where it ends' (1989: 245) – concatenates allusions to numerous films, many of them obscure, culminating in an encounter with the giant ants he first saw, aged six, in *Them!*: 'it's all over for man', he realises, 'but there are still some things left. Like choices ... A choice of personal monsters' (246).

Many of Waldrop's stories are overtly concerned with textuality and mediation, with the complex layerings of fiction and reality in everyday life. 'The Passing of the Western' (1989) is presented as three contributions to a special issue of *Film Review World* on the largely forgotten *Cloudbusters* westerns which, in this alternate history, depicted the transformation of the American west by nineteenth-century rainmaking technologies; one essay is an exuberant introduction to the films by Formalhaut J. Amkermackam, a nod to influential fan and editor of *Famous Monsters of Filmland* magazine, Forrest J. Ackerman. 'Thirty Minutes over Broadway' (1987) is the opening story in George R.R. Martin's still-ongoing *Wild Cards* series of shared-world, superhero anthologies. It depicts the return of Jetboy, a pilot hero who, near the end of WWII, was marooned on an island and presumed dead. His childhood sweetheart has moved on. He is in dispute with Cosh Comic over royalties, and dislikes the changes they have made to *Jetboy* comic, abandoning 'flying and combat and cleaning up spy rings – real stuff' (1990: 97) for more fantastical plots. He spends most of his time watching movies and failing to write his memoirs, finding that 'what had seemed just like the facts when he told them to the G-2 boys during the war looked like bragging on paper' (108) and wondering 'who needs this stuff?' (109). He is saved from this banal fate by the reappearance of the evil Dr Tod, equipped with crashed alien technology, which requires him to save the day again one last time.

Newman similarly parodies, pastiches and pays homage to SF and other genres across media, mixing, for example, Lovecraft's cosmic horror with Raymond Chandler's hard-boiled crime fiction in 'The Big Fish' (*Interzone* 1993). A number of his stories map the history of twentieth-century racial prejudice through its popular fiction or critique contemporary right-wing politics. 'Famous Monsters' (*Interzone* 1988), an alternate history in which H.G. Wells' *The War of the Worlds* and *The First Men in the Moon* actually happened, is the memoir of a Martian who became a minor Hollywood actor. Despite being born on Earth to refugees from the Martian dictatorship, he is subjected to marginalisation, discrimination and abuse because of his race. Generally stuck in comedy sidekick roles of the sort played by African Americans in the 1930s, he finds himself (like such anti-Nazi German émigrés as Peter Lorre and Conrad Veidt) in demand to play villains when the Second War of the Worlds breaks out. After the war ends, this work dries up and he ends up performing in low-budget drive-in SF-horror movies. 'Pitbull Brittan' (1991) – written for the *Temps* shared-world anthologies (1991–1992) about bureaucratised British superheroes – imagines a superhero whose 'musculature is composed entirely of erectile tissue' which, when 'aroused, physically or emotionally' produces 'pronounced turgidity of the surface flesh, extraordinary muscular strength, limited invulnerability and psychological capacity for feats of selfless heroism' (1995a: 82). It derives most of its humour from depicting as literally true everything British right-wing tabloids claimed about miners during the 1984–1985 strike, and from bigoted Pitbull needing to go beyond heteronormative sexuality to avoid death from unrelieved arousal. 'Übermensch!' (*New Worlds* 1991), littered with allusions to German expressionist cinema, imagines that Superman crashed in Germany rather than Kansas and grew up to serve the Reich in his familiar costume: 'light brown body-stocking, with black trunks, boots and cloak. A black swastika in the red circle on the chest' (1995b: 219). However, sickened by his masters' Final Solution, he refused to intervene in the D-Day landings and, after the war, voluntarily confined himself to Spandau Prison. Years later, an elderly Jewish Nazi-hunter, concerned by the resurgence of fascism, persuades him to commit suicide.

These ironic exercises in allusion are dwarfed by Gene Wolfe's critically renowned, if politically conservative, *The Book of the New Sun* (1980–1983), a series characterised by recursion, remembrance and reverberation, by relics and resurrections. It is set on the medieval-seeming, far future Urth, which might be

Earth and which, since these novels concern the revival of its dying sun, might equally be set in our distant past. This uncertainty is reinforced by Wolfe's archaic vocabulary, which emphasises the belatedness of the setting, and by his mythic imagery, particularly of the Fisher King, Christ, Theseus and Oedipus. Typical of Wolfe's symbolism is the Citadel's library, whose shelves perhaps extend indefinitely, meaning the world is in the library as much as the library is in the world. The four volumes follow Severian, a young member of the Torturer's Guild, who is banished from Nessus, the capital city, for helping Thecla, a prisoner with whom he has become involved, to commit suicide. Presented as Severian's memoirs, written after he has ascended to the rank of Autarch, the novels frequently draw attention to the act of narration and the unreliability of narrators: events are sometimes recounted out of chronological order, and the belated revelation of crucial information requires the reader to reconsider the meaning of earlier events; accounts of dreams and visions often leave it unclear whether certain events have actually happened; some information, such as the identity of Severian's mother, is withheld completely. The reader is also denied any sense of the stability of Severian's own identity: long before telling his story, he consumed some of Thecla's flesh along with a drug which gives him access to her memories and on occasion allows her to take over his body, and by similar means now possesses the memories of all the previous Autarchs.

The Book of the New Sun was followed by *The Urth of the New Sun* (1987) and two related series, *The Book of the Long Sun* (1994–1996) and *The Book of the Short Sun* (1999–2001). Dan Simmons' four-volume *Hyperion Cantos* (1989–1997), laden with allusions to John Keats' poetry, is similarly immense. *Hyperion* (1989) replicates the structure of Chaucer's *Canterbury Tales*, bringing together pilgrims who in turn tell of their previous encounters with the Shrike, a monstrous creature connected to the Time Tombs to which they journey. This episodic structure enables Simmons to use different kinds of story to comment on the diverse forms SF has taken historically, including anthropological SF (the Priest, Lenar Hoyt, tells of a colleague who discovered an ancient tribe, each of its members repeatedly resurrected by a cruciform parasite that clings to their chests) and cyberpunk (the Detective, Brawne Lamia, gives a hard-boiled account of how she was hired by a cybrid, an AI entity in a human body whose persona is a reconstruction of Keats, to investigate his temporary murder). The Scholar, Sol Weintraub, tells the most personal and emotional tale: his archaeologist daughter, Rachel, transformed by the Time Tombs, is ageing in reverse; now an infant, she is nearing her birth, perhaps to disappear. He is plagued by dreams in which he sees himself as the biblical Abraham, ordered to offer Rachel to the Shrike in order to save humankind. The pilgrims' stories flesh out the detail of the interstellar human Hegemony and develop the series' concern with redemption and spiritual truth.

In *Fall of Hyperion* (1990), we learn that Sol wrote a book, *The Abraham Dilemma*, which argued for 'refusing all sacrifice, refusing any relationship with God except one of mutual respect and honest attempts at mutual understanding' (1990: 150). Simmons repeatedly alludes to the Catholic philosopher

Pierre Teilhard de Chardin, who argued that divinity was an emergent phenomenon and that 'every level of organic consciousness was part of a planned evolution towards ultimate mergence with the Godhead' (108). Autonomous AIs, secretly engaged in trying to create an Ultimate Intelligence, discover that another Ultimate Intelligence has evolved from human consciousness on the quantum level of the universe. Aenea, Brawne's daughter by the Keats cybrid, is the Christ-like protagonist of *Endymion* (1996) and *The Rise of Endymion* (1997), set 250 years later, when the Hegemony is dominated by a Catholic theocracy. Her blood contains a virus that enables her to communicate through quantum telepathy with everyone infected by it. She submits to torture and death at the hands of the new Inquisition so as to reveal the true nature of the theocracy and create a space for genuine spirituality to emerge.

The *Hyperion* novels emphasise textuality and narration through their structure, the *Endymion* novels frequently remind the reader that they are a written narrative, and both pairs are concerned with the relationship between reality and representation. For example, one of the pilgrims, Martin, wrote an epic poem, *The Hyperion Cantos*, about events related in the *Hyperion* novels, but by the time of the *Endymion* novels it has taken on the status of myth. In a similar vein, former truths are revealed as lies and the basic premises of the setting are repeatedly revised. As Simmons proliferates detail and narrative strands, the series moves further into the adventurous terrain of space opera.

The new space opera

Space opera was among the most successful SF of this period, as influential as cyberpunk but not as quickly embraced by academics. The critical commentary that has emerged is most frequently associated with a sense that the best SF of the 1990s was by British authors. Among the reasons for 'the British boom' was the regular appearance of *Interzone*, now the longest-running British SF magazine, and the sense that British culture was distinguished from American culture in its relationship to the idea of empire. While the US was expanding its global influence through neoliberal economic empire, Britain was characterised by an ambivalent, post-imperial melancholy, mourning its post-war loss of stature and colonial empire. Space opera was not the only form British boom SF took, and many non-Britons have participated in the space-opera renaissance, but the fiction of Colin Greenland, Ken MacLeod and Iain M. Banks was vital to both.

Greenland's space operas teem with allusions to earlier SF and other literary texts, from Edgar Rice Burroughs to the *Dan Dare* comic strip (1950–1967), from Jean-Jacques Rousseau to Charles Dickens. *Take Back Plenty* (1990) was noted for its protagonist, Captain Tabitha Jute, maverick owner of the independent spaceship *Alice Lidell*: 'not as the net media show her, heroine of hyperspace, capable, canny and cosmetically enhanced ... but a small, weary young woman in a cracked foil jacket and oil-stained trousers' with skin the colour 'of an ordinary milky coffee' and hair of 'darkest ginger' (1990: 6), given to enthusiastic sex with both men and women and to drinking until she passes out. Nevertheless, no matter how high the stakes become, she exasperatedly saves the day. *Harm's Way* (1993) depicts a steampunk solar system criss-crossed by the vessels that resemble the sailing ships of the British Empire. Urchin Sophie Farthing stows away to Earth to discover the real identity and fate of her mother. Her picaresque adventures include the discovery that she really is the long lost heir to Lord Lychworthy, head of the powerful, all male Pilot's Guild. Into this generic blend are also mixed traces of colonial adventure fiction, nineteenth-century novels of social hardship and gothic mysteries. Lychworthy thought that Sophie's mother, a prostitute with whom he fell in love, posed a threat to his position and had her murdered. Believing the same of Sophie, he orders her death, but the assassin, the son of her mother's killer, falls in love with her and helps her to uncover the truth. She kills Lychworthy and becomes head of the Guild, opening it to women. The novel ends with Sophie's wedding, surrounded by the idiosyncratic friends she made during her adventure.

MacLeod's novels, characterised by political and technological speculations, are less whimsical, but far from humourless. The *Fall Revolution* quartet (1995–1999) explores the different futures that could emerge from competing political ideologies and considers the contingencies of individual, human lives that shape the outcomes of major historical events. The *Engines of Light* trilogy (2000–2002) imagines a future polarised between a new, socialist Soviet Union, which includes Europe, and the capitalist US, working through the implications of how this would shape interstellar trade with alien species. In contrast, Banks' *Culture* novels (1987–) combine the serious with the capricious in their depiction of a eutopian, post-scarcity, galactic civilisation called the Culture. In the Culture, labour is performed by non-sentient machines, freeing humankind to pursue artistic and intellectual endeavours or whatever playful diversions they choose. AIs have evolved into superior intelligences, but neither resent nor fear humans, instead serving humanity by piloting immense starships, managing vast space stations and so on. Human bodies contain glands that enable the harmless consumption of recreational drugs, can be easily modified into various forms and can be restored from almost any injury. Despite all the wonders that such a future proffers, the novels tend to focus on characters marginal to or outside of the Culture. Frequently they work for Special Circumstances, an agency that directly intervenes in the Culture's relationships with other civilisations so as to produce politically desirable outcomes. Thus, although free from the inequities of capitalist social organisation, the Culture has a sinister side. Echoing US economic and cultural imperialism, the Culture seeks to convert rather than conquer its others. Superficially, this conversion seems to be benevolent since rival civilisations are typically inequitable, caste-ridden and violent, but the Culture's help carries a price that Banks questions as much as endorses.

Consider Phlebas (1987) strings together action set-pieces against vast backdrops, enabling Banks to recapture a sense of awe and immensity. Protagonist Horza is a Changer, able to reshape his body so as to take on other identities. He sides with the Idirans, a genocidal, totalitarian theocracy, in a war against the Culture, who consider the Idirans to pose such a threat to all other life that destroying them is the only reasonable option. Fully aware of Idiran atrocities, Horza insists that the Culture is worse:

> On a straight head count [of those killed] the Idirans no doubt do come out in front ... and I've told them I never did care for some of their methods, or their zeal. I'm all for people being allowed to live their own lives. But now they're up against [the Culture], and that's what makes the difference to me. Because I'm against [the Culture], rather than for [the Idirans] ... I don't care how self-righteous the Culture feels, or how many people the Idirans kill. They're on the side of life – boring, old-fashioned, biological life; smelly, fallible and short-sighted, God knows, but *real* life. You're ruled by your machines. You're an evolutionary dead end.... The worst thing that could happen to the galaxy would be if the Culture wins this war.
>
> (1987: 26)

However, the Culture does win, and despite the enormous scale evoked throughout the novel, an appendix notes the relative insignificance of it all: 'A small, short war that rarely extended throughout more than .02% of the galaxy by volume and .01% by stellar population' (490).

Taken as a whole, the new space opera seems concerned with restoring the sense of human agency and purpose denied to many in the era of neoliberal globalisation. Horza's objection to the centrality of machines in the Culture might, then, be understood as expressing anxiety about the degree to which the global economy, and the systems of global governance supporting it, are not only difficult to comprehend but impossible to bring to account. In contrast, the Culture's benevolent machines put human happiness at the centre of the social order. Despite such accomplishments as C.J. Cherryh's *Union-Alliance* (1976–), David Brin's *Uplift* (1980–1998) and Vernor Vinge's *Deep* (1992–1999) series, American space opera of this period was still typically characterised by militaristic storylines and themes that did not significantly differ from the space opera of earlier decades, although characterisation often challenged previous assumptions. For example, the protagonists of David Weber's *Honor Harrington* (1993–) and Lois McMaster Bujold's *Miles Vorkosigan* (1988–) series are, respectively, female and physically-impaired. On television, the various new *Star Trek* series asserted multicultural, liberal humanist values, and often organised stories around ethical issues related to the Prime Directive of non-intervention, struggling to balance a respect for cultural autonomy with a commitment to universal rights. *Babylon 5* (1994–1998) was groundbreaking not just in bringing huge, CGI space battle sequences to the medium and in mapping out a five-season story arc before the first episode was broadcast (thus breaking with episodic television's traditional structure of more-or-less standalone episodes and requiring the viewers' ongoing attentiveness), but also in the complexity with which it engaged with space opera's predilection for warfare. Consciously informed by conflicts in the former Yugoslavia (1990–1992), it tells of the intersecting fates of four space-faring species – humans, Centauri, Minbari and Narn – during and after a war between two ancient and more powerful alien species, the Vorlon and the Shadows. The eponymous human space station serves as neutral ground for the different species to meet and negotiate, enabling the series to explore the politics of multiculturalism, while the galactic backdrop produces a sense of sublime scale (the series consciously alludes to E.E. Smith's space opera and H.P. Lovecraft's cosmic horror). The Vorlon and the Shadows are initially understood as the forces, respectively, of light and darkness, possibly the source of human myths about God and Satan. The series slowly reveals the inadequacy of such binary oppositions to understanding political realities. The narrative strand about the long-term antagonism between Centauri and Narn sees allies become enemies, and vice versa, as characterisation and politics are allowed to become increasingly, and realistically, complex. The final season involves the birth of a new, interstellar political order after Babylon 5 declares independence from Earth. Founded on ideals of cooperation and mutual respect, it values individuality and difference, but *Babylon 5* also imagines the problematic continuation and expansion of capitalism, resisting *Star Trek*'s magical erasure of economics.

Multiculturalism and identity

Throughout this period, SF explored and elaborated upon the idea of multicultural community, fostering the growing interest in gender, race and sexuality in fan and academic communities. Elizabeth Moon, author of the *Serrano* (1993–2000) series, moved away from space opera to explore gender and agency in *Remnant Population* (1996). When the Sims Bancorp Ltd. colony on an alien world is an economic failure, the corporation orders the removal of its settlers, who are little more than indentured labourers. The elderly Ofelia realises that Sims Bancorp will expect her son to cover the expense of her relocation even though she will probably die *in cryo* transit, so she hides rather than being evacuated. Freed from the resented authority of her son and his wife, she is independent and utterly competent, caring for herself, the remaining livestock, the crops and the abandoned town's physical infrastructure. When rival corporation Zeoteka O.S. attempt to establish a colony nearby, Ofelia's radio picks up the sound of their slaughter by a hitherto unknown indigenous species (she later learns that the landing party provoked the attack by inadvertently destroying a nesting ground). When Ofelia encounters a party of the indigenous People, one of whom is injured, her compassion overcomes her fear as she invites them to shelter with her from a storm. Interacting with them as she would with pre-linguistic toddlers, Ofelia establishes interspecies communication and friendship, validating the pragmatic, domestic knowledge of an elderly woman whose life had always been tightly constrained. She is eventually made a 'click-kaw-keerrrr' (1996: 224) to a newly hatched group of People. Moon's refusal to translate the People's speech underlines the ability to communicate through cultural bonds of caring outside of full linguistic comprehension.

A team of human experts arrives to determine whether the People are sentient, as this will then dictate colonial policy. They treat Ofelia as a senile irritation: 'she didn't matter; she didn't count, she was nothing. Exactly right, the old voice said to her. This is how it is; this is how it has always been. Accept it, and they will accept you as what you are. Old woman. Nothing' (263). The People, however, insist on placing her wisdom and experience at the centre of cultural and political exchange: 'She was worth it; she was their nest-guardian, and the nest-guardian was the most important position the People had' (290). The People prove to be intellectually superior to humans, and dictate the terms of continued contact, which results in the recruitment of other older human women, open to difference, as interspecies ambassadors.

Octavia Butler, one of the few African Americans consistently working in SF, came to prominence for her representation of racial identity as a complex phenomenon intersecting with other identities, particularly gender and sexuality. Her *Xenogenesis* trilogy (1987–1989) mixes the hard SF of genetic determinism with a concern for just communities and respecting cultural difference. The few survivors of a global nuclear war are rescued by the alien Oankali, genetic traders who mix their genes with those of other species to produce an ever-evolving community. They find in humans a mismatched pair of genetic tendencies towards intelligence and hierarchy, with the latter too-often dominating: 'When human intelligence served it instead of guiding it, when human intelligence did not even acknowledge it as a problem, but took pride in it or did not notice it at all ... That was like ignoring cancer' (1987: 40). The Oankali therefore insist that interbreeding is essential, and render sterile all humans who refuse to engage in genetic exchange. The Oankali's alien appearance provokes fear responses in humans, who must learn to accept and embrace difference, but Resister humans insist that genetic mixing is a form of genocide. Although sceptical, the Oankali eventually grant the Resisters a colony on Mars where they can try to build a civilisation of unaltered humans that does not repeat the destructive errors of the past. Despite foregrounding the role genetics plays in culture and identity, Butler insists that human intelligence means that we are not doomed merely to play out instructions encoded in our genes.

Gwyneth Jones' *Aleutian* trilogy (1991–1997) also uses aliens to explore notions of human community and difference, demonstrating how preconceptions about otherness can hinder rather than enable communication. *White Queen* (1991) focuses on the period of first contact, and the misconceptions and misunderstandings that arise when each species reads the other through their own cultural norms. Humans assume that Aleutians are superior beings who arrived by faster-than-light travel, an error compounded by the continuity of Aleutian subjectivity: humans think that the Aleutians are the same *physical* individuals who departed from their distant planet, while Aleutians presume that humans understand that the same personality is reincarnated across generations. Aleutians see humans as potential trading partners, an opportunity for profit, while humans fear invasion and interpret Aleutian behaviour in terms of interplanetary intrigue. Human culture is irrevocably transformed by the encounter with the aliens, their technology greatly improving the lives of the poor but having terrible consequences elsewhere. Many humans begin to imitate alien ways, provoking anxieties about the disappearance of 'true' human culture.

Aleutians communicate in the Common Tongue, a combination of body language and cultural training developed among the limited number of personalities who recur in each generation. Failing to observe this non-verbal communication, humans think Aleutians are telepathic and are unaware of their own unconscious, non-verbal communications. The Aleutian Clavel believes she is in love with the human Johnny. Because of misunderstandings about Common Tongue, Clavel misreads Johnny's desire for the aliens to cure him of a virus as a reciprocation of his own desire for Johnny and responds to Johnny's apparent request for sexual fulfilment. Clavel's 'rape' of Johnny becomes an important first contact incident, returned to in *North Wind* (1994) and *Phoenix Café* (1997), as the reincarnated Clavel personality tries to make sense of this personal history and as both cultures struggle to understand how disastrous exploitation can occur between those with good intentions towards each other. Aleutians are baffled by human ideas of gender, a complication compounded by mistaking the World Conference of Women for a global government. Aleutians decide that humans are divided between 'childbearers' and 'parasites'. Political conflict develops between Traditionalist humans, associated with men, and Reformers, associated with women, although 'there are biological males on the Woman's side, and biological females on the Men's side' (1994: 17). Humans who try to adapt Aleutian biological weapons risk eradicating all humans since the 'Weapons attack biochemical identity. They can't distinguish between *political parties*!' (1998: 298).

Aleutian embodiment and culture – they believe that 'everything that lives on this whole planet belongs to ... the same brood. Sharing life, sharing self' (1998: 298) – thus challenges ideas about the biological differences that humans use to distinguish among ourselves. The consequences, both positive and negative, of encountering the alien critically reflect upon first contact stories and colonial adventure fiction. Nicola Griffith's *Ammonite* (1992) similarly rewrites narratives of colonisation with a particular emphasis on gender and sexuality. Anthropologist Marghe is sent to investigate Jeep (Grenchstrom's Planet, or GP), where a virus eliminated male colonists but enabled women to reproduce and build an all-female culture that has been out of contact with the rest of humanity for several hundred years. The Company, who want to extract Jeep's resources, has developed a potential antidote to the virus, which if successful would genocide the female colony. Simultaneously, Company personnel based on the planet know that if the antidote fails, it will be more cost effective to abandon them there than to quarantine them offworld.

Leaving the Company beachhead, Marghe comes into contact with two communities, the nomadic Echraidhe, who effectively abduct her, and the small settlement that takes her in after she escapes. She is healed of injuries sustained in her flight by Thenike, who becomes her lover, and discovers that Jeep reproduction occurs during a joint meditative state that enables lovers to engage in biofeedback changes to each other's body, stimulating the production of zygotes. The Echraidhe are dying out because their social structure has become insular and rigid, isolated from others; echoing this, Marghe learns she needs to stop studying '*people like shells found on a beach*' (1992: 179) and engage with the lives of others. She stops taking the antidote, is transformed by the virus and becomes, like Thenike, a viajera – an itinerant entertainer, oral historian, news reporter, judge and repository of communal knowledge. She is instrumental in ending Echraidhe aggression, integrating them and the remaining Company personnel into Jeep's wider community.

While *Ammonite*'s SF apparatus enables Griffith to normalise lesbian identity and community to such an extent that the word 'lesbian' never actually needs to be used, Maureen F. McHugh's *China Mountain Zhang* (1992) depicts queer identity in a Chinese-dominated future, in which racialised hierarchies privilege the Chinese and homosexuality is criminalised. Prenatal genetic modifications enable the Chinese-Hispanic Zhang Zhong Shan, also known as Rafael, to pass as full Chinese. Although he thus avoids overt racial discrimination, he runs into difficulties when his traditional Chinese boss wants Zhang to court his daughter, San-xiang. Zhang is uninterested, but cannot reveal the truth about his origins or his sexuality. He eventually goes to study organic Daoist engineering in China, where his sexual identity becomes more perilous than his ethnic passing. His tutor, who becomes his lover, commits suicide when the authorities discover that he is gay.

Zhang returns to New York and, rather than accept a job in the isolated compounds of corporations eager to hire him, establishes his own engineering company. Echoing the other, minor narrative strands – one follows San-xiang, who agitates for social revolution; the other, Martian colonists, struggling equitably to organise a society with limited resources – Zhang renovates his depressing apartment according to Daoist engineering principles, and begins to do so for others in the rundown block. These processes orient him towards a new kind of socialism related to the idea of history as a complex, chaotic system that, like the weather, is 'sensitive, dependent on initial conditions' (1992: 295) and thus open to multiple possible outcomes.

Ecological SF

SF continued to explore the relationships between social structures and physical environments. In *The Drylands* (1994), Mary Rosenblum extrapolates from the ongoing depletion of aquifers and from models of global warming to depict a desiccated future US in which the power of the Water Policy board exceeds that of the president. A conspiracy narrative charts struggles among politicians, the Army Corps of Engineers charged with guarding water pipelines but unable to set policy and a group of subsistence farmers dependent on the pipeline. This complicated set of interconnections is matched by an ecological sensitivity to the non-linear dynamics of complex systems: on the one hand, short-term reliance on genetically engineered crops that can be irrigated with sea water produces long-term consequences for soil fertility; on the other, the environment seems to be responding to increased stresses by producing a generation of children with extrasensory abilities, a possible site of hope for the future.

Other examples of ecological SF rethink the narratives of colonisation. In Molly Gloss' *The Dazzle of Day* (1997), a multi-racial group of Quakers arrive, after generations of travel, at a planet they might colonise. They debate whether it is better to remain on the starship or venture onto this new world. They left Earth because of a 'dream of a world in which people respectfully take part in their landscape, and go on doing it generation after generation' (1997: 13). Pata Vilasensor argues that life aboard the starship enables them to fulfil human potentialities denied to people on Earth because the ship's closed biosystem requires everyone always 'to be mindful of every detail of their living environment, their souls and minds put to work always in keeping the whole world from collapsing', making daily life an 'act of conscious worship ... loving and protecting this soil, these trees, these animals, against the void of space' (210). Others believe this will give them a greater appreciation of and sensitivity to the planet's biosphere, and that they will not repeat the mistakes of Earth: 'It's so obvious we're in control, I guess we may have forgotten we're not in control. ... those people on the Earth, because it was so clear they weren't in control, forgot that they were' (215).

Sheri S. Tepper's fiction explores environmental devastation, human–animal relations and gender discrimination, creating worlds that demonstrate that the exploitation of humans and other animals is part of a wider, patriarchal logic. She specifically identifies male control of female bodies as the cause of overpopulation amid finite resources. She emphasises kindness and the harmony among species that can grow from recognising the autonomy of all beings. In *Grass* (1989), the eponymous planet, governed by an aristocracy organised around a version of foxhunting, is the only world not affected by a plague sweeping through human civilisation. Olympic horse rider Marjorie and her politically-connected, upper-class family are sent to investigate. They take horses with them in the hope that a shared equestrian culture will give Marjorie vital access to Grass' aristocrats, but while Marjorie feels for her horses and is trusted by them, the hunt is rather different than expected: the mounts are Hippae, huge indigenous beasts with spiky barbs and glowing red eyes; the ferocious hounds are the size of horses; and their quarry, the barely-glimpsed foxen, is 'an explosion of what might have been fur or scales or fangs, talons ... the size of half a dozen tigers' (1989: 108). Marjorie immediately determines not to participate in the dangerous, addictive hunt, unlike her husband, Rigo, who wishes to assert his masculinity and gain the aristocrats' respect.

Marjorie's investigation reveals the origin of the plague and uncovers a complicated life-cycle in which non-sentient Peepers are the larval stage of a species that metamorphoses into hound, then partially-sentient Hippae, then sentient foxen. A genetic aberration generations earlier gave the Hippae numerical advantage over the foxen, whom they pursue as enemies, not acknowledging their relationship. Although powerful, the foxen are deeply troubled because they did not prevent the Hippae's genocide of the Arbai, gentle alien creatures who once lived on Grass and sought to establish community with them. Marjorie eventually convinces the foxen of the importance of acting for the future. She kills two of her enemies, explaining that mercy is a limited, naïve solution to antagonistic difference:

> The Arbai were merciful, but when confronted with evil, mercy becomes an evil. It got the Arbai killed, and it could get us killed because these two might

simply come back and murder us. The question is, are they evil? If they are, it doesn't matter how they got that way.... If we forgive these two, we may actually cause another killing.... Do we have the right to be fools if we want to? No. Not at someone else's expense.

(433)

Such zealous polemics about the relative ease with which good can be distinguished from evil and the importance of eradicating the latter recur in Tepper's novels, earning her as many critics as admirers.

Kim Stanley Robinson shares an equally strong commitment to environmental – and social – justice. Although undeniably Marxist and Green, his work has proven less contentious, perhaps because of the inclusion of diverse politics among his main characters. The *Three Californias* trilogy imagines three different futures for Orange County: in *The Wild Shore* (1984), the survivors of nuclear war rebuild society around subsistence agriculture; the dystopian *The Gold Coast* (1988) extrapolates the worst problems of contemporary, neoliberal Los Angeles; and *Pacific Edge* (1990) presents an ecotopia that has grown out of incremental shifts in policy and law. The *Mars* trilogy (1993–1996) traces the colonisation of Mars, from the first human colonists in the early twenty-first century to the full independence of a sovereign, partially-terraformed Mars by the late twenty-second century. The length and complexity of the trilogy enable Robinson to present a longer view of history but defy easy summary. Each novel ends with a revolution that marks a new stage for the Martian social order, creating a sense that the future is open, while detailed descriptions of political processes demonstrate the responsibility of all humans to make the future we want. Like other works of the period, the trilogy alludes to previous SF, but Robinson also refers overtly to critical thinkers, including Thomas Kuhn, Louis Althusser, A.J. Greimas and Raymond Williams.

Red Mars (1993) introduces the First Hundred, the original colonists, about ten of whom reappear in the subsequent novels. As they travel to Mars and establish the first settlement, the political differences emerge that will result, at the end of the novel, in the First Martian Revolution. While Sax Russell advocates the fastest possible transformation of the planet to make it habitable for humans, Ann Clayborne becomes associated with the politics of Red Mars, resisting terraforming and asking others to appreciate the unmodified environment. Sax supports the influx of terrestrial capital that will enable his plans, but John Boone and others are concerned that this will recreate on Mars the pursuit of profit over sustainability that plagues an environmentally devastated Earth. A Green Mars position gradually evolves, insisting that 'we must terraform not only Mars, but ourselves' (1993: 89), producing a genuinely new culture and social order. The colonists develop a system of eco-economics based on the premise that 'everyone should make their living ... based on a calculation of their real contribution to the human ecology. Everyone can increase their ecological efficiency by efforts to reduce how many kilocalories they use' (298). The novel ends with the first revolution crushed by Earth's military strength.

By the time of *Green Mars* (1994), a generation born on Mars see themselves as indigenous Martians and have only minimal interest in Earth. They are physically transformed by living in Mars' lesser gravity and socially transformed by existing outside the structures of capitalism and patriarchy. Many are conceived by IVF, some are brought to term in artificial wombs, and it is not uncommon to be raised collectively within a community, not knowing the identity of one's father. Political struggles are now largely concerned with the nature of the relationship between planets. The climate has begun to change, with temperature and atmospheric pressure increasing, partly because damage during the suppression of the revolution released masses of water into the environment. The original treaty for Martian colonisation included significant environmental protections and prevented private ownership of the land. Pressures to produce financial returns on infrastructural investments result in frequent treaty violations by corporations. A Free Mars movement, associated with the murdered Green moderate Boone, develops among native-born Martians. On Earth, the depredations of meta-national corporations prompts growing unrest among the disenfranchised Southern nations. The situation worsens when volcanic activity causes the West Antarctic ice sheet to melt, causing global sea levels to rise by several metres, resulting in massive population displacements and social disruption. The military might of the G7 nations protects corporate interests, pressurising Mars to accept more colonists and to flout environmental constraints on resource extraction. One corporation, Praxis, looking for alternative responses to this crisis, becomes interested in Martian eco-economics and sustainability strategies. On Earth, Praxis uses a 'Country Future Index … taking into account debt, political stability, environmental health and the like. A useful cross-check on the GNP, and it helps tag countries that could use our help. We identify those, go to them and offer them a massive capital investment, plus political advice, security, whatever they need. In return we take custody of their bioinfrastructure. We also have access to their labor' (1994: 86). Praxis seeks such a partnership with Mars, participating in a conference that writes a declaration of the principles shared by Mars' settlers and upon which the new constitution will be based when Mars declares its independence from Earth. These principles not only assert human rights, autonomy and diversity and the common stewardship of 'land, air, and water', effectively outlawing capitalism, but also Mars' own 'rights of place', mandating environmental respect and 'a spirit of reverence for this planet and for the scarcity of life in the universe' (389–390).

Blue Mars (1996) works through the difficulties of writing and enforcing the constitution and retaining independence. Various political factions eventually accept compromise, mediation and a collective vision as the best way for all to achieve their goals. Ann and Sax, who along with others of the First Hundred have survived into this period thanks to longevity treatments, are reconciled into a new brown politics that combines aspect of the earlier Red and Green positions. Humans, bioengineered to have a higher carbon dioxide tolerance, can now live openly in the terraformed atmosphere. On Earth, environmental devastation has provided an opportunity to rebuild social, economic and political structures so as to produce a more just society. An economic history written in this future argues that history is the dialectical interaction of residual and emergent systems: *'capitalism was … composed of clashing elements in the residual feudalism, and an emergent future order that was only now being defined in their own time, which Charlotte called democracy'* (1996: 482). Despite emerging more or less simultaneously, capitalism and democracy were ideologically opposed, as is evident from the way that capitalist democracy 'was able to turn so quickly into the metanational system, in which democracy grew ever weaker and capitalism ever stronger. In which one percent of the population owned half of the wealth, and five percent of the population owned ninety-five percent of the wealth' (143). Mars is now the location where humans can observe *'some emergent aspects of an order beyond democracy – one that could not be fully characterized yet, as it had never existed, but which Charlotte ventured to call Harmony, or General Goodwill'* (483).

Conclusion

- Although SF magazine circulation declined further in this period, the audience for SF in other media expanded massively. The growing influence of non-print media in shaping SF was acknowledged by authors who situated their fiction in relation to SF film, television, comics and music.
- Major SF traditions, such as space opera, were revitalised, their renewal emphasised by a foregrounded intertextuality that signalled self-reflexive confidence about developing and deploying generic material.
- The normatively heterosexual and patriarchal visions of earlier SF, that could at best imagine a 'colour-blind' future, gave way to a recognition of the importance of gender, race, sexuality and other identities, including those of non-human subjects, in everyday life and imagined worlds.
- Some complained about SF's hybridisation with and dissolution into other genres, but this apparent end of the genre can also be understood as a move towards greater inclusivity. Such enrolments restored SF to the rich mixture of the fantastic that existed before the establishment of genre niches in specialised pulps, and have given SF vast new resources.

10 Possible futures

Overview

In recent years, many critics have argued, whether anxiously or with anticipation, that SF is disappearing, its images diffusing into contemporary culture and the boundaries that once kept it 'pure' and 'separate' eroding. One might see this as a return to a broader tradition of the fantastic that was carved up into niche categories by Hugo Gernsback and other actants; but even if this is the case, that broader tradition has been radically transformed by a century of generic distinctions, in which its component parts have developed in unique ways. It is much too soon to claim any kind of consensus over which texts from the early twenty-first century have been, or will be, successfully enough enrolled to be deemed central to SF even a decade from now. Instead, this final chapter will outline observable trends in contemporary SF under six headings, while recognising that these are contingent groupings and that the texts discussed under one heading could as easily appear under another. It is through such endeavours that the process of enrolment continues.

Changing times

By the start of the twenty-first century, SF's repertoire of images, ideas and techniques are no longer the sole property – if they ever were – of the magazine and paperback tradition, and the genre itself might even be seen as *passé*. This is certainly one implication of 2009's rebranding of the SciFi channel (launched in 1992) as SyFy, a name that phonetically invokes the genre for one audience while downplaying generic affiliations in an attempt to reach a mass audience. SF film is now a mainstay of Hollywood, which seems intent on remaking formerly successful titles with up-to-the-minute effect technologies, many of them simultaneously adaptations of literary sources. Philip K. Dick's fiction, with its pessimism about progress and confusions of reality and virtuality, continues to be both a source and an inspiration. Comic book adaptations have proliferated, with *X-Men* (Singer 2000), *Spider-Man* (Raimi 2002), *Batman Begins* (Nolan 2005), *Fantastic Four* (Story 2005) and *Iron Man* (Favreau 2008) all spawning sequels; adaptations of digital games, such as *Resident Evil* (Anderson 2002) and its sequels, have also been financially successful. The importance to global entertainment industries of

The influence of Philip K. Dick on cinema

Dick film adaptations	Dickian films
Blade Runner (Scott 1982)	*They Live* (Carpenter 1988)
Total Recall (Verhoeven 1990)	*Dark City* (Proyas 1998)
Confession d'un Barjo (Boivin 1992)	*eXistenZ* (Cronenberg 1999)
Screamers (Duguay 1995)	*Avalon* (Oshii 2001)
Impostor (Fleder 2001)	*Donnie Darko* (Kelly 2001)
Minority Report (Spielberg 2002)	*Cypher* (Natali 2002)
Paycheck (Woo 2003)	*Eternal Sunshine of the Spotless Mind* (Gondry 2004)
A Scanner Darkly (Linklater 2006)	*Renaissance* (Volckman 2006)
Next (Tamahori 2007)	*Mock-up on Mu* (Baldwin 2008)
The Adjustment Bureau (Nolfi 2011)	*Inception* (Nolan 2010)

building SF franchises around cross-marketable titles is perhaps best demonstrated by *AVP: Aliens vs. Predator* (Anderson 2004), based on a game which was in turn based on a comic which brought together two film franchises, both of which had only ever been moderately successful financially; it not only prompted a sequel, *AVPR: Alien vs. Predator – Requiem* (Strause brothers 2007), but also returns to the original individual franchises, with *Predators* (Antal 2010) and with Ridley Scott announcing his intention to make prequels to *Alien* (Scott 1979). Blockbusters – the *Star Wars* prequels (Lucas 1999, 2002, 2005), *Avatar* (Cameron 2009), *Tron: Legacy* (Kosinski 2010) – continue to push technical achievements, while more modestly budgeted films – *CSA: The Confederate States of America* (Willmott 2004), *Primer* (Carruth 2004), *Special* (Haberman/Passmore 2006) and *Moon* (Jones 2009) – have succeeded not least as social commentary.

Perhaps the most significant political event of the decade was the terrorist attacks on the US on September 11, 2001. Cast by some as a rupture in history, it heightened paranoia about enemies hidden within and provoked a discourse about irreconcilable ideological differences that ignored the ongoing economic inequities that drive much of the discontent with the present world order. Protests against the organisations governing the global economy gained great momentum with the demonstrations at the G8 summits in Seattle (1999) and Genoa (2001), but the so-called War on Terror, including US-led invasions and occupations of Afghanistan and Iraq, has largely succeeded in making such issues less visible. A sense of aftermath preoccupies much subsequent SF, including *Lost* (2004–2010), *Doctor Who* (2005–) and *Heroes* (2006–2010), and there has been a rise of apocalyptic visions, often inflected by the Christian Right's sensibility that grew in political influence after George W. Bush's controversial 2000 election. Near-future fictions about high-tech terrorist attacks, often with nuclear or biological weapons, have proliferated, some overtly science-fictional, such as *Jericho* (2006–2008) and Brian D'Amato's *In the Courts of the Sun* (2009), others more marginally so, such as *24* (2001–2010). John Birmingham's *Axis of Time* trilogy (2004–2006) and Eric Flint's *1632* series (2000–) replay aspects of American history and reboot the American republic on more egalitarian grounds, while L. Timmel Duchamp's *Marq'ssan Cycle* (2005–2007), Marvel Comics' *Civil War* storyline (2006–2007), Ken MacLeod's *The Execution Channel* (2007) and Cory Doctorow's *Little Brother* (2008) depict increasingly tyrannical curtailments of civil liberties. *Battlestar Galactica* (2003–2009) successfully transformed the camp 1970s series into a dark political drama about living under occupation, enemy infiltration of civilian populations, the use of torture and struggles between church and state. Anxieties about infiltration were expressed through viral narratives – *Survivors* (2008–), Nancy Kress' *Dogs* (2009) and numerous zombie fictions – which are often also related to such real-world viral pandemics as SARS (2002–2003) and H1N1 (2009).

Noting that any genre is a historical phenomenon that is 'bound to its time and must pass with it', Istvan Csicsery-Ronay, Jr wonders whether SF 'is a twentieth-century form so characteristic of it that we may come to view that period as the Science-Fiction Century' (2008: 265–266). In contrast, this chapter will consider six trends in contemporary SF that suggest some possible and promising futures for the genre.

Near futures

Since the end of the Cold War, many feel that it is easier to imagine the end of the world than the end of capitalism. This certainly seems to be true of this period's near-future SF. Kim Stanley Robinson's *Science in the Capital* trilogy (2004–2007) extrapolates from relatively conservative models of global warming a future in which humanity barely, and only provisionally, survives. Gwyneth Jones' *Bold as Love* series (2001–2006) depicts the dissolution of the UK in revolutions and counter-revolutions and the massive reorganisations of social life necessary to survive. In both examples, the only imaginable end of capitalism lies in the approach to the end of the world itself; and the only solutions we are likely to find are 'partial, fucked-up and temporary' (Jones 2001: 82). When the end of the world, or something like it, does come, its cause – whether genetic engineering (Margaret Atwood's *Oryx and Crake* (2003)), a zombie pandemic (Max Brooks' *World War Z* (2006)) or becoming the target of US ire (James Lovegrove's *Untied Kingdom* (2003)) – is frequently connected to global capitalism. While many SF writers merely assume without thinking the perpetuation of capitalism, those novels that do engage with the economics of their future worlds, such as Cory Doctorow's *Down and Out in the Magic Kingdom* (2003), Tricia Sullivan's *Maul* (2004) and David Marusek's *Counting Heads* (2005), typically have a comical or satirical edge. William Gibson retreated from depicting cyberpunk futures, developing his concern with the ongoing commodification of human subjectivity and everyday life in *Pattern Recognition* (2003), which is set several months before its publication.

One of cyberpunk's now rather clichéd legacies is the corporate-dominated dystopia. Paolo Bacigalupi's *The Windup Girl* (2009), set in Thailand, re-enlivens such material by extrapolating from trends in the corporate ownership and engineering of genetic foodstuffs. During the Contraction, oil reserves dried up, global warming caused sea levels to rise and the 'rust plague' devastated genetically-modified monocultures; now, in a new period of expansion, energy is measured in calories and the main power-source is the kinetic energy stored in kink-springs wound by humans or animals. The Ministry of the Environment, which enforces stringent import laws, thus protecting Thailand's people and ecosystem from biological contamination and economic colonisation, is in conflict with the Ministry of Trade, who wish to re-enter the global economy more fully. Anderson Lake, working undercover for AgriGen, is trying to locate Thailand's seedbank, one of the few remaining sources of uncorrupted genetic material for crops.

Emiko, the windup girl of the title, is an artificial person combining human and animal DNA. Engineered to be submissive and obedient, she was created in Japan, an ageing country that needs young workers, but abandoned in Thailand, where such technology is illegal, because it was cheaper for her owner to replace her than to ship her home with him. She found shelter, of sorts, with Raleigh, a pimp who also makes her perform nightly in abusive sex shows. Should she, the novel asks, be considered an unnatural threat like GM crops that force out indigenous species, or the genetically engineered Cheshire cats, that have displaced other cats, devastating bird and rodent populations with wide-reaching ecosystem consequences? Should such beings be regarded as natural, part of a continually evolving ecology that now includes human technoscientific interventions? Or are they all merely vermin? Emiko has been taught that she should eschew her animal appetites and embrace 'the civilized self' that 'knows the difference between niche and animal urge' (2009: 154). While the novel's ecological sentiments support this idea, it is also painfully aware that 'natural' humans do not respect this distinction.

This bleak vision, however, is not without elements of hope. Emiko learns to use her superior speed and strength to rebel against the men who hurt her (with unforeseen consequences for all of Thailand). When Jaidee, a fiercely incorruptible Ministry of Environment officer, takes revenge on the conspirators who murdered his wife, the Ministry of Trade are able to destroy their rival agency and gain political power. However, Jaidee's example inspires Kanya, a Ministry of Trade agent placed as his second-in-command, to defy her masters. She aids the monks guarding the seedbank to flee with it, dispersing it throughout the country, rather than capitulate to Western hegemony. *The Windup Girl* envisions a complexly overdetermined world in which individual decisions, as well as the constraints of capitalist socio-economic structures, can produce unexpected outcomes: as Gibbons, an outlaw genetic engineer, tells Emiko, 'nothing about you is inevitable' (358). As the novel ends, US expansionism has failed, at least in Thailand, at least for a time, and suddenly the defeated Ministry of

Environment's 'white shirts, so despised and disgraced just days before, are every-where' (355).

In contrast, Robert Charles Wilson's *Julian Comstock* (2009) contains no trace of cyberpunk. Following the collapse produced by the 'Years of Vice and Profligacy' (2009: 18) under the 'Efflorescence of Oil' (20), America, now extending from the pole to the equator, has reverted to feudalism. The novel is presented as Adam Hazzard's memoir of his friendship with Julian Comstock between 2172 and 2175. President Deklan Comstock, fearing that his nephew might challenge his rule, places Julian in situations of increasing danger in the war against Mitteleuropa for control of the newly extant Northwest Passage, increasingly important since global warming enabled agriculture to expand northwards. Julian survives, returns a war hero and displaces Deklan before being undone by the extent of the reforms he pursues.

Adam is a naïve and thus unreliable narrator, failing even to realise that Julian is gay. Wilson manipulates Adam's perspective to reveal the gulf that can lie between political rhetoric and reality. For example, although Adam believes America to be democratic, it is obviously an absolutist, theocratic state. Indentured labour is regarded as patriotic, since it emerged during the economic collapse when landowners realised that even though they could not pay to have their crops harvested, destitute people would labour in exchange for food and shelter. The landowners subsequently formed the hereditary aristocracy that now governs the US through their workers' proxy votes. Three branches of government remain, but they are now the Executive, the Military and the Dominion, which licenses valid Christian denominations, punitively taxes other sects and stamps out heresy. A version of the Bill of Rights persists, but it is concerned with 'Freedom of Pious Assembly', 'Freedom of Acceptable Speech' (119) and the right 'to worship at any church we please, as long as it's a genuine Christian congregation and not some fraudulent or satanistic set' (24). Wilson satirises 'War on Terror' rhetoric and the influence of the Christian Right in contemporary America: in the 'battle between Good and Evil', Adam explains, 'What was good was full ownership of North America by its natural masters; and what was evil was the claim of "territorial interest" advanced by that ungodly commonwealth of nations known as Mitteleuropa' (82).

Julian, a rebellious freethinker, believes in evolution rather than creationism. As president, he challenges the power of the Dominion, which he considers responsible for most of the excesses and inequities of his realm. He sees god as conscience rather than a supernatural entity: 'Conscience isn't the mean-spirited overseer so many people seem to think it is. Genuine Conscience speaks to all people in all tongues, and it can do so because it has just a few simple things to say: "Love your neighbor as your brother," and do all that that entails – visit the sick, refrain from beating wives and children, don't murder people for profit, etc.' (373). However, his legislative efforts to curtail the Dominion's power, and his refusal to send troops to crush a workers' uprising, ensure another coup. The novel ends quite pessimistically, with religious intolerance and class privilege proving frighteningly tenacious.

Hard SF

Eight years after editing *The Ascent of Wonder* (1994), the first anthology to map out the evolution of hard SF from the nineteenth century, through the magazine-and-paperback tradition to the early 1990s, David G. Hartwell and Kathryn Cramer note in *The Hard SF Renaissance* (2002) that hard SF has suddenly become fashionable. They attribute this largely to British boom authors who shifted hard SF's political orientation, emphasising the political and social contexts and consequences of scientific and technological developments. For example, Paul J. McAuley's *White Devils* (2004) depicts a future Africa, subjected once more to Western colonialism as multinational corporations plunder its biodiversity for commodifiable genetic materials. However, this shift was not restricted to British authors. In Peter Watts' *Starfish* (1999), psychologically-damaged individuals bio-engineered to maintain the machinery drawing power from a deep-sea hyper-thermal vent discover ßehemoth, a primeval template for life more efficient at absorbing nutrients than the template that populates the surface world. The *Rifters* trilogy (2001–2005) charts the transformation of the biosphere once ßehemoth finds its way out of the ocean depths. In Julie E. Czerneda's *Species Imperative* series (2004–2006), biologist Mackenzie Connor uses her expertise to understand the evolution of a region of space called the Chasm and to fight the destructive advance of the alien Dhryn. Only her comprehension of the relationship among species, ecosystems and migratory routes enables her to save the Earth and assist the Dhryn in disconnecting biological imperatives from political structures. Among the many movements and manifestoes of recent years, one of the most intriguing was Geoff Ryman's 2002 call for a 'Mundane SF', which urged authors to reject the unlikely SF fantasies (faster-than-light travel, parallel universes) that imply that the Earth is something disposable that humankind could escape from once it has been used up and made uninhabitable. Mundane SF would instead focus on plausible science and real-world problems, such as climate change, species' extinction and the imminent end of oil, and through this self-discipline restore a sense of wonder to encountering new ideas. *When It Changed* (2009), edited by Ryman, presents the results of a related project to encourage writers to develop new stories from discussions with scientists about their current research in nanotechnology, particle physics, genomics, imaging, computer science, neuroscience, astrophysics, climate adaptation and artificial photosynthesis.

Anna Senoz, the protagonist of Gwyneth Jones' *Life* (2004), is modelled in part on Barbara McClintock, the female geneticist who discovered transposition (the jumping of controlling genes from one part of the chromosome to another), but whose research was ignored for 15 years. Anna is a self-possessed, dedicated and intelligent undergraduate studying genetics. On the fast track to a brilliant career, she is diverted and derailed by the structural and institutional sexism she encounters, both as a female scientist and as a researcher into human genetic difference. Each person normally has two sex chromosomes: females usually two X chromosomes, males usually one X and one Y chromosome. Anna's work uncovers a process in which parts of the Y chromosome jump to the X chromosome, enabling XX males to be fertile. She predicts that this will result in the elimination of the Y chromosome and a future in which all humans will have two X chromosomes. Jones is careful to insist that this chromosomal change does not necessarily or inevitably mean that all humans will become androgynous. Nevertheless, Anna's research is controversial 'Because it's about sex, and that means trouble. ... There are significant people in life science who would react very poorly, although they'd never admit they were personally upset about the daft "death of the male chromosome" aspect' (2004: 206).

Anna struggles with cultural expectations about gender in her personal life as well as in her work. She and Spence start a relationship on the rational grounds that the best way to enjoy sex and avoid disease is to pursue monogamy with a partner one likes. She is unaware that he feels diminished by this loss of romance, as if 'his birthright was being ripped from him' (37). She is also unaware of the degree to which she has internalised sexist ideas, blaming herself for being raped by a lab partner who misinterpreted her behaviour for a sexual invitation. She feels that

> he'd done nothing specially terrible. It was Anna who had been unforgivably careless. She had answered him back in seminars, making him feel she was a challenge.... She had let him touch her shoulder, squeeze her waist, so he would do the work: imagining she was being clever. To Charles it was as if she'd been saying *please fuck me*. And he had.
>
> (81)

Reunited some years after university, Anna and Spence marry, but it is not until he almost has an affair with a woman who embodies all the stereotypes of female dependence eschewed by Anna, that she realises that affect and cultural heritage shape human sexual behaviour in ways that exceed reason. She eventually comes to understand human sexuality as a kind of power relationship that is only partly to do with personal choice, and that it is so essential to Western constructions of humanity that it shapes everyone, including herself, in often unacknowledged ways.

Some welcome Anna's Transferred Y findings, such as the self-proclaimed Transformationists who have been experimenting with gender roles and sexual diversity and who claim 'We knew what was happening, we were *living it*. But you've given us ... a *rationale*. A scientific explanation' (349). However, Anna insists that 'there is *no* straightforward match between variations in chromosomal sex and the behavior of the individual' (304). Rigorous in its portrayal of scientific research, *Life* is equally exacting in its insistence on the complex, nonlinear relationship between scientific facts and the cultural and political systems built upon them. Its incisive treatment of gender extends the critical vision of feminist SF.

Greg Egan's *Schild's Ladder* (2001) is similarly concerned with the relationship between science and the social world. It explores what it would mean to be human if humanity were able to relate to the quantum mechanics that govern the subatomic scale of the universe rather than remain trapped in the phenomenological experience of the Newtonian physics of the observable, macroscopic scale. Some 20,000 years in the future, humans have long since moved out into the galaxy. Interstellar travel is now achieved by encoding the self as information to be transmitted across space; when the signal is received at its destination, the information can either be uploaded into a virtual construct or downloaded into a physical body. Some people prefer to be entirely acorporeal, rejecting physical embodiment as mere nostalgia. Regularly updated digital backups of the self produce a kind of immortality in which the local death of any single instantiation of self is at most an inconvenience.

Since the twenty-first century, physics has been understood in terms of Sarumpaet rules of Quantum Graph Theory, which reconcile general relativity and quantum mechanics mathematically to explain the underlying structure of reality. (Although QGT is Egan's invention, an appendix notes that loop quantum gravity, from which he derived it, is an ongoing research field.) An experiment intended to verify QGT unintentionally creates a novo-vacuum, whose front, expanding at half the speed of light, is consuming the physical universe. The novel follows the efforts of scientists, 600 years later, to understand and possibly intervene in this phenomenon. The Yielder faction contends that it should not be feared, but examined, explored and, if possible, inhabited under new conditions of embodiment. The Preservationists argue that, although inhabited planets in the novo-vacuum's path can be evacuated, the loss of specific physical locations is a tragedy and that therefore, even if the novo-vacuum contains life, it should be stopped or destroyed.

Egan uses this scenario to explore questions of embodiment, identity and permanence. The humans of this era, aware of the relationship between quantum physics and the observer, have installed quantum processors, Qusps, in their brains that isolate consciousness from the physical world during any calculation, 'a condition lasting just microseconds at a time, but rigidly enforced for the duration – only breaking quarantine when its state vector described *one outcome*' (2001: 17), thus producing humans that are, for the first time, what they 'they'd believed themselves to be for most of their history: a creature of choice, capable of doing *one thing and not another*' (18). Anachronaut remnants of pre-Qusp civilisation 'still chugged between the stars in spluttering contraptions, … taking thousands of years for every journey' (52). The posthumans amuse themselves by telling the anachronauts wild stories about social developments while they were in suspended animation, emphasising the 'eternal struggle between men and women' (99), a topic that obsesses anachronauts. The truth is, however, that gender has long ago disappeared and that otherwise neuter humans generate new and novel genitals through chemical and biological feedback between mutually attracted individuals. The anachronauts are profoundly xenophobic, and when evidence of extremely small-scale life is found in the novo-vacuum, they advocate complete and immediate annihilation since anything so alien can only be planning the same for them.

The title refers to a mathematical process – described to a child concerned that as he grows up he will change into someone else – by which one can map the path necessary to carry an arrow across a curved surface, such as a planet, and ensure that it is pointing in the same direction when one arrives at the destination. This involves ensuring that at each point en route the arrow is parallel to its previous position; but, as the child's father explains, a different route will produce a different map. One will

> never stop changing, but that doesn't mean you have to drift in the wind. Every day, you can take the person you've been and the new things you've witnessed and make your own, honest choice as to who you should become.
>
> (184)

In the quantum space of the novo-vacuum, decoherence – which collapses the hesitation between quantum states into one perceivable outcome – is a much weaker force, enabling multiple quantum potentialities to exist simultaneously. Only some humans are able to adjust to the radically different embodiment this involves, others to return to ordinary space, to reconnect with kinds of embodiment that are more obviously *Homo sapiens'* heritage. Neither is the wrong or lesser choice.

Singularity fiction

Schild's Ladder might also be considered a singularity fiction, a kind of SF that extends cyberpunk's fascination with digital consciousness and mutable embodiment. The 'singularity' refers to the point at which technological change becomes so accelerated that it is impossible to predict what will happen next or to understand the lives of those entities that exist after it. In more paranoid scenarios, machines not only become sentient but also see humankind as an impediment to their own future; or perhaps worse, they so far surpass their creators as to render humankind irrelevant even in their own eyes. The concept was first popularised by computer scientist and SF writer Vernor Vinge's influential essay, 'The Coming Technological Singularity' (1993); more recently, Ray Kurzweil's *The Singularity Is Near* (2005) champions a future in which humans, augmented by intelligent machines, can exceed the limitations of nature. Much SF has been rather sceptical about the prospect, including Ken MacLeod's *The Cassini Division* (2000), Ted Chiang's 'Liking What You See: A Documentary' (2002), Alastair Reynolds' *Revelation Space* series (2000–2007) and Elizabeth Bear's *Jacob's Ladder* trilogy (2008–2011).

Singularity fiction often focuses on the interpenetrations of globalised capital and information networks. In Karl Schroeder's *Permanence* (2002), the Rights Economy literally maps capitalist ideology onto perceptions of the material world through a neural interface that tags all objects with information indicating ownership and value, making 'it appear that the essence of things is money – that a thing only really exists if it can be bought or sold' (2002: 223). Vernor Vinge's *Rainbow's End* (2006), dedicated to 'the Internet-based cognitive tools that are changing our lives – Wikipedia, Google, eBay, and the others of their kind', features a digitisation project intended to make information from the 'whole premodern world' (344) up to 2000 AD widely available. However, the scanning process destroys the physical books, meaning that publicly-owned libraries will be superseded by private, for-profit ownership of the digital texts. In *Makers* (2009), Cory Doctorow (who is active in the OpenSource, Copyleft and Creative Commons movements that resist the privatisation of knowledge by granting liberal copyright permissions to use, remix and share creative works) imagines the collapse of the American economy and its innovative reinvention by hacker designers.

Charles Stross' *Accelerando* (2005) traces the evolution of the human into the posthuman by focusing on Manfred Macx and his family. Manfred is a prodigy of the new digital age. Continually tied into the Net through external augmentations that seem like parts of himself, he inhabits a kind of cash-free, gift economy. Each chapter, set in consecutive decades of the twenty-first century, introduces techno-logical innovations that enable the rise of digital consciousness, which is linked to both a new economic order and a new kind of human identity. When the neural pathways of lobsters are uploaded in experiments on digital consciousness transfer, the emergent consciousness asks for his help in being transmitted offworld; repre-senting them, he insists that they must be treated as labour rather than software: 'Leave uploads covered by copyrights not civil rights and where will we be in fifty years?' (2006: 101).

Manfred's daughter, Amber, heads a space expedition to investigate the origin of what seems to be a message from another sentient race. Her crew debate whether there is such a thing as the singularity, whether this 'rapture of the nerds' (190) has happened and, if so, when. They discover a system of routers that are able to transfer uploaded consciousnesses across the galaxy, and send versions of themselves through it. Among their discoveries is 'a life-form [that] is an incredi-bly ornate corporate ecosphere, legal instruments breeding and replicating' that 'mug[s] passing sapients and use them as currency' (249). It has dismantled the physical mass of its solar system to produce a vast computing network that enables an exponentially larger number of consciousnesses to exist as uploads than could be supported in material bodies on planets, but is trapped there by bandwidth limitations.

Returning to our solar system, Amber's crew find several planets already dis-mantled in this manner and Earth a dying biosphere polluted by out-of-control nanotechnology. *Homo sapiens* are being made obsolete by 'self-aware corpora-tions. The phrase "smart money" has taken on a whole new meaning, for the collision between international business law and neurocomputing technology has given rise to a whole new family of species – fast-moving corporate carnivores in the net' (251). The economy evolves into Economics 2.0, which proceeds at a speed and complexity impossible for even posthumans to comprehend, leaving Amber in backwater poverty that is nonetheless unimaginable luxury compared to the lives of most humans throughout history.

Justina Robson's *Natural History* (2003) is similarly interested in the long-term evolution of the human species and the implications of shifting embodiment and digital environments. The solar system is divided between the Unevolved, unmodi-fied humans who have remained on Earth and at the top of the social hierarchy, and the Forged, beings raised in virtual environments whose cyborg bodies are designed to exist in a variety of off-Earth environments and to perform particular kinds of labour. Some of the Forged challenge the Unevolveds' innate sense of superiority and their right to goven.

Following an encounter with an alien artefact, which seems to give her a means of instantaneous travel across galactic distances, the Forged explorer Isol discovers a new planet, orbiting the star Zia Di Notte more than 27 light years from Earth (although it might in fact be much further away). She wishes to claim it as a home-land for the Forged, somewhere they can live free from Unevolved domination and liberate themselves from the engineered destiny of form matching function. Cultural anthropologist Zephyr is sent to investigate whether there is alien life on the planet, while others examine the Stuff that provided Isol's new propulsion system. Defying conventional description or categorisation, the Stuff seems to be a kind of collective consciousness that exists in 11-dimensional space, not a tech-nology as such but an ever-changing entity that 'responds to sentient intent. It can change its structure according to whatever purpose the observer has in mind. It doesn't require anything like a specific design. It makes itself into the right tool for the right job' (2004: 237). The Stuff absorbs those who interact with it; as the Forged Corvax tries to explain, 'It's like a technology that's eaten people and they're still alive inside it, but they're all one, or none, or else ... it reacts to the observer' (302, original ellipsis).

The focus of the novel thus alternates between political struggles. Are the Forged slaves to be emancipated? How far should they go to emancipate them-selves? Do they need, and should they have, a homeland? And if so, is this new world it? – and question about the nature of identity – is it a kind of death to be absorbed into the Stuff? Why is it that the Stuff will absorb Unevolved and Forged but not AIs? What significance does this distinction hold? Isol desperately resists what she fears will be the erasure of her self, but others claim that absorption by the Stuff is an expansion of self:

> I am Tom Corvax. And there is no 'I' – there is a greater mind, a superposition of all minds that have ever entered this state of being Stuff. These two states exist simultaneously because the mind that is Tom is here, made of this body, but the matter of this body is a part of a greater ocean of matter interpenetrated by the minds of the others who live within imaginary time, volumeless and occupying the whole universe.
>
> (347)

The planet Isol discovered 'was the home of the "First to Translate Into Other Space"' (349), preserved as a library so that the disembodied beings do not forget their origins. A reconciliation between beings and their tools, the Stuff promises to heal the rift between Unevolved and Forged by enabling all humans to function without being trapped in a particular form. For Zephyr, it represents an opportunity not merely to study different lives but to live in 'a universe of history and life, living it all, from every angle' (369).

Engaging with histories

Interest in how the past produces the future, and in the difficulty of imagining futures that consist of anything other than endless capitalism, wars and environmental degradation, have seen a substantial increase in alternate histories and other fiction that combines elements of SF and historical fiction. In Kim Stanley Robinson's *The Years of Rice and Salt* (2002), bubonic plague eradicates 99 per cent of the European population in the early fifteenth century, producing a world without the influence of Christianity and European culture. Michael Chabon's murder mystery, *The Yiddish Policeman's Union* (2007), is set in a Jewish State established in Alaska in 1941 whose lease is about to expire, returning the land to US control. In contrast to such major historical divergences, Kathleen Ann Goonan's *In War Times* (2007) presents a world subtly different from our own 1940s, 1950s and 1960s, in which a blend of quantum physics and genetics might radically alter the human propensity for violence. Neal Stephenson's *Baroque Cycle* (2003–2004) is a historical romp set in the seventeenth and eighteenth centuries, its major science-fictional characteristic being its anachronistic perspective, which imagines the development of mercantile capital as the emergence of an information technology. Connie Willis' *Blackout* (2010) and *All Clear* (2010) follows a group of mid-twenty-first-century historians who conduct primary research by visiting the past – here, the London Blitz – to add detail and texture to the historical record by living among the 'contemps'. The twenty-fourth-century, time-travelling cyborgs of Kage Baker's *Company* series (1997–2010) snatch valuable artefacts before they are, according to the historical record, destroyed and hide them where they can be 'discovered' in the future. In contrast to such fastidious efforts at historical accuracy, Cherie Priest's *Boneshaker* (2009) happily acknowledges the 'particularly grievous and shameless warping of history, geography, and technology' (2009: 415) necessary to produce a steampunk romp about zombies and dirigibles.

Jo Walton's *Farthing* (2006), *Ha'penny* (2007) and *Half a Crown* (2008) are set in a Britain that made peace with Hitler, withdrawing from the war in 1941. Fascism dominates Europe, and anti-Semitism is an accepted part of daily life. Although Britons generally frown upon such extremes as labour camps, many of those who realise their full import are complacent about it. Beyond this alternative reality, there is nothing science-fictional about the novels, which read like period crime fiction not only in terms of being set in the past but also of their indebtedness to such authors as Agatha Christie and Dorothy L. Sayers. Each novel contains two narrative strands that work to evoke the experience of ethical individuals struggling to find their way in a morally ambiguous world: a first-person account by a female narrator involved in the events being investigated; and a third-person account of the investigation by Peter Carmichael, who during the course of series is promoted from Scotland Yard inspector to head of the newly-formed Watch, a British version of the Gestapo.

Farthing, set in 1949, concerns the murder of a relatively liberal aristocrat, James Thirkie, in the Farthing family's country house. It is eventually revealed to be part of a conspiracy by British fascists to secure a vote of no confidence in the Prime Minister. He is replaced by their own Mark Normanby, who manipulates popular fears of Bolshevism to impose political reforms that erode the democratic institutions of government and concentrate increased power in the Prime Minister – a manoeuvre that recalls Hitler's own ascendancy under democratic forms that were then replaced by dictatorial structures and is perhaps a critique of the extensions of executive power by recent US presidents.

Farthing's female narrator is Lucy, the Farthings' daughter, who renounced her heritage to marry Jewish David Kahn. David served during the war with her brother, who was killed. Lucy accepts that they were also lovers, although the regime condemns homosexuality and bisexuality. Through David's influence she has begun to realise the monstrous intolerance of her family and their circle:

> I might have carried on thinking all these people were basically good people, with odd little quirks perhaps, but I'd never have understood how foul they were. David took the blinkers off me and I've never been sorry, because who would want to go around in a world that's like a very thin strip of pretty flower garden surrounded by fields and fields of stinking manure that stretch out as far as the eye can see?
>
> (2006: 74)

David is slow to realise the danger he faces. When a Jewish refugee from the continent warns him that his good citizenship will ultimately count for nothing as the tide of fascism rises, he insists that 'she's wrong about England. People care about liberty and justice, and there's resentment, but not that buried hatred. That kind of thing would never happen here' (234). Neither he nor Lucy is able to guess the depth of her family's hatred, never suspecting that they were invited to the weekend party specifically to frame David for Thirkie's murder and thus inflame anti-Semitic feeling.

Carmichael uncovers the truth, and helps Lucy and David to escape to Canada, but his findings are suppressed and a Bolshevik is framed for Thirkie's murder. His superiors, who have hitherto overlooked his circumspect homosexuality, use this knowledge to leverage his silence and his cooperation in the creation of the Watch. As *Farthing* ends, Carmichael remembers that he used to wonder how the Gestapo 'could live with themselves and do some of the things they were to do. Now he knew' (317).

Larissa Lai's *Salt Fish Girl* (2002) mixes SF with historical fiction and folkloric fantasy, alternating between China in the late-nineteenth and early-twentieth centuries and the mid-twenty-first-century American Pacific Northwest. The novel begins with Nu Wa, an aquatic immortal, creating beings from the mud of the Yellow River. When they laugh at her, she dashes them to the ground, their injuries producing either a bifurcated tail or legs. To compensate for these injuries, she invents erotic pleasure, which she later connects to sexual reproduction, itself a compensation for sickness and death. Nu Wa is swallowed by a woman and born in nineteenth-century China. In adolescence, she falls for the daughter of a salt fish vendor, who disapproves of their illicit love. Nu Wa flees with the Salt Fish Girl, but life in the impoverished margins of the city strains their relationship. The Salt Fish Girl, working for a pittance in a toy factory, falls sick. Nu Wa goes to buy medicine, but an English woman lures her to the Island of Mist and Forgetfulness, which seems to be in both the sky and the future and where time works differently. When she returns to China, the Salt Fish Girl is an old woman who barely recognises her. Nu Wa visits her family, who pretend she is her brother's daughter and marry her to the elderly brother of the Salt Fish Girl in order to preserve a lucrative business relationship that has developed between the families. When Nu Wa dies, she returns to the water and is taken up by a durian tree.

This fantastical-historical narrative alternates with the more conventional SF story of Miranda in a corporate-feudalist future. On the night Miranda was conceived, her mother ate a durian fruit grown in the Unregulated Zone without a corporate seal of approval, and from birth a weird smell – like cat urine or a durian – has emanated from Miranda's skin. As she grows up, her father seeks cures from traditional Chinese medicine and the labs of a rival corporation. Rumours begin to circulate about other children with similar symptoms. The Contagion, as it is known, appears to be absorbed from the ground through bare soles, and there are '*some who believe these symptoms to be peculiar to a new breed of auto-immune diseases, related to genetic and other industrial modifications to our food supply, that may prove quite devastating in the decades to come*' (2002: 69).

After Miranda and her family are evicted from Saturna corporation's Serendipity enclave, she starts to encounter a familiar-seeming girl, Evie, but can never quite fathom from where she knows her. It becomes clear that Evie and Miranda are versions of the Salt Fish Girl and Nu Wa. Although this reincarnation is primarily the stuff of fantasy and myth, a potential – but at best partial – scientific rationale is hinted at by the two women's origins. Human genes have been implanted in durian fruit 'as fertility therapy for women who could not conceive', but these trees cross pollinated with others 'bred for other purposes – trees bred to withstand cold climates, trees bred to produce fruit that would strengthen the blood' (258). It is perhaps through the fruit of one of these wild trees that Nu Wa entered Miranda's mother. Evie, on the other hand, is one of the 'Sonia' series of clones. Years earlier, the corporations took over the Diverse Genome Project 'focused on the peoples of the so-called Third World, Aboriginal peoples, and people in danger of extinction', and thus all cloned workers have 'brown eyes and black hair, every single one' (160), embodying the North–South and ethnic divisions between varieties of labour in our own world. The Sonia clones are part fish, their DNA 'point zero three per cent *Cyprinus carpio* – freshwater carp', making them a 'patented new fucking life form' (158) and not, technically, human. Consequently, the few remaining legal protections for labour do not apply to them. However, since clones are not supposed to be sufficiently intelligent to resent their circumstances, Evie's choice of a name other than Sonia is a potent symbol of her rebellion. The novel ends with a further evasion of capitalist-patriarchal control over women's bodies, as Evie gives birth to a daughter.

Globalised SF

Cyberpunk was criticised for exoticising and denying subjectivity to non-Western peoples, particularly the Japanese, and ignoring large parts of the world, such as Africa and Latin America. More recently, Fredric Jameson described Bruce Sterlings and William Gibson's subsequent fiction as 'global tourism' SF (2005: 385), a phrase that captures their fuller engagement with, yet persistent distance from, other cultures. In this vein, Jon Courtenay Grimwood's *Arabesk* series (2001-2003) reworks cyberpunk in the twenty-first-century North Africa of an alternate world in which WWI ended in 1915 and the Ottoman Empire survived; and Ian McDonald's *River of Gods* (2004), *Brasyl* (2007) and *The Dervish House* (2010) imagine the impact of new technologies in near-future India, Brazil and Turkey. Alongside such work, more and more foreign-language SF is appearing in English translation. Wesleyan University Press' *Early Classics of Science Fiction* have published critical editions of new translations of Jules Verne, Albert Robida and other non-Anglophone authors, and Black Coat Press numerous never-before translated works by Robida, J.H. Rosny-aîné, Maurice Renard and other French authors. Translations of contemporary Japanese SF are available from Haikasoru and Kurodahan, and in 2010 the Science Fiction and Fantasy Translation Awards were launched. Perhaps most significant, though, is the growing visibility of SF by diasporic peoples and peoples of colour, including Aliette de Bodard, Tananarive Due, Nalo Hopkinson, Anthony Joseph, Rushir Joshi, Nnedi Okorafor, Nisi Shawl and Vandana Singh. Rimi B. Chatterjee's *Signal Red* (2005) depicts a near-future India of increasingly belligerent Hindu nationalism and geopolitical ambition. In an isolated, high-security compound, Gopal Chandran, a scientist working on 'novel glass applications', including 'nano-wires, photonic computing, various kinds of shields and sensors' (2005: 16), finally begins to question the ethics of conducting research that will lead to military applications. Walter Mosley's *Futureland* (2001) collects nine stories set in a dystopian future in which the un-employed, known as White Noise, are subject to an endless boredom that under-lines the meaninglessness of their lives. In 'The Nig in Me', a white supremacist group's attempt to create a race-specific virus to eradicate peoples of colour leads to the accidental release of a version that kills off everyone without black ancestry; but conflict with 'white' survivors and over resources continues. In 'Whispers in the Dark', Chill sells his organs, including his penis, so as to buy an education for his child-prodigy nephew. Chill's sacrifice is not much different from that of ear-lier African Americans who 'often sold pieces of themselves to the rich in order to give their children a chance' (2001: 22).

Geoff Ryman's *Air* (2004) is set in Kizuldah, a village in Karzistan, one of the last places in the world not yet online. It opens with a test of Air, a wireless net-work service that interfaces directly with the brain, permitting global connectivity without hardware infrastructure. During the test, Chung Mae's mind fuses with that of Mrs Tung, killing the elderly woman and transforming Mae. Recognising the profound changes that Air will mean for Kizuldah, she immediately begins to pre-pare for them, struggling against a traditional, patriarchal hierarchy that discounts her insight. Despite her illiteracy, she uses the internet-connected television in Kizuldah's school to educate villagers on the opportunity Air represents, and globally to extend her local fashion business, selling the traditional embroidery of the Eloi ethnic minority to which she belongs.

The novel explores issues of cultural specificity and hegemony. In order to use educational software, the villagers must overcome their prejudice against its symbol of an owl – which signals knowledge and wisdom to Westerners, but death to Karzistanis. Indeed, this software does bring a kind of death, ending Kizuldah's relative isolation and potentially destroying its way of life. Mae therefore urges the villagers not to be passive victims of a system that will be imposed regardless of their wishes but to seek ways to shape it, to retain Kizuldah's identity through the coming transformation. Her business exemplifies this dual position: she uses inter-active software to understand business plans and thus secure a bank loan, and communications software to display her wares online and communicate with buyers; yet she also ensures that her designs reflect Eloi tradition and identity, thus countering the government's negative stereotypes of her people. There is also a political struggle over whether to adopt the UN format or the corporate-backed Gates format of Air, which will make a crucial difference to future autonomy: 'Did we want big companies, rich men, making the shapes of people's minds?' (2004: 123). Bugsy, Mae's New York buyer, publishes two widely circulated newspaper articles based on their conversations, enabling a rural villager to disseminate her perspective more widely and ensuring the implementation of the UN format.

Like cyberpunk and singularity fiction, *Air* addresses the transformative effects of information technologies and economic globalisation on human social exist-ence, but it significantly decentres the perspective of Western, technological elites. It also complicates the empiricist epistemology underpinning much SF by combin-ing realist speculation about plausible, near-future technologies with fantastic ele-ments that are not merely symbolism. When Mae is imprisoned, she escapes by using the power of her mind to seize 'reality, as she herself had been seized, and very simply, very easily, [rip] the metal of the fence apart' (214). By the novel's end, technology itself seems to have become equally magical: Mae gives birth from her stomach to a damaged but viable son. Courtesy of Air, he will 'not need to see, for we can all see for [him], and sights and sounds will pass through to [him] from us', he 'will not need hands, for [his] mind will control the machines, and they will be as hands' and despite his ruined ears he 'will hear more in one hour than we heard in all of our lifetimes' (389). This strange but happy baby signifies a future in which we might all be hopeful monsters.

Nalo Hopkinson's *Midnight Robber* (2000) blends myth and history with SF, challenging and rewriting the Western cultural forms that have shaped the genre's visions of technology and the future. Combining English with Jamaican and Trinidadian creole, it intersperses an account of protagonist Tan-Tan's life with sections that transform her experience into folklore. As a young girl, Tan-Tan lives on the planet Toussaint, named after Haitian revolutionary Toussaint L'Ouverture, which was colonised by 'Taino Carib and Arawak; African; Asian; Indian; even the Euro, though some wasn't too happy to acknowledge that-there bloodline' (2000: 18). The colonists celebrate the legend of the Robber King, based on the life of Olaudah Equiano, the son of a noble African family who wrote a famous narrative about his enslavement and became prominent in British abolitionism; on Toussaint, Robber King tales 'always told of escaping the horrors of slavery and making their way into brigandry as a way of surviving in the new and terrible white devils' land in which they'd found themselves' (57). Tan-Tan, in contrast, is obsessed with the related figure of the Robber Queen.

Toussaint has a complex technological infrastructure. An AI called Eshu, after the Yoruba trickster deity, runs the protagonist's household (the computer language is called Eleggua, after an aspect of Eshu). The colony's central AI is called 'Nansi, after another trickster god of West African and Caribbean tradition, or Granny Nanny, after an eighteenth-century Jamaican revolutionary. When Tan-Tan's father, Antonio, is exiled to New Half-Way Tree, an alternative, unterraformed version of Toussaint where there is no advanced technology, he takes her with him. Her life changes radically. The colonisation of Toussaint involved the destruction or modification of many life forms, but on her new world, the Douen, sentient avians, have not been exterminated and the mako-jumbo birds are not a genetically altered and domesticated food source but creatures the size of dinosaurs. Tan-Tan is sexually abused by Antonio, whom she kills on her 16th birthday. Pregnant by him, she goes into exile to avoid execution. She learns from the Douen how to live as part of a cooperative ecosytem and to question the ease with which humans categorise others as people or animals. Visiting outlying communities, she begins to play the role of Robber Queen, challenging injustices and bringing secrets to light in carnivalesque suspensions of conventional authority.

The novel is primarily concerned with Tan-Tan's need to reconcile conflicting aspects of her identity: the 'good' Tan-Tan who obeys authority and thus allows Antonio's abuse, and the 'bad' Tan-Tan who learns from it to distrust and lash out at others. As the Robber Queen, she mediates her 'bad' empowerment through a 'good' sense of justice; but it is not until she confronts the accusation that she is a murderer and reveals her history of abuse that she is able to behave justly towards her self and to love rather than resent her coming child. The resonance this has with those affected by histories of slavery and colonisation are complex, subtle and oblique.

Alternative worlds

James Patrick Kelly and John Kessel argue that 'traditional SF is today broken into pieces' and that if it 'ever had a consistent core, … that time has long since passed' (2009: 16). One of the ways in which actants have responded to this apparent passing is to utilise Bruce Sterling's notion of slipstream fiction, in much the same way as John W. Campbell used *Unknown*, to create a boundary zone between 'real' SF and other fiction that violates, disrupts or refuses hegemonic varieties of literary realism. Other actants have embraced opportunities for boundary-breaking, interstitiality, transgression, hybridity, fusion and mash-up. However it is viewed, such fiction distinguishes itself from earlier and more overtly experimental postmodern metafiction by retaining a commitment to story-telling. Broadly speaking, such fiction is produced by two overlapping groups: those associated with contemporary literary fiction, such as Aimee Bender, Michael Chabon, Rebecca Goldstein, Jonathan Lethem, Steven Millhauser, David Mitchell, Richard Powers and George Saunders, and those with closer ties to genre fiction, such as Ted Chiang, Kelly Link, China Miéville, Benjamin Rosenbaum, Steph Swainston and Jeff VanderMeer. It is affiliated with a number of movements, such as the New Weird, and has been fostered in both SF and literary magazines, including *Conjunctions* (1981–), *The Third Alternative/Black Static* (1994–), *Lady Churchill's Rosebud Wristlet* (1996–) and *McSweeney's Quarterly Concern* (1998–). Although critical discussions have concentrated on prose fiction, one might also enrol a number of films into this tendency, including *Possible Worlds* (Lepage 2000), *A Snake of June* (Tsukamoto 2002), *Time of the Wolf* (Haneke 2003), *Nothing* (Natali 2003), *4* (Khrjanovsky 2005), *The Wild Blue Yonder* (Herzog 2005), *The Bothersome Man* (Lien 2006) and *La Antena* (Sapir 2007).

New Weird fiction

China Miéville, *Perdido Street Station* (2000)

Kelly Link, *Stranger Things Happen* (2001)

Jeff VanderMeer, *City of Saints and Madmen* (2001)

M. John Harrison, *Light* (2002)

K.J. Bishop, *The Etched City* (2003)

Steph Swainston, *The Year of Our War* (2004)

Susanna Clarke, *Jonathan Strange & Mr Norrell* (2004)

Hal Duncan, *Ink* (2006)

Such genre-blurring fiction also exists far beyond the traditional audiences for SF and literary fiction. The *In Death* (1995–) series of mid-twenty-first-century police procedurals by best-selling romance writer Nora Roberts under her J.D. Robb pseudonym, has reached nearly forty volumes, while Michel Faber's *Under the Skin* (2000), a serial killer thriller with an SF rationale, and Kit Whitfield's *Benighted* (2006), a conspiracy thriller set in an alternate reality in which 99 per cent of the population are werewolves, have been critically acclaimed. Joss Whedon successfully blended horror, SF, comedy, teen romance and drama in *Buffy, the Vampire Slayer* (1997–2003) and *Angel* (1999–2004), while his space opera/western *Firefly* (2002–2003) attracted a cult audience. J.J. Abrams' *Lost* (2004–2010) incorporated major SF elements into a prime-time drama that consistently attracted high ratings, prompting numerous other big-budget drama series with fantastic elements.

Shelley Jackson's *Half Life* (2006) is set in an alternative present in which atomic tests produced so many genetic mutations that conjoined twins, or 'twofers', now form a substantial minority of the population. The novel begins as a narrative told by Nora, who wants to be separated from her unconscious twin, Blanche, in an illegal surgical procedure. Nora recounts her life story while she searches for a radical doctor to perform the operation, reflecting on their childhood when Blanche was conscious and they had to learn how to share the body, sometimes as comrades, more often as rivals. Nora includes in her manuscript pages from her 'Siamese Twin Reference Guide', a compilation of newspaper clippings, fliers and other found documents, which conveys the complexities of twofer culture. For example, prosthetics and surgery are available for those who feel that they are truly twofers but were wrongly born into a singleton body, and some regard twofers as sacred, believing

> government forces and no-nuke activists alike have misconstrued the purpose of nuclear testing, which was neither to atone nor prepare for war but to prevent it by engendering a mutant strain of homo sapiens with the capacity to see both sides of an issue at one time.
>
> (2006: 112)

An area of the desert irradiated by nuclear tests is designated as the National Penitence Ground, and the tests themselves are seen as a kind of mourning in which America attacked an image of itself by bombing replicas of American homes and citizens. However, it seems likely that 'The National Penitence activity has not destroyed sadness, but split it from its source. Sadness survives but cannot be understood, except by animals, ghosts, and the body, where it takes the form of disease. What cannot be understood, cannot be cured. The Device refigures sadness by painstakingly crocheting together the knowledge that Penitence had erased and dispersed' (431).

In this way, the title refers both to Nora and Blanch's situation and to the decay of radioactive materials. Nora and Blanche's doubled body is a literalised metaphor for the split consciousness of America, and Nora's refusal to accept Blanche as part of herself becomes an image of America's refusal to accept its responsibility for developing – and using against another nation – weapons whose radioactive by-products and Cold War proliferation cast a dual and deadly shadow over the post-war world. Thus, when Audrey argues against Nora's separation surgery, her words have multiple meanings:

> Actually I *believe* what you told me is that Blanche is in charge of the past and you're in charge of the future, but that's NOT talking. The past is part of the future, you know, which is why you have more in common with Blanche than you want to think, and it might behoove you to get to know her. That's not charity, that's self-preservation. Cutting off your past is like cutting off, I don't know, your own *head*.
>
> (334)

Nora begins to add footnote commentary to the account she is writing, to wonder whether her words represent her own thoughts and to worry that Blanche is altering the text while she is asleep. Nora becomes obsessed with writings and erasures, elaborating strategies to ensure that the text is true, including 'to write what I believe, in such a context of suspicion that it appears to be what I do not believe' and 'to write what I believe, but leave gaps' (353). She concludes that the 'blank spaces aren't just empty' but 'stained with words I've taken back'; thus the 'larger part' of the book, 'like an iceberg's, is invisible' and '*that* is the real book. The words you are actually reading are just a sort of erased erasing, a cautiously omitted omission' (355). She tells herself to consider the possibility that 'Blanche is my invention' or that 'I am Blanche … In which case I am being haunted by my own rejected experience' (373). Images of Venn diagrams organised by Boolean operators have been used throughout the novel to represent various ways of dealing with the experience of duality, encouraging more complex ways of relating to otherness than simple opposition; this is matched by Jackson's refusal to resolve whether the novel represents an alternative world or our world seen through a troubled psyche. *Half Life* is, therefore, simultaneously both SF and not SF.

China Miéville's police procedural *The City & the City* (2009) takes place in a world that is inconsistent with our own in only some details. Inspector Tyador Borlú is a detective in the Extreme Crime Squad in Besźel, a country whose location is unspecified but appears to be in Eastern Europe. His efforts to identify a murdered woman lead him to uncover a far-reaching political conspiracy. However, the novel's appeal has less to do with its narrative than with the presentation of its setting. Initially, some sentences do not seem to make sense, as when Borlú's description of a woman seen in the distance is followed by: 'With a hard start, I realised that she was not on GunterStrász at all, and that I should not have seen her' (2009: 12). Borlú repeatedly uses the verb 'to unsee' and distinguishes between things that are 'in' Besźel, and hence can be seen, and things that are elsewhere – in the twin city of Ul Qoma, which occupies the same physical space as Besźel but is in a separate country. Citizens of both countries are trained from youth to recognise the semiotic distinctions – in dress, comportment, architecture, language, even colour palettes – that keep the city and the city distinct, and to not notice or to promptly unsee things from the other city. When Borlú's investigation takes him across the border to Ul Qoma, he experiences the same physical locations in radically different ways and notices, for example, things that are 'grosstopically close' (66) to his apartment but which he has never before seen.

The solution to the murder seems like it will involve Orciny, a mysterious third city believed by some to exist in the unclaimed, ambiguous spaces between Besźel and Ul Qoma, but this is just a red herring in a rather more ordinary conspiracy. Similarly, Breach, an apparently supernatural agency that invisibly polices the border between the cities, appearing only to punish those who violate the rules of perception and behaviour that separate city from city, is also ultimately revealed to be mundane. Borlú, in Ul Qoma, deliberately breaches the border by shooting the killer, who is just feet away but in Besźel and bound to escape before Borlú can legally enter the other country. Subsequently recruited by Breach, he learns that their 'invisibility' is accomplished by moving in such a way as to never clearly signify whether one is in Besźel or Ul Qoma, thus remaining unseen by the citizens of both.

The murder, it transpires, was related to a foreign corporation's interest in ancient artefacts. When confronted by a Breach agent, the American executive behind it all reveals his contempt for the locals of whichever city, sneering 'What do you think would happen if you provoked my government?' (287). While Besźel and Ul Qoma have been distinguished by their different technological levels, which are explicitly related to the extent of their respective integration into the global economy, the executive's attitude makes it clear that their cultural specificities are irrelevant to capitalism's homogenising drive, concerned only with markets rather than peoples or communities.

Borlú is compelled to join Breach since the border between the city and the city, maintained by 'everyone in Besźel and everyone in Ul Qoma', only

> works because you don't blink. That's why unseeing and unsensing are so vital. No one can admit it doesn't work. So if you don't admit it, it does. But if you breach, even if it's not your fault, for more than the shortest time … you can't come back from that.
>
> (310, original ellipsis)

One might regard *The City & the City* as being beyond the genre of SF, since its bizarre, alternative geography is the product of ideological rather than material difference. However, it also exemplifies the qualities that have always animated the best of the genre, enabling us to see that the material and the ideological always-already permeate each other, that other worlds are always our own.

And once you blink, once you recognise how tenuous is the border between either/or, there is no going back.

Conclusion

- SF is proliferating globally across media. Its images, ideas and techniques are now commonly found outside of traditional venues, while writers who identify strongly with the genre nonetheless draw increasingly on other genres, including literary fiction.
- SF's engagement with science has developed in new ways as the contingency of paradigms and the ideological contexts in which science takes place have been recognised.
- SF's engagement with historical questions and its own history has been accompanied by a growing recognition that there is not a single, true history of the genre but a rich diversity of possible science fictions and experiences of SF.

Works cited

Aldiss, Brian (1975) *Billion Year Spree: The History of Science Fiction*. London: Corgi.

Altman, Rick (1999) *Film/Genre*. London: BFI.

Ashley, Mike (2000) *The Time Machines: The Story of the Science-Fiction Pulp Magazines from the Beginning to 1950*. Liverpool: Liverpool University Press.

Ashley, Mike (2005) *Transformations: The Story of the Science Fiction Magazines from 1950 to 1970*. Liverpool: Liverpool University Press.

Asimov, Isaac (1970) 'Nightfall', in Robert Silverberg (ed.) *The Science Fiction Hall of Fame, volume one*. New York: Doubleday. 112–143.

Asimov, Isaac (2004a) *Foundation*. New York: Bantam Dell.

Asimov, Isaac (2004b) *Foundation and Empire*. New York: Bantam Dell.

Asimov, Isaac (2004c) *Second Foundation*. New York: Bantam Dell.

Asimov, Isaac (2008a) 'Little Lost Robot', *I, Robot*. New York: Bantam. 112–143.

Asimov, Isaac (2008b) 'Runaround', *I, Robot*. New York: Bantam. 25–45.

Attebery, Brian (2005) 'Science Fiction, Parables, and Parabolas', *Foundation*, 95: 7–22.

Bacigalupi, Paolo (2009) *The Windup Girl*. San Francisco: Night Shade.

Ballard, J.G. (1968) 'You and Me and the Continuum', in Judith Merril (ed.) *England Swings SF*. New York: Ace. 95–102.

Ballard, J.G. (1990) 'Why I Want to Fuck Ronald Reagan', *The Atrocity Exhibition*. San Francisco: Re/Search. 105–207.

Baltadonis, John V. (1939) Letter, *Unknown*, 1(3) (May): 155–156.

Banks, Iain M. (1987) *Consider Phlebas*. New York: Bantam.

Barth, John (1984) 'The Literature of Exhaustion', *The Friday Book: Essays and Other Nonfiction*. New York: G.P. Putnam's Sons. 62–76.

Bear, Greg (1985) *Blood Music*. New York: Ace.

Bellamy, Edward (1951) *Looking Backward, 2000–1887*. New York: Modern Library.

Benford, Gregory (1980) *Timescape*. New York: Bantam.

Benoît, Pierre (2005) *Queen of Atlantis*. Trans. Arthur Chambers. Lincoln: University of Nebraska Press.

Benson, Allan Ingvald (1939) Letter, *Amazing Stories*, 13(1) (January): 139.

Benton, Mike (1992) *Science Fiction Comics: The Illustrated History*. Dallas: Taylor.

Beresford, J.D. (1999) *The Wonder*. Lincoln: University of Nebraska Press.

Bleiler, Everett F. with Richard J. Bleiler (1990) *Science-Fiction: The Early Years*. Kent: Kent State University Press.

Bleiler, Everett F. (1998) *Science-Fiction, The Gernsback Years: A Complete Coverage of the Genre Magazines Amazing, Astounding, Wonder, and Others from 1926 Through 1936*. Kent: Kent State University Press.

Bova, Ben (1977) *Millennium*. New York: Dell.

Bova, Ben (1981) *Kinsman*. New York: Dell.

Brackett, Leigh (1963) 'All the Colors of the Rainbow', in Allen DeGraeff (ed.) *Human and Other Beings*. New York: Collier. 219–240.

Brackett, Leigh (1975) *The Long Tomorrow*. New York: Ballantine.

Brackett, Leigh (2005a) 'Enchantress of Venus', *Sea-Kings of Mars and Otherworldly Stories*. London: Gollancz. 421–489.

Brackett, Leigh (2005b) 'Queen of the Martian Catacombs', *Sea-Kings of Mars and Otherworldly Stories*. London: Gollancz. 359–420.

Brackett, Leigh (2005c) 'The Sorcerer of Rhiannon', *Sea-Kings of Mars and Otherworldly Stories*. London: Gollancz. 1–30.

Bradbury, Ray (1963) 'Way in the Middle of the Air', in Allen DeGraeff (ed.) *Human and Other Beings*. New York: Collier. 63–75.

Bralley, Ross L. (1926) Letter, *Weird Tales*, vii(4) (April): 567.

Bringwald, Henry E. (1939) Letter, *Amazing Stories*, 13(3) (March): 143.

Brown, Fredric and Mack Reynolds (1963) 'Dark Interlude', in Allen DeGraeff (ed.) *Human and Other Beings*. New York: Collier. 15–22.

Brunner, John (1978) *Stand on Zanzibar*. London: Arrow.

Brunner, John (2003) *The Sheep Look Up*. Dallas: BenBella.

Bulwer-Lytton, Edward (1989) *The Coming Race*. Santa Barbara: Woodbridge.

Burdekin, Katharine (1993) *Proud Man*. New York: The Feminist Press at The City University of New York.

Butler, Octavia (1987) *Dawn*. London: Gollancz.

Cadigan, Pat (1992) *Fools*. New York: Bantam.

Callenbach, Ernest (1977) *Ecotopia*. New York: Bantam.

Campbell, Jr, John W. (1939) '*Unknown*', *Astounding Science Fiction*, xxii.6 (February): 72.

Campbell, Jr, John W. (1975) 'The Battery of Hate', in Damon Knight (ed.) *Science Fiction of the Thirties*. New York: Avon. 117–153.

Campbell, Jr, John W. (2003a) 'The Escape', in James A. Mann (ed.) *A New Dawn: The Complete Don A. Stuart Stories*. Framingham: NESFA. 131–147.

Campbell, Jr, John W. (2003b). 'Twilight', in James A. Mann (ed.) *A New Dawn: The Complete Don A. Stuart Stories*. Framingham: NESFA. 19–37.

Cantril, Hadley (1966) *The Invasion from Mars: A Study in the Psychology of Panic*. New York: Harper Torchbooks.

Čapek, Karel (2004) *R.U.R. (Rossum's Universal Robots)*. Trans. Claudia Novack. London: Penguin.

Carter, Angela (2005) *The Passion of New Eve*. London: Virago.

Castells, Manuel (2000) *The Information Age: Economy, Society and Culture, volume I: The Rise of the Network Society*, second edition. Oxford: Blackwell.

Castillo, Greg (2010) *Cold War on the Home Front: The Soft Power of Midcentury Design*. Minneapolis: University of Minnesota Press.

Chatterjee, Rimi B. (2005) *Signal Red*. New Delhi: Penguin.

Chesney, General Sir George Tomkyns (1995) *The Battle of Dorking: Reminiscences of a Volunteer*, in I.F. Clarke (ed.) *The Tale of the Next Great War, 1871–1914: Fictions of Future Warfare and Battles Still to Come*. Liverpool: Liverpool University Press. 27–73.

Christopher, John (1958) *The Death of Grass*. Harmondsworth: Penguin.

Clarke, Arthur C. (2002a) 'Breaking Strain', *The Collected Stories of Arthur C. Clarke*. New York: Orb. 169–190.

Clarke, Arthur C. (2002b) 'History Lesson', *The Collected Stories of Arthur C. Clarke*. New York: Orb. 92–98.

Clarke, Arthur C. (2002c) 'Rescue Party', *The Collected Stories of Arthur C. Clarke*. New York: Orb. 35–55.

Clute, John and Peter Nicholls (eds) (1993) *The Encyclopedia of Science Fiction*. London: Orbit.

Conover, Jr, Willis C. (1937) Letter, *Amazing Stories*, 11(3) (June): 132.

Corelli, Marie (1890) *A Romance of Two Worlds*. New York: F.M. Lupton.

Cottrell, C. (1939) Letter, *Unknown*, 1(3) (May): 159–160.

Cowan, Aaron (1926) Letter, *Weird Tales*, vii(4) (April): 567.

Csicsery-Ronay, Jr, Istvan (1991) 'The SF of Theory: Baudrillard and Haraway', *Science-Fiction Studies*, 55: 387–404.

Csicsery-Ronay, Jr, Istvan (2008) *The Seven Beauties of Science Fiction*. Middletown: Wesleyan University Press.

Delany, Samuel R. (1976) *Triton*. New York: Bantam.

Delany, Samuel R. (2001) *Dhalgren*. New York: Vintage.

del Rey, Lester (1979) *The World of Science Fiction: The History of a Subculture, 1926–1976*. New York: Del Rey.

Dick, Philip K. (1990a) 'The Defenders', *Beyond Lies the Wub, volume 1 of the Collected Stories of Philip K. Dick*. London: Grafton. 95–119.

Dick, Philip K. (1990b) 'Exhibit Piece', *The Father-Thing, volume 3 of the Collected Stories of Philip K. Dick*. London: Grafton. 199–213.

Dick, Philip K. (1990c) 'Foster, You're Dead', *The Father-Thing, volume 3 of the Collected Stories of Philip K. Dick*. London: Grafton. 280–300.

Dick, Philip K. (1990d) 'The Hanging Stranger', *The Father-Thing, volume 3 of the Collected Stories of Philip K. Dick*. London: Grafton. 28–43

Dick, Philip K. (1990e) 'Tony and the Beetles', *The Father-Thing, volume 3 of the Collected Stories of Philip K. Dick*. London: Grafton. 161–74.

Dick, Philip K. (1991) *A Scanner Darkly*. New York: Vintage.

Disch, Thomas M. (1968) 'The Squirrel Cage', in Judith Merril (ed.) *England Swings SF*. New York: Ace. 125–139.

Disch, Thomas M. (1980) *Camp Concentration*. New York: Bantam.

Donnelly, Ignatius (1960) *Caesar's Column: A Story of the Twentieth Century*. Cambridge: The Belknap Press of Harvard University Press.

Dorman, Sonya (2009) 'Go, Go, Go, Said the Bird', in Harlan Ellison (ed.) *Dangerous Visions*. New York: Edgeworks Abbey. 447–452.

Durant, Sam (ed.) (2007) *Black Panther: The Revolutionary Art of Emory Douglas*. New York: Rizzoli.

Easley, Nivi-Kofi A. (1974) *The Militants*. New York: Carlton.

Egan, Greg (2001) *Schild's Ladder*. London: Gollancz.

Elliott, George P. (1963) 'The NRACP', in Allen DeGraeff (ed.) *Human and Other Beings*. New York: Collier. 141–172.

Ellison, Harlan (2009a) 'Afterword', in Harlan Ellison (ed.) *Dangerous Visions*. New York: Edgeworks Abbey. 165–169.

Ellison, Harlan (2009b) 'The Prowler in the City at the Edge of the World', in Harlan Ellison (ed.) *Dangerous Visions*. New York: Edgeworks Abbey. 144–165.

Enstice, Andrew and Janeen Webb (2003) 'Introduction' in Kenneth Mackay, *The Yellow Wave: A Romance of the Asiatic Invasion of Australia*. Middletown: Wesleyan University Press. xi–xxxiv.

Fairbairns, Zöe (1979) *Benefits*. London: Virago.

Firestone, Shulamith (1988) *The Dialectic of Sex: The Case for Feminist Revolution*. London: The Women's Press.

Fischer, Jr, Fred W. (1926) Letter, *Weird Tales*, (April): 567.

Foster, Thomas (2005) *The Souls of Cyberfolk: Posthumanism as Vernacular Theory*. Minneapolis: University of Minnesota Press.

Frank, Pat (2005) *Alas, Babylon*. New York: Harper Perennial.

Franklin, H. Bruce (1982) 'America as Science Fiction: 1939', *Science-Fiction Studies*, 26: 38–50.

Gernsback, Hugo (1926) 'A New Sort of Magazine', *Amazing Stories* 1(1) (April): 3.

Giunta, John (1939) 'COMICS CRAZY', *Fantasy News*, 3(13) (September 17): 5.

Gloss, Molly (1997) *The Dazzle of Day*. New York: Tor.

Goodwin, Archie (1972) *Luke Cage, Hero for Hire 2* (August).

Greenland, Colin (1990) *Take Back Plenty*. London: Unwin Hyman.

Griffith, Nicola (1992) *Ammonite*. New York: Ballantine.

Gunn, James (1975) *Alternate Worlds: The Illustrated History of Science Fiction*. New York: A&W Visual Library.

Haldeman, Joe (1976) *The Forever War*. London: Orbit.

Hamilton, Edmond (2009a) 'The Comet-Drivers', *The Star-Stealers: The Complete Tales of the Interstellar Patrol*. Royal Oak: Haffner. 293–330.

Hamilton, Edmond (2009b) 'The Star Stealers', *The Star-Stealers: The Complete Tales of the Interstellar Patrol*. Royal Oak: Haffner. 53–90.

Haraway, Donna (1991) 'A Cyborg Manifesto: Science, Technology, and Socialist-Feminism in the Late Twentieth Century', *Simians, Cyborgs and Women: The Reinvention of Nature*. New York: Routledge. 149–181.

Harrison, Harry (2008) *Make Room! Make Room!* New York: Orb.

Hartwell, David G. and Kathryn Cramer (2006) 'Introduction: How Shit Became Shinola: Definition and Redefinition of Space Opera', in David G. Hartwell and Kathryn Cramer (eds) *The Space Opera Renaissance*. New York: Tor. 9–18.

Harvey, David (2004) 'The Languages of Science', in Michael Moorcock (ed.) *New Worlds: An Anthology*. New York: Thunder's Mouth. 380–386.

Heinlein, Robert A. (1967a) 'The Black Pits of Luna', *The Past Through Tomorrow*. New York: Berkley Medallion. 287–300.

Heinlein, Robert A. (1967b) 'Blowups Happen', *The Past Through Tomorrow*. New York: Berkley Medallion. 73–120.

Heinlein, Robert A. (1967c) 'The Green Hills of Earth', *The Past Through Tomorrow*. New York: Berkley Medallion. 363–373.

Heinlein, Robert A. (1967d) '*If This Goes On—*', *The Past Through Tomorrow*. New York: Berkley Medallion. 449–584.

Heinlein, Robert A. (1967e) 'Logic of Empire', *The Past Through Tomorrow*. New York: Berkley Medallion. 375–421.

Heinlein, Robert A. (1967f) 'The Roads Must Roll', *The Past Through Tomorrow*. New York: Berkley Medallion. 35–72.

Heinlein, Robert A. (1971) *Stranger in a Strange Land*. New York: Berkley Medallion.

Hoban, Russell (1998) *Riddley Walker*, expanded edition. Bloomington: Indiana University Press.

Hopkins, Pauline (1996) *Of One Blood*. London: The X Press.

Hopkinson, Nalo (2000) *Midnight Robber*. New York: Warner.

Hubbard, L. Ron (1996) *Final Blackout*. Los Angeles: Bridge.

Hubbard, L. Ron (2007) *Dianetics: The Evolution of a Science*. Los Angeles: Bridge.

Jackson, Blyden (1973) *Operation Burning Candle: A Novel*. New York: Third Press.

Jackson, Shelley (2006) *Half Life*. New York: HarperCollins.

Jacobs, Harvey (2004) 'Gravity', in Michael Moorcock (ed.) *New Worlds: An Anthology*. New York: Thunder's Mouth. 1–11.

Jameson, Fredric (1991) *Postmodernism, or, The Cultural Logic of Late Capitalism*. Durham: Duke University Press.

Jameson, Fredric (2005) *Archaeologies of the Future: The Desire Called Utopia and Other Science Fictions*. London: Verso.

Jones, Gordon (1904) 'Jules Verne at Home', *Temple Bar* 129: 664–671.

Jones, Gwyneth (1991) *White Queen*. New York: Tor.

Jones, Gwyneth (1994) *North Wind*. New York: Tor.

Jones, Gwyneth (1998) *Phoenix Café*. New York: Tor.

Jones, Gwyneth (2001) *Bold as Love*. London: Gollancz.

Jones, Gwyneth (2004) *Life*. Seattle: Aqueduct.

Kadrey, Richard and Larry McCaffery (1991) 'Cyberpunk 101: A Schematic Guide to *Storming the Reality Studio*', in Larry McCaffery (ed.) *Storming the Reality Studio: A Casebook of Cyberpunk and Postmodern Science Fiction*. Durham: Duke University Press. 17–29.

Kelly, James Patrick and John Kessel (2009) 'Introduction', in James Patrick Kelly and John Kessel (eds) *The Secret History of Science Fiction*. San Francisco: Tachyon. 7–17.

Kilgore, De Witt Douglas (2003) *Astrofuturism: Science, Race, and Visions of Utopia in Space*. Philadelphia: University of Pennsylvania Press.

Knight, Damon (1967) *In Search of Wonder: Essays on Modern Science Fiction*, second edition. Chicago: Advent.

Knight, Damon (1977) *The Futurians: The Story of the Great Science Fiction 'Family' of the 30's That Produced Today's Top SF Writers and Editors*. New York: John Day.

Kornbluth, C.M. (1939) 'Cyril's Very Own Department', *Escape*, 1(4) (October): 7–8.

Kress, Nancy (2004) *Beggars in Spain*. New York: EOS.

Kuttner, Henry (1984) 'Camouflage', in Isaac Asimov and Martin H. Greenberg (eds) *Isaac Asimov Presents the Golden Years of Science Fiction, Fourth Series*. New York: Bonanza. 211–245.

Lai, Larissa (2002) *Salt Fish Girl*. Toronto: Tom Allen.

Lane, Mary E. Bradley (1999) *Mizora: A World of Women*. Lincoln: University of Nebraska Press.

Latham, Rob (2010) '"A Rare State of Ferment": SF Controversies from the New Wave to Cyberpunk', in Graham J. Murphy and Sherryl Vint (eds) *Beyond Cyberpunk: New Critical Perspectives*. New York: Routledge. 29–45.

Latour, Bruno (1996) *Aramis or The Love of Technology*. Trans. Catherine Porter, Cambridge: Harvard University Press.

Latour, Bruno (1999) *Pandora's Hope: Essays on the Reality of Science Studies*. Cambridge: Harvard University Press.

Lefanu, Sarah (1988) *In the Chinks of the World Machine: Feminism & Science Fiction*. London: The Women's Press.

Le Guin, Ursula K. (1982) *The Word for World Is Forest*. New York: Berkley.

Le Guin, Ursula K. (2003) *The Left Hand of Darkness*. New York: Ace.

Leinster, Murray (1978a) 'First Contact', in John J. Pierce (ed.) *The Best of Murray Leinster*. New York: Del Rey. 131–166.

Leinster, Murray (1978b) 'A Logic Named Joe', in John J. Pierce (ed.) *The Best of Murray Leinster*. New York: Del Rey. 219–237.

Leinster, Murray (1978c) 'Proxima Centauri', in John J. Pierce (ed.) *The Best of Murray Leinster*. New York: Del Rey. 59–115.

Leinster, Murray (1978d) 'Sidewise in Time', in John J. Pierce (ed.) *The Best of Murray Leinster*. New York: Del Rey. 1–58.

Lewis, C.S. (1996) *Out of the Silent Planet*. New York: Scribner.

Lewis, C.S. (2003a) *Perelandra*. New York: Scribner.

Lewis, C.S. (2003b) *That Hideous Strength*. New York: Scribner.

Lightner, A.M. (1969) *The Day of the Drones*. New York: Norton.

Lorraine, Lilith (1929) *The Brain of the Planet*. New York: Stellar.

Lorraine, Lilith (1930) 'Into the 28th Century', *Science Wonder Quarterly*, 1(2) (Winter): 250–267, 276.

Lovecraft, H.P. (2005) *At the Mountains of Madness*. New York: Modern Library.

Lucanio, Patrick and Gary Coville (2002) *Smokin' Rockets: The Romance of Technology in American Film, Radio and Television, 1945–1962*. Jefferson: McFarland.

Luckhurst, Roger (2005) *Science Fiction*. Cambridge: Polity.

McHale, Brian (1989) *Postmodernist Fiction*. London: Routledge.

McHugh, Maureen F. (1992) *China Mountain Zhang*. New York: Tor.

Mackay, Kenneth (2003) *The Yellow Wave: A Romance of the Asiatic Invasion of Australia*. Middletown: Wesleyan University Press.

MacLean, Katherine (1973a) 'Defense Mechanism', *The Diploids and 7 Other Stories*. New York: Manor. 185–192.

MacLean, Katherine (1973b) 'Feedback', *The Diploids and 7 Other Stories*. New York: Manor. 138–156.

Malzberg, Barry N. (1975) *Galaxies*. New York: Pyramid.

Matheson, Richard (1987) *I Am Legend*. London: Robinson.

Merrick, Helen (2009) *The Secret Feminist Cabal: A Cultural History of Science Fiction Feminisms*. Seattle: Aqueduct.

Merril, Judith (2005a) 'Barrier of Dread', *Homecalling and Other Stories: The Complete Solo Short Science Fiction of Judith Merril*. Framingham: NESFA. 31–42.

Merril, Judith (2005b) 'That Only a Mother', *Homecalling and Other Stories: The Complete Solo Short Science Fiction of Judith Merril*. Framingham: NESFA. 11–19.

Merril, Judith and J.G. Ballard (1968) 'J.G. Ballard ...', in Judith Merril (ed.) *England Swings SF*. New York: Ace. 103–206.

Miéville, China (2009) *The City & the City*. London: Macmillan.

Miller, Jr, Walter M. (1988) *A Canticle for Leibowitz*. New York: Bantam.

Mitchison, Naomi (1985) *Memoirs of a Spacewoman*. London: The Women's Press.

Moon, Elizabeth (1996) *Remnant Population*. New York: Ballantine.

Moore, C.L. (1987) *Doomsday Morning*. New York: Popular Library.

Moore, C.L. (1995) 'No Woman Born', in Pamela Sargent (ed.) *Women of Wonder, The Classic Years: Science Fiction by Women from the 1940s to the 1970s*. San Diego: Harvest. 21–64.

Moore, C.L. (2002a). 'Black Thirst', *Black Gods and Scarlet Dreams*. London: Gollancz. 196–233.

Moore, C.L. (2002b) 'Shambleau', *Black Gods and Scarlet Dreams*. London: Gollancz. 165–195.

Moore, C.L. (2002c) 'The Tree of Life', *Black Gods and Scarlet Dreams*. London: Gollancz. 234–262.

More, Max (1995) 'The Extropian Principles, v2.6', http://www.maxmore.com/extprn26. htm, accessed July 5, 2010.

Moreau, Julian (1967) *The Black Commandos*. US: privately printed.

Moskowitz, Sam (1963) *Explorers of the Infinite: Shapers of Science Fiction*. Cleveland: World Publishing.

Mosley, Walter (2001) 'Whispers in the Dark', *Futureland: Nine Stories of an Imminent World*. New York: Warner. 1–25.

Newman, K. (1995a) 'Pitbull Britain', *Famous Monsters*. London: Pocketbooks. 81–161.

Newman, K. (1995b) 'Übermensch!', *Famous Monsters*. London: Pocketbooks. 213–231.

Niven, Larry (2009) 'Afterword', in Harlan Ellison (ed.) *Dangerous Visions*. New York: Edgeworks Abbey. 252–253.

Niven, Larry and Jerry Pournelle (1981) *Oath of Fealty*. New York: Pocketbooks.

Nowlan, Philip Francis (2005) 'Armageddon – 2419 AD', *Wings over Tomorrow: The Collected Science Fiction of Philip Francis Nowlan*. Rockville: Wildside. 25–105.

Nowlan, Philip Francis and Dick Calkins (2008) *Buck Rogers in the 25th Century: The Complete Newspaper Dailies, volume one, 1929–1930*. Neshannock: Hermes.

O'Donnell, Lawrence [Henry Kuttner and C.L. Moore] (1984) 'Vintage Season', in Isaac Asimov and Martin H. Greenberg (eds) *Isaac Asimov Presents the Golden Years of Science Fiction, Fourth Series*. New York: Bonanza. 548–591.

Orwell, George (1987) *Nineteen Eighty-four*. New York: Signet.

Padgett, Lewis [Henry Kuttner and C.L. Moore] (1984) 'The Piper's Son', in Isaac Asimov and Martin H. Greenberg (eds) *Isaac Asimov Presents the Golden Years of Science Fiction, Fourth Series*. New York: Bonanza. 37–64.

Padgett, Lewis [Henry Kuttner and C.L. Moore] (1988) 'Private Eye', in Isaac Asimov and Martin H. Greenberg (eds) *Isaac Asimov Presents the Golden Years of Science Fiction, Sixth Series*. New York: Bonanza. 45–72.

Palmer, Raymond A. (1939) 'The Observatory', *Amazing Stories*, 13(2) (February): 7, 135.

Piercy, Marge (1991) *Woman on the Edge of Time*. New York: Fawcett Crest.

Platt, Charles (2004) 'The Disaster Story', in Michael Moorcock (ed.) *New Worlds: An Anthology*. New York: Thunder's Mouth. 280–282.

Poe, Edgar Allan (1976a) 'A Descent into the Maelström' in Harold Beaver (ed.) *The Science Fiction of Edgar Allan Poe*. Harmondsworth: Penguin. 72–88.

Poe, Edgar Allan (1976b) 'The Facts in the Case of M. Valdemar', in Harold Beaver (ed.) *The Science Fiction of Edgar Allan Poe*. Harmondsworth: Penguin. 194–203.

Poe, Edgar Allan (1976c) 'MS. Found in a Bottle' in Harold Beaver (ed.) *The Science Fiction of Edgar Allan Poe*. Harmondsworth: Penguin. 1–11.

Poe, Edgar Allan (1976d) 'The Unparalleled Adventure of One Hans Pfaall' in Harold Beaver (ed.) *The Science Fiction of Edgar Allan Poe*. Harmondsworth: Penguin. 12–64.

Pohl, Frederik and C.M. Kornbluth (1955) *Gladiator-at-Law*. New York: Ballantine.

Pohl, Frederik and C.M. Kornbluth (1981) *The Space Merchants*. New York: Ballantine.

Pournelle, Jerry and Dean Ing (1984) *Mutual Assured Survival*. New York: Baen.

Priest, Cherie (2009) *Boneshaker*. New York: Tor.

Price, E. Hoffman (1926) Letter, *Weird Tales*, vii(4) (April): 567–568.

Rieder, John (2008) *Colonialism and the Emergence of Science Fiction*. Middletown: Wesleyan University Press.

Roberts, Adam (2006) *The History of Science Fiction*. London: Palgrave.

Roberts, Keith (1968) 'Manscarer', in Judith Merril (ed.) *England Swings SF*. New York: Ace. 143–164.

Robida, Albert (2004) *The Twentieth Century*. Trans. Philippe Willems. Middletown: Wesleyan University Press.

Robinson, Kim Stanley (1993) *Red Mars*. New York: Bantam.

Robinson, Kim Stanley (1994) *Green Mars*. New York: Bantam.

Robinson, Kim Stanley (1996) *Blue Mars*. New York: Bantam.

Robson, Justina (2004) *Natural History*. London: Pan.

Roshwald, Mordecai (2004) *Level 7*. Madison: The University Press of Wisconsin.

Ross, Andrew (1991) *Strange Weather: Culture, Science, and Technology in an Age of Limits*. London: Verso.

Russ, Joanna (1977) *We Who Are About To....* New York: Dell.

Russ, Joanna (1978) 'When It Changed', in Pamela Sargent (ed.) *The New Women of Wonder*. New York: Vintage. 227–239.

Russ, Joanna (1986) *The Female Man*. Boston: Beacon.

Russell, Eric Frank. (1966) *Sinister Barrier*. New York: Paperback Library.

Rydell, Robert W., John E. Findling and Kimberly D. Pelle (2000) *Fair America: World's Fairs in the United States*. Washington: Smithsonian Institute Press.

Ryman, Geoff (2004) *Air*. New York: St. Martin's Griffin.

Sargent, Pamela (1978) 'Introduction', in Pamela Sargent (ed.) *The New Women of Wonder*. New York: Vintage. xii–xxxiv.

Schaeffer, Harold G. (1939) Letter, *Amazing Stories*, 13(6) (June): 143.

Schroeder, Karl (2002) *Permanence*. New York: Tor.

Scott, Jody (1977) *Passing for Human*. New York: DAW.

Scott-Heron, Gil (1970) 'Whitey on the Moon', *Small Talk at 125th and Lenox*. Flying Dutchman.

Shiel, M.P. (1963) *The Purple Cloud*. London: Gollancz.

Shiner, Lewis (1991) 'Confessions of an Ex-Cyberpunk', *New York Times* (7 January): A17.

Silverberg, Robert (1972) *Dying Inside*. London: Sidgwick & Jackson.

Simak, Clifford D. (1971a) 'Aesop', *City*. London: Sphere. 188–222.

Simak, Clifford D. (1971b) 'Desertion', *City*. London: Sphere. 103–116.

Simak, Clifford D. (1971c) 'Paradise', *City*. London: Sphere. 119–144.

Simmons, Dan (1989) *Hyperion*. New York: Bantam.

Simmons, Dan (1990) *The Fall of Hyperion*. New York: Bantam.

Sladek, John T. (2004) 'Masterson and the Clerks', in Michael Moorcock (ed.) *New Worlds: An Anthology*. New York: Thunder's Mouth. 191–234.

Slonczewski, Joan (1986) *A Door into Ocean*. New York: Avon.

Smith, E.E. (1972) *First Lensman*. London: Grafton.

Smith, E.E. (1973) *Second Stage Lensman*. London: Panther.

Smith, E.E. (1977) *The Skylark of Space*. London: Panther.

Smith, E.E. (1978) *Skylark of Valeron*. London: Panther.

Smith, George O. (1976) 'Beam Pirate', *The Complete Venus Equilateral*. New York: Ballantine. 202–242.

Spinrad, Norman (1972) *Bug Jack Barron*. London: Panther.

St. Clair, Margaret (1967) *The Dolphins of Altair*. New York: Dell.

Stapledon, Olaf (1972) *Odd John and Sirius*. Mineola: Dover.

Stapledon, Olaf (2004) *Star Maker*. Middletown: Wesleyan University Press.

Stephenson, Neal (1992) *Snow Crash*. New York: Bantam.

Sterling, Bruce (1986) 'Preface', in Bruce Sterling (ed.) *Mirrorshades: The Cyberpunk Anthology*. New York: Ace. ix–xvi.

Sterling, Bruce (1989) 'CATSCAN: Slipstream', *Science Fiction Eye*, 1(5) (July): 77–80.

Stern, Roger (2006) 'Introduction', *Superman: Sunday Classics 1939–1943*. New York: Sterling. ix–xv.

Stewart, George R. (2006) *Earth Abides*. New York: Del Rey.

Stone, Leslie F. (1932) 'The Hell Planet', *Wonder Stories*, 4(1) (June): 14–27.

Stross, Charles (2006) *Accelerando*. London: Orbit.

Sturgeon, Theodore (1984) 'Memorial', in Isaac Asimov and Martin H. Greenberg (eds) *Isaac Asimov Presents the Golden Years of Science Fiction, Fourth Series*. New York: Bonanza. 346–360.

Sturgeon, Theodore (1999) *Venus Plus X*. New York: Vintage.

Sturgeon, Theodore (2009) 'If All Men Were Brothers, Would You Let One Marry Your Sister?', in Harlan Ellison (ed.) *Dangerous Visions*. New York: Edgeworks Abbey. 382–424.

Suvin, Darko (1979) *Metamorphoses of Science Fiction: On the Poetics and History of a Literary Genre*. New Haven: Yale University Press.

Tepper, Sheri S. (1989) *Grass*. London: Gollancz.

Tiptree, Jr, James [Alice Sheldon] (1978) 'Beam Us Home', *Ten Thousand Light-Years from Home*. New York: Ace. 354–374.

Tiptree, Jr, James [Alice Sheldon] (1995) 'The Women Men Don't See', in Pamela Sargent (ed.) *Women of Wonder: The Classic Years*. San Diego: Harvest. 308–334.

Tucker, Wilson (1972) *The Year of the Quiet Sun*. London: Arrow.

Unwin, Timothy (2000) 'The Fiction of Science, or the Science of Fiction', in Edmund Smyth (ed.) *Jules Verne: Narratives of Modernity*. Liverpool: Liverpool University Press. 46–59.

Vance, James (2006) 'A Job for Superman', *Superman: The Dailies 1939–1942, volumes 1–3*. New York: Sterling. Volume 1, 6–11.

Van Houten, Raymond (1938) 'Van Houten Says', *New Fandom*, 1(1) (September–October 1938): 5.

Van Houten, Raymond (1939) 'What Science Fiction Could Be', *New Fandom*, 1(3) (January): 7–10.

van Vogt, A.E. (1966) *The Players of Null-A*. New York: Berkley Medallion.

van Vogt, A.E. (1981) *The Voyage of the Space Beagle*. New York: Pocket Books.

van Vogt, A.E. (1969) *The Weapon Shops of Isher*. London: NEL.

van Vogt, A.E. (1970) *The Weapon Makers*. London: NEL.

van Vogt, A.E. (2002) *The World of Null-A*. New York: Orb.

Varley, John (1983) 'Manikins', *The Barbie Murders*. London: Orbit. 132–145.

Verne, Jules (1978) *From the Earth to the Moon Direct in Ninety-seven Hours and Twenty Minutes*. Trans. Walter James Miller. New York: Thomas Y. Crowell.

Verne, Jules (1992) *Journey to the Centre of the Earth*. Trans. William Butcher. Oxford: Oxford University Press.

Villiers de l'Isle-Adam (2001) *Tomorrow's Eve*. Trans. Robert Martin Adams. Urbana: University of Illinois Press.

Vinge, Vernor (2006) *Rainbows End*. New York: Tor.

'The Visascreen' (1939) *Fantasy News*, 3(4) (July 19): 3.

Vonnegut, Kurt (1988) *Player Piano*. New York: Dell.

Waldrop, Howard (1989) 'All About Strange Monsters of the Recent Past', *Strange Things in Close Up*. London: Arrow. 237–246.

Waldrop, Howard (1990) 'Thirty Minutes over Broadway', *Night of the Cooters*. New York: Ace. 83–125.

Walton, Jo (2006) *Farthing*. New York: Tor.

Warner, Jr, Harry (1969) *All Our Yesterdays: An Informal History of Science Fiction Fandom in the Forties*. Chicago: Advent.

Warner, Jr, Harry (1976) *A Wealth of Fable: The History of Science Fiction Fandom in the 1950's, volume 1*. New York: Fanhistorica.

Warner, Jr, Harry (1977) *A Wealth of Fable: The History of Science Fiction Fandom in the 1950's, volume 2*. New York: Fanhistorica.

Weinstein, Lee (2005). 'Introduction', *Wings over Tomorrow: The Collected Science Fiction of Philip Francis Nowlan*. Rockville: Wildside Press. 17–23.

Wells, H.G. (2002) *The War of the Worlds*. New York: The Modern Library.

Williams, John A. (1971) *The Man Who Cried I Am*. Harmondsworth: Penguin.

Williamson, Jack (1984) *Darker Than You Think*. New York: Bluejay.

Wilson, Robert Charles (2009) *Julian Comstock: A Story of 22nd Century America*. New York: Tor.

Wolfe, Bernard (1963) *Limbo*. New York: Ace.

Wright, Sydney Fowler (2003) *Deluge*. Middletown: Wesleyan University Press.

Wyndham, John (1987) *The Chrysalids*. London: Penguin.

Yaszek, Lisa (2008) *Galactic Suburbia: Recovering Women's Science Fiction*. Columbus: Ohio State University Press.

Zoline, Pamela (1971) 'The Holland of the Mind', in Langdon Jones (ed.) *The New SF*. London: Arrow. 175–215.

Zoline, Pamela (2004) 'The Heat Death of the Universe', in Michael Moorcock (ed.) *New Worlds: An Anthology*. New York: Thunder's Mouth. 131–144.

Guide to further reading

Chapter 1

Histories and overviews

Aldiss, Brian (1973) *Billion Year Spree: The True History of Science Fiction*. London: Weidenfeld & Nicolson. Emphasises role of European fiction; revised as *Trillion Year Spree* in 1986.

Clute, John and Peter Nichols (eds) (1993) *The Encyclopedia of Science Fiction*. London: Orbit.

Csicsery-Ronay Jr, Istvan (2008) *The Seven Beauties of Science Fiction*. Middletown: Wesleyan University Press.

James, Edward (1994) *Science Fiction in the Twentieth Century*. Oxford: Oxford University Press. Emphasises the American magazine tradition.

Luckhurst, Roger (2005) *Science Fiction*. Cambridge: Polity. Links SF to technologically saturated societies and thus dates it from the late nineteenth century.

Roberts, Adam (2007) *The History of Science Fiction*. New York: Palgrave. Includes extensive coverage of pre-nineteenth-century fiction.

On pulp magazines

Ashley, Mike (2001) *Time Machines: The Story of Science Fiction Pulp Magazines from the Beginning to 1950*. Liverpool: Liverpool University Press.

Ashley, Mike and Robert A.W. Lowndes (2004) *The Gernsback Days: A Study of the Evolution of Modern Science Fiction from 1911 to 1936*. Holicong: Wildside.

Westfahl, Gary (1998) *The Mechanics of Wonder*. Liverpool: Liverpool University Press.

On Suvin

Bould, Mark and China Miéville (eds) (2009) *Red Planets: Marxism and Science Fiction*. London: Pluto.

Freedman, Carl (2000) *Critical Theory and Science Fiction*. Hanover: Wesleyan University Press.

Parrinder, Patrick (ed.) (2001) *Learning from Other Worlds: Estrangement, Cognition, and the Politics of Science Fiction and Utopia*. Durham: Duke University Press.

Chapter 2

On eutopia and dystopia

Kumar, Krishan (1987) *Utopia and Anti-Utopia in Modern Times*. Oxford: Basil Blackwell.
Wegner, Philip E. (2002) *Imaginary Communities: Utopia, the Nation and Spatial Histories of Modernity*. Berkeley: University of California Press.

On colonial adventure fiction

Rieder, John (2008) *Colonialism and the Emergence of Science Fiction*. Middletown: Wesleyan University Press.

On future war stories

Clarke, I.F. (1992) *Voices Prophesying War: Future Wars 1763–3749*, second edition. Oxford: Oxford University Press.
Clarke, I.F. (ed.) (1996) *The Tale of the Next Great War, 1871–1914: Fictions of Future Warfare and Battles Still to Come*. Liverpool: Liverpool University Press. Fiction collection.
Clarke, I.F. (ed.) (1997) *Great War with Germany, 1890–1914: Fictions and Fantasies of the War-to-Come*. Liverpool: Liverpool University Press. Fiction collection.

On apocalyptic fiction

Ketterer, David (1974) *New Worlds for Old: The Apocalyptic Imagination, Science Fiction, and American Literature*. Garden City: Anchor.
Sharp, Patrick (2007) *Savage Perils: Racial Frontiers and Nuclear Apocalypse in American Culture*. Norman: University of Oklahoma Press.

On prehistoric and evolutionary romances

Ruddick, Nicholas (2009) *The Fire in the Stone: Prehistoric Fiction from Charles Darwin to Jean M. Auel*. Middletown: Wesleyan University Press.

On tales of science and invention

Willis, Martin (2006) *Mesmerists, Monsters, and Machines: Science Fiction and the Cultures of Science in the Nineteenth Century*. Kent: Kent State University Press.

On other contemporary fiction

Alkon, Paul K. (1987) *Origins of Futuristic Fiction*. Athens: University of Georgia Press.
Alkon, Paul K. (2002) *Science Fiction Before 1900: Imagination Discovers Technology*. New York: Routledge.
Bould, Mark (2010) 'Revolutionary African American SF before Black Power SF', *Extrapolation*, 51(1) (Spring): 53–81. Overview of African-American SF before WWII.

Clareson, Thomas D. (1985) *Some Kind of Paradise: The Emergence of American Science Fiction*. Westport: Greenwood.

Fitting, Peter (2004) *Subterranean Worlds: A Critical Anthology*. Middletown: Wesleyan University Press.

Franklin, H. Bruce (ed.) (1995) *Future Perfect: American Science Fiction of the Nineteenth Century: An Anthology*. Revised and expanded edition. New Brunswick: Rutgers University Press.

Nicolson, Marjorie Hope (1948) *Voyages to the Moon*. London: Macmillan.

Stableford, Brian (1985) *Scientific Romance in Britain, 1890–1950*. London: Palgrave Macmillan.

Chapter 3

On early media SF

Benton, Mike (1992) *Science Fiction Comics: The Illustrated History*. Dallas: Taylor.

Sadowski, Greg (2009) *Supermen!: The First Wave of Comic Book Heroes, 1936–1941*. Seattle: Fantagraphics.

Telotte, J. P. (1999) *A Distant Technology: Science Fiction Film and the Machine Age*. Hanover: Wesleyan University Press.

On gender

Attebery, Brian (2002) *Decoding Gender in Science Fiction*. New York: Routledge. Analysis of gender in pulp magazines that includes advertisements as well as stories.

Donawerth, Jane L. and Carol A. Kolmerten (eds) (1994) *Utopian and Science Fiction by Women: Worlds of Difference*. Syracuse: Syracuse University Press.

Roberts, Robin (1993) *A New Species*: *Gender and Science in Science Fiction*. Champaign: University of Illinois Press.

Three critical responses to Campbell's 'Who Goes There?'

Pearson, Wendy (1999) 'Alien Cryptographies: The View from Queer', *Science Fiction Studies*, 77 (March): 1–22. Queer reading.

Rieder, John (1982) 'Embracing the Alien: Science Fiction in Mass Culture', *Science-Fiction Studies*, 26 (March): 26–37. Marxist reading.

Vint, Sherryl (2005) '*Who Goes There?* "Real" Men, Only', *Extrapolation*, 46(4) (Winter): 421–438. Feminist reading.

Chapter 4

On Golden Age SF

Berger, Albert I. (1993) *The Magic That Works: John W. Campbell and the American Responses to Technology*. San Bernadino: Borgo.

Hartwell, David G. and Kathryn Cramer (eds) (1994) *The Ascent of Wonder: The Evolution of Hard SF*. New York: Orb. Fiction collection.

Huntington, John (1989) *Rationalizing Genius: Ideological Strategies in the Classic American Science Fiction Story*. New Brunswick: Rutgers University Press.

Knight, Damon (1956) *In Search of Wonder: Essays on Modern Science Fiction*. Chicago: Advent. Credited with launching serious SF criticism.

On specific authors

Gunn, James (1982) *Isaac Asimov: The Foundations of Science Fiction*. Oxford: Oxford University Press.

Franklin, H. Bruce (1980) *Robert A. Heinlein: America as Science Fiction*. Oxford: Oxford University Press.

Olander, Joseph D. and Martin H. Greenberg (eds) (1977) *Arthur C. Clarke*. New York: Taplinger.

Chapter 5

On 1950s SF

Ashley, Mike (2005) *Transformations: The Story of the Science-Fiction Magazine from 1950 to 1970*. Liverpool: Liverpool University Press.

Booker, M. Keith (2001) *Monsters, Mushroom Clouds and the Cold War: American Science Fiction and the Roots of Postmodernism, 1946–1964*. Westport: Greenwood.

Hendershot, Cyndy (1999) *Paranoia, the Bomb and 1950s Science Fiction Films*. Bowling Green: Bowling Green State University Popular Press.

Jancovich, Mark (1996) *Rational Fears: American Horror in the 1950s*. Manchester: Manchester University Press.

Seed, David (1999) *American Science Fiction and the Cold War: Literature and Film*. Edinburgh: Edinburgh University Press.

Yaszek, Lisa (2008) *Galactic Suburbia: Recovering Women's Science Fiction*. Columbus: Ohio State University Press.

On the relationship between science and cultural politics

Harding, Sandra (2008) *Sciences from Below: Feminisms, Postcolonialities, and Modernities*. Durham: Duke University Press.

Hayles, N. Katherine (1999) *How We Became Posthuman: Virtual Bodies in Cybernetics, Literature, and Information*. Chicago: Chicago University Press.

Latour, Bruno (1999) *Pandora's Hope: Essays on the Reality of Science Studies*. Harvard: Harvard University Press.

Chapter 6

On the New Wave

Ashley, Mike (2007) *Gateways to Forever: The Story of the Science-Fiction Magazines from 1970 to 1980*. Liverpool: Liverpool University Press.

Greenland, Colin (1983) *The Entropy Exhibition: Michael Moorcock and the British 'New Wave' in Science Fiction*. London: Routledge and Kegan Paul.

Latham, Rob (2005) 'The New Wave', in David Seed (ed.) *A Companion to Science Fiction*. London: Blackwell. 202–216.

Moorcock, Michael (ed.) (1983) *New Worlds: An Anthology*. New York: Thunder's Mouth. Fiction collection.

On specific authors

Cortiel, Jeanne (1999) *Demand My Writing: Joanna Russ, Feminism, Science Fiction*. Liverpool: Liverpool University Press.
Luckhurst, Roger (1998) *'The Angle between Two Walls': The Fiction of J.G. Ballard*. Liverpool: Liverpool University Press.
Mendlesohn, Farah (ed). (2009) *On Joanna Russ*. Middletown: Wesleyan University Press.
Mullen, R.D., Arthur B. Evans, Veronica Hollinger and Istvan Csicsery-Ronay Jr. (eds) (1992) *On Philip K. Dick: 40 Articles from Science Fiction Studies*. Terra Haute and Greencastle: SF-TH.
Palmer, Christopher (2003) *Philip K. Dick: Exhilaration and Terror of the Postmodern*. Liverpool: Liverpool University Press.
Sallis, James (1996) *Ash of Stars: On the Writing of Samuel R. Delany*. Jackson: University Press of Mississippi.

Chapter 7

On race

Greene, Eric (1998) *Planet of the Apes as American Myth: Race, Politics and Popular Culture*. Middletown: Wesleyan University Press.
Kilgore, De Witt Douglas (2003). *Astrofuturism: Science, Race and Visions of Utopia in Space*. Philadelphia: University of Pennsylvania Press. Provides a critique of hard SF responses to the limits to growth hypothesis; also relevant to chapter four.
Science Fiction Studies, 102 (July 2007). Special issue on Afrofuturism.
Social Text, 71 (Summer 2002). Special issue on Afrofuturism.
Spaulding, A. Timothy (2005) *Re-Forming the Past: History, the Fantastic and the Postmodern Slave Narratives*. Columbus: Ohio State University Press.

On gender and sexuality

Barr, Marleen S. (1981) *Future Females: A Critical Study*. Bowling Green: Bowling Green State University Popular Press.
Donawerth, Jane (1997) *Frankenstein's Daughters: Women Writing Science Fiction*. Syracuse: Syracuse University Press.
Lefanu, Sarah (1988) *In the Chinks of the World Machine: Feminism and Science Fiction*. London: The Women's Press.
Merrick, Helen (2009) *The Secret Feminist Cabal: A Cultural History of Science Fiction Feminisms*. Seattle: Aqueduct.
Moylan, Tom (1987) *Demand the Impossible: Science Fiction and the Utopian Imagination*. New York: Routledge.

On environmentalism

Haraway, Donna J. (1989) *Primate Visions: Gender, Race and Nature in the World of Modern Science*. New York: Routledge.

Latham, Rob (2007) 'Biotic Invasions: Ecological Imperialism in New Wave Science Fiction', *Yearbook of English Studies*, 37(2): 103–119.

Science Fiction Studies 105 (July 2008). Special issue on Animals and Science Fiction.

Vint, Sherryl (2010) *Animal Alterity: Science Fiction and the Question of the Animal*. Liverpool: Liverpool University Press.

Chapter 8

On cyberpunk and cyborgs

Balsamo, Anne (1996) *Technologies of the Gendered Body*. Durham: Duke University Press.

Featherstone, Mike and Roger Burrows (eds) (1995) *Cyberspace/Cyberbodies/Cyberpunk*. New York: Sage.

Foster, Thomas (2005) *The Souls of Cyberfolk: Posthumanism as Vernacular Theory*. Minneapolis: University of Minnesota Press.

Haraway, Donna J. (1991) *Simians, Cyborgs, and Women: The Reinvention of Nature*. New York: Routledge.

McCaffery, Larry (ed.) (1991) *Storming the Reality Studio: A Casebook of Cyberpunk and Postmodernism*. Durham: Duke University Press.

Murphy, Graham J. and Sherryl Vint (eds) (2010) *Beyond Cyberpunk: New Critical Perspectives*. New York: Routledge.

Nixon, Nicola (1992) 'Cyberpunk: Preparing the Ground for Revolution or Keeping the Boys Satisfied', *Science Fiction Studies*, 57 (July): 219–235.

Ross, Andrew (1991) 'Cyberpunk in Boystown', *Strange Weather: Culture, Science, and Technology in an Age of Limits*. London: Verso. 137–167.

Slusser, George and Tom Shippey (1992) *Fiction 2000: Cyberpunk and the Future of Narrative*. Athens: University of Georgia Press.

Springer, Claudia (1996) *Electronic Eros: Bodies and Desire in the Postindustrial Age*. Austin: University of Texas Press.

Stone, Allucquère Rosanne (1996) *The War of Desire and Technology at the Close of the Mechanical Age*. Cambridge: MIT Press.

Wolmark, Jenny (1994) *Aliens and Others: Science Fiction, Feminism, and Postmodernism*. Iowa City: University of Iowa Press.

On postmodernism

Broderick, Damien (1994) *Reading by Starlight: Postmodern Science Fiction*. New York: Routledge.

Bukatman, Scott (1993) *Terminal Identity: The Virtual Subject in Postmodern Science Fiction*. Durham: Duke University Press.

Kuhn, Annette (1990) *Alien Zone: Cultural Theory and Contemporary Science Fiction*. London: Verso.

Landon, Brooks (1992) *The Aesthetics of Ambivalence: Rethinking the Science Fiction Film in the Age of Electronic (Re)Production*. Westport: Greenwood.

Latham, Rob (2002) *Consuming Youth: Vampires, Cyborgs and the Culture of Consumption*. Chicago: University of Chicago Press.

Science Fiction Studies 55 (November 1991): special issue on Science Fiction and Postmodernism.

Sobchack, Vivian (1987) *Screening Space: The American Science Fiction Film*. New Brunswick: Rutgers University Press.

On hard SF

Franklin, H. Bruce (2008) *War Stars: The Superweapon and the American Imagination*. Revised and expanded edition. Amherst: University of Massachusetts Press.

Hartwell, David G. and Kathryn Cramer (eds) (2002) *The Hard SF Renaissance*. New York: Toe. Fiction collection.

Science Fiction Studies 60 (July 1993): special section on Hard Science Fiction.

Westfahl, Gary (1996) *Cosmic Engineers: A Study of Hard Science Fiction*. Westport: Greenwood.

Chapter 9

On the politics of contemporary SF

Foundation 86 (Autumn 2000): special issue on Gay and Lesbian Science Fiction.

Griffith, Nicola and Stephen Pagel (eds) (1999) *Bending the Landscape: Original Gay and Lesbian Writing: Science Fiction*. New York: Overlook. Fiction collection.

Helford, Elyce Rae (2000) *Fantasy Girls: Gender in the New Universe of Science Fiction and Fantasy Television*. Lanham: Rowman & Littlefield.

Hollinger, Veronica and Joan Gordon (eds) (2002) *Edging into the Future: Science Fiction and Contemporary Cultural Transformation*. Pittsburgh: University of Pennsylvania Press.

Hollinger, Veronica, Wendy Pearson and Joan Gordon (eds) (2008) *Queer Universes: Sexualities and Science Fiction*. Liverpool: Liverpool University Press.

Moylan, Tom (2000) *Scraps of the Untainted Sky: Science Fiction, Utopia, Dystopia*. Boulder: Westview.

Science Fiction Studies 77 (March 1999): special section on Queer Theory and Science Fiction.

Shaviro, Steve (2003) *Connected, or What It Means to Live in the Network Society*. Minneapolis: University of Minnesota Press.

Vint, Sherryl (2007) *Bodies of Tomorrow: Technology, Subjectivity, Science Fiction*. Toronto: University of Toronto Press.

On specific authors

Burling, William J. (ed.) (2009) *Kim Stanley Robinson Maps the Unimaginable: Critical Essays*. Jefferson: McFarland.

Extrapolation 49(2) (Summer 2008): special issue on Geoff Ryman.

Extrapolation 50(2) (Summer 2009): special issue on China Miéville.

Chapter 10

Diasporic SF anthologies

Bell, Andrea L. and Yolanda Molina-Gavilán (eds) (2003) *Cosmos Latinos: An Anthology of Science Fiction from Latin America and Spain*. Middletown: Wesleyan University Press.

Hopkinson, Nalo and Uppinder Mehan (eds) (2004) *So Long Been Dreaming: Postcolonial Science Fiction and Fantasy*. Vancouver: Arsenal Pulp Press.

Mak, Derwin and Eric Choi (2010) *The Dragon and the Stars*. New York: DAW.

Thomas, Sheree R. (ed.) (2000) *Dark Matter: A Century of Speculative Fiction from the African Diaspora*. New York: Warner.

Thomas, Sheree R. (ed.) (2005) *Dark Matter: Reading the Bones*. New York: Warner.

Tidhar, Lavie (ed.) (2009) *The Apex Book of World SF*. Lexington: Apex.

Glossary of terms

Actant: a term used by Bruno Latour to refer to any entity (human, animal, machine, object, organisation) that is involved in the ongoing project of creating meanings and events. It is intended to avoid the word 'actor' and the divisions that often attach to ideas of who or what can be considered to act.

Discursive, discourse: 'discursive' refers to things that are in the realm of discourse, that is, which come from thought, writing or speaking; the 'discursive' in this sense is typically opposed to the 'material', which refers to things in the physical realm that are concrete rather than abstract.

Enrolment: a term used by Bruno Latour and in Actor-Network Theory to designate the way that a project or concept comes into existence and changes by convincing various actants to join. Actants are enrolled by believing their interests to coincide with the aims of the project/concept. Thus each enrolment both expands the project/concept by widening its network of actants and simultaneously changes the project/concept towards the newly enrolled interests of these added actants.

First/Third World: terms introduced in the 1950s to distinguish between nations. The First World consists of capitalist, industrialised nations (typically, successful colonisers during previous centuries); the Second World of communist, industrialised nations; and the Third World of nations (typically the victims of colonialism) that were perceived to be in need of development so that their economies would better fit into global capitalism. Following the end of the Cold War (and thus of the Second World), the First World and Third World have been more commonly described as 'developed' and 'developing' nations. Many critique these terms for implying that there is a single model of cultural and technological change. Some prefer 'Global North' and 'Global South' so as to emphasise the vast inequities in resources and material wealth that persist between former colonising and colonised nations.

Gender/Sex: terms used to differentiate between those qualities of men and women perceived to be natural and biological (sex) and those which are the products of social structures and rules (gender). Originally, this distinction was considered helpful in separating qualities pertaining to fixed, physical bodies and their capacities (male/female) and those related to fluid, cultural roles and their stipulations (masculine/feminine). More recent research challenges the idea that differences in sex are any more natural or fixed than those in gender.

Hegemony: a term used by Antonio Gramsci to describe rule by the consent of the governed, that is achieved through influence rather than overt oppression and dominance. Ideas or procedures that have achieved hegemony often present themselves as the only possible or reasonable ones and hence are consented to even by those whose interests they do not serve.

Hyperreal: a term used by Umberto Eco and Jean Baudrillard to describe the postmodern experience of reality in which it is no longer possible to distinguish 'plain' reality from its representation since our experience is constantly permeated by and mediated through strategies and technologies of representation. The hyperreal thus seems more real than reality.

Ideology, ideological: the body of beliefs, ideas and assumptions that shapes how we perceive the world and thus opportunities for action within it. Ideology is always partial and limited (i.e., we see and understand from a particular historical and cultural location) and often unconscious. This term was once used to designate a distinction between a biased or partial view (ideology) and a neutral or complete one (just 'reality' or 'truth') but contemporary criticism refuses this binary and reminds us that all perceptions and ideas are partial, contingent and located in specific identities and experiences.

Latent content/Manifest content: terms drawn from psychoanalysis to distinguish between hidden or not-immediately-apparent meanings (latent content; in psychoanalysis the wish that the dream strives to represent through the manifest content) and the evident, on-the-surface meaning of things and images (manifest content; in psychoanalysis the actual images or events in dreams).

Material: see **discursive**

Neoliberalism: a style of governance and economic policy that emerged in the 1960s. It returns to classical economic paradigms (theorised by Adam Smith in the eighteenth century to explain the distributions of goods and services through market mechanisms of supply and demand) but extends this logic to all aspects of social life and political governance. Neoliberalism stresses the role of the private sector in determining economic and political priorities and presumes not only that efficiency is the most important outcome of such transactions but also that it can be best achieved through competition in a free market. It minimises the role of the state in providing social and other services to citizens in the belief that the market and private enterprise can more effectively provide these services and that governments can best serve their citizens by prioritising economic growth and profitability. Neoliberal governance is characterised by the privatisation of public services (utilities, education, healthcare, transportation), which were once considered the responsibility of the state, and the refusal to allow legislation to interfere with the independent functioning of the market (except when it will privilege the free flow of capital across national and other boundaries).

Ontology, ontological: the branch of philosophy pertaining to the nature of being or existence. It is frequently contrasted with epistemology, the branch of philosophy pertaining to the nature of knowledge.

Orientalist, orientalism: terms used by Edward Said to refer to the production of knowledge or ideas about people from Asia, India and the Middle East, specifically in opposition to the Occidental or Western nations. Orientalism designates the creation of a kind of knowledge by projection rather than by observation and has little or no material basis in reality.

Paradigm: a term used by Thomas Kuhn to refer to the ways in which a structure of assumptions shapes the way new data can be perceived and understood by scientists. A shift of paradigm allows the perception of new possibilities about how the physical world might work.

Post-imperial melancholy: a perceived sense of persistent loss, particularly of identity or meaning, that is sometimes taken to be typical of the UK after losing its status as the most significant imperial power.

Pulps: a term used to refer to the inexpensive periodicals published weekly, monthly or quarterly in the late-nineteenth and early-twentieth centuries that were printed on cheap, wood pulp paper. More prestigious magazines, or 'slicks', were printed on a higher grade of paper, implying that they were not so disposable. The term has come to refer to formulaic fiction, regardless of where or how it is published.

Rhizomatic: a term used by Gilles Deleuze and Félix Guattari to refer to associations of ideas and events that are organised by a chaotic, branching network pattern without a centre rather than by the more linear, structured and hierarchical metaphor of branching from a single trunk.

Semiotics: the study of systems of signs and meanings.

Sex: see **gender**

Signification: the production of meaning through sign systems, with signs being understood to refer to any organised representational system, including language.

Sublime: a term used by philosophers to refer to a combined feeling of awe and terror that accompanies overwhelming perceptions, usually of physical magnitude (such as standing before a mountain) or scope (such as the number of stars in the universe). Specific definitions vary among philosophers, but all include this sense of scale and a (perhaps temporary) feeling of inadequacy in the face of the sublime.

Technocracy: a model of governance in which skilled engineers and scientists hold political power and are trusted to make decisions based on the assumption that their knowledge and reason best suits them to rule. During the early-twentieth century, a Technocracy movement was influential in US culture.

Third World: see **First World**

Translation: a term used by Bruno Latour, who rejects a fixed opposition between the discursive and the material, to refer to the various stages, chains of meaning and negotiations through which 'things' in the material world are translated into 'ideas' in the discursive realm. For Latour, the two are connected through an unbroken chain of links which may be perceived in both directions (material to discursive and the reverse) and thus there is no gap, as semiotics implies, between reality and its representation.

Index